PENGUIN ⊕ CLASSICS

THE SATYRICON AND THE APOCOLOCYNTOSIS

ADVISORY EDITOR: BETTY RADICE

TITUS PETRONIUS ARBITER is reputedly the author of the *Satyricon*. Historical and literary evidence confirms that he is the same Petronius whose character and strange death in A.D. 66 are so graphically described in Tacitus' *Annals*. As governor of Bithynia and as consul he showed vigour and ability, but his chief talent lay in the pursuit of pleasures, in which he displayed such exquisite refinement that he earned the unofficial title of the emperor Nero's 'arbiter of elegance' (*arbiter elegantiae*). Court rivalry and jealousy contrived to cast on Petronius the suspicion that he was conspiring against the emperor, and he was ordered to commit suicide. He gradually bled to death, opening his veins, binding and re-opening them, passing his last hours in social amusement and the composition of a catalogue of Nero's debaucheries. Petronius is also the author of a small collection of lyric and elegiac poems.

The *Apocolocyntosis* is generally attributed to Seneca and there are good political and personal grounds for giving it a place among his more serious prose works and verse tragedies. It deals with the frustrated attempt of the unpopular emperor Claudius to claim his place among the Olympian Gods. A tissue of irony, parody and satire in a Menippean miscellany of prose and verse, it is a slight but highly artistic creation only understandable against the literary and political background of the age of Nero.

•

J. P. SULLIVAN has held appointments in Classics or Arts and Letters at the Universities of Oxford, Cambridge, Texas, Buffalo, Minnesota and Hawaii. He is presently Professor of Classics at the University of California, Santa Barbara. He is the author of *The Satyricon of Petronius: A Literary Study* and *Literature and Politics in the Age of Nero*.

PETRONIUS

THE SATYRICON

AND

SENECA

THE APOCOLOCYNTOSIS

Revised edition

TRANSLATED
WITH INTRODUCTIONS AND NOTES BY
J. P. SULLIVAN

PENGUIN BOOKS

PENGUIN BOOKS

Published by the Penguin Group
27 Wrights Lane, London w8 5TZ, England
Viking Penguin Inc., 40 West 23rd Street, New York, New York 10010, USA
Penguin Books Australia Ltd, Ringwood, Victoria, Australia
Penguin Books Canada Ltd, 2801 John Street, Markham, Ontario, Canada L3R 1B4
Penguin Books (NZ) Ltd, 182–190 Wairau Road, Auckland 10, New Zealand

Penguin Books Ltd, Registered Offices: Harmondsworth, Middlesex, England

This translation of *The Satyricon* published 1965
Reprinted with revisions 1969
Reprinted 1971, 1972
Reprinted with revisions 1974
Reprinted 1976
Reprinted with *The Apocolocyntosis* 1977
Reprinted 1979, 1981, 1983, 1984
Revised Edition 1986
Reprinted 1987, 1988

This translation of *The Apocolocyntosis* first published
in the United States of America in *Arion*, University of Texas, 1966

Copyright © J. P. Sullivan, 1965, 1969, 1974, 1977, 1986
All rights reserved

Made and printed in Great Britain by
Richard Clay Ltd, Bungay, Suffolk
Filmset in Monophoto Ehrhardt

CONTENTS

PETRONIUS

Introduction
    The Authorship and Date of the *Satyricon*   11
    The Extent of the Work and the Plot   16
    The Literary Qualities of the *Satyricon*   18
    On the Text and Translation   26

Acknowledgements   33

THE SATYRICON
    PUTEOLI   37
    DINNER WITH TRIMALCHIO   51
    EUMOLPUS   92
    THE ROAD TO CROTON   126
    CROTON   141

THE FRAGMENTS AND THE POEMS   163

List of Characters   181
Notes on the *Satyricon*   185
Notes on the Fragments and Poems   204

SENECA

Introduction
    The Authorship and Date of the *Apocolocyntosis*   209
    The Place of the Work in Seneca's Writings   212
    The Literary Qualities of the *Apocolocyntosis*   214
    On the Text and Translation   218

THE APOCOLOCYNTOSIS OF THE DIVINE CLAUDIUS   221

Notes on the *Apocolocyntosis*   234

PETRONIUS

INTRODUCTION

The Authorship and Date of the *Satyricon*

The *Satyricon* has been traditionally, and rightly, attributed to the courtier of Nero whose downfall and death in A.D. 66 are described by Tacitus (*Annals* 16.17–20):

17. So the space of a few days saw the fall, in the same bloody action, of Annaeus Mela, Cerialis Anicius, Rufrius Crispinus, and Petronius, Mela and Crispinus being Roman knights of senatorial status...

18. Gaius Petronius deserves a further brief notice. He spent his days sleeping and his nights working and enjoying himself. Industry is the usual foundation of success, but with him it was idleness. Unlike most people who throw away their money in dissipation, he was not regarded as an extravagant sensualist, but as one who made luxury a fine art. His conversation and his way of life were unconventional with a certain air of nonchalance, and they charmed people all the more by seeming so unstudied. Yet as proconsul in Bithynia and later as consul, he showed himself a vigorous and capable administrator. His subsequent return to his old habits, whether this was real or apparent, led to his admission to the small circle of Nero's intimates, as his Arbiter of Elegance. In the end Nero's jaded appetite regarded nothing as enjoyable or refined unless Petronius had given his sanction to it. Consequently the jealousy of Tigellinus was aroused against him: he saw in Petronius a rival, someone superior to himself in the whole art of pleasure. So he worked upon the Emperor's cruelty, his master-passion, to which all his other lusts were subordinate. Accusing Petronius of being an intimate of Scaevinus, he bribed a slave to give evidence against him. Petronius did not have a chance to reply and Tigellinus threw most of his household into prison.

19. The Emperor at that time happened to be on a visit to Campania. Petronius got as far as Cumae and was prevented from going any further. He refused to prolong the suspense that hope or fear involved. Not that he was hasty in taking leave of his life. On the contrary, he opened his veins and then, as the fancy took him, he bound them up or re-opened them, and all the while talked with his friends, but not on serious topics or anything calculated to win

admiration for his courage. He listened to their contributions – not discussions about the immortality of the soul or the opinions of philosophers, but simply gay songs and light verses. He dealt out rewards to some of his slaves and floggings to others. He began a lavish dinner and took a nap, so that his death, although forced on him, should appear natural. Even in the codicils to his will, unlike most of the victims, he refused to flatter Nero or Tigellinus or anyone else powerful. Instead he wrote out a full description of the Emperor's vicious activities, giving the names of his male and female partners, and specifying the novel forms his lust had taken. This document he sent under seal to Nero. Then he broke his signet ring in case it should be used later to endanger others.

20. Nero's puzzlement as to how his nocturnal ingenuities were known was resolved by blaming Silia. This was a not insignificant person, a senator's wife, in fact, who had been a chosen partner in all the Emperor's vices and also a close friend of Petronius. She was exiled, an example of personal hatred, for her lack of discretion about what she had seen and experienced.

Plutarch, in his essay *On the Distinction Between Flattery and Friendship* (60 d–e), adds an anecdote which may throw some light on Petronius' character and the methods by which he retained for a time his position with Nero:

These are minor faults. Next, however, comes that unscrupulous practice which has such a damaging effect on silly people. This consists in accusing them of tendencies and weaknesses the very opposite of their real failings ... This may take the form of sneering at reckless and extravagant spenders for their petty-minded and sordid ways – Titus Petronius did this with Nero.

Finally the elder Pliny in his *Natural History* (37.20) tells us that

T. Petronius, a consular, when he was going to die through Nero's malice and envy, broke his fluorspar wine-dipper so that the Emperor's table would not inherit it. It had cost 300,000 sesterces.

It is likely that Pliny and Plutarch are right in giving his praenomen as Titus, and that Tacitus, who occasionally slips in such matters, was wrong to call him Gaius. The name 'Arbiter' given him in the MSS was probably not his real cognomen, but a soubriquet with which Tacitus too was familiar. He has been most convincingly identified with T. Petronius Niger, who was consul in July–August A.D. 62.[1]

However this may be, for centuries the dating of the *Satyricon* to Neronian times and the attribution of the work to Nero's courtier has

---

1. K. F. C. Rose, *The Date and Author of the Satyricon* (Leiden, 1971), pp. 47 ff.

been hotly disputed, and counter-suggestions range from the time of Augustus to the late second century A.D., but there has been no consensus among the opponents of a Neronian dating. It would be temerarious to consider the whole discussion closed, but for the general reader, the main arguments for accepting this dating and attribution may be summarized as follows. The historical and economic references in the work point to the first century A.D.[1] The language and style belong to the same period: for example, the vulgarisms introduced into the speech of Trimalchio and his circle may be paralleled not only in the Senecan *Apocolocyntosis* (a work which surely belongs to the Neronian era),[2] but also in the wall-inscriptions preserved at Pompeii, all of which must belong to the period before A.D. 79. The literary criticism in the work is very like the criticism (particularly of rhetoric) that we find in other writings of the first century. And, in particular, the criticism prefacing the *Carmen de Bello Civili* (118 ff.), which seems directed at Lucan (d. 30 April A.D. 65) without mentioning his name, can only be appropriate to the few years during which the *Pharsalia* was written and partially published. The literary sources of the work, including the imitation of Senecan tragedy in c. 89, the citations from other authors, arguably the literary intentions (which I shall discuss below), all fit this dating. The author of the work was obviously a highly literary and literate man; the court circle of Nero, with an Emperor of such literary ambitions, would be naturally interested in criticism and literature. Consequently it is difficult to believe that the courtier Petronius became *elegantiae arbiter* (Arbiter of Elegance) simply because he knew which end of a spoon was which or how best to flavour wine, although it is perhaps significant that much of the satire directed against Trimalchio is satire of manners, not excluding table manners. The psychological similarity so frequently alleged between the man and the work, even if this is extended to the voyeurism which seems a characteristic of both, is perhaps too dubious to argue from,[3] but in addition to the considerations adduced above, one or two detailed

1. Rose, op. cit., pp. 20 ff. Rose's penetrating and exhaustive study supersedes most previous work on the subject. A detailed discussion of the economic background, which takes account of Petronius' fictional purposes, is to be found in R. Duncan, *The Economy of the Roman Empire* (Cambridge, 1974), pp. 238 ff.

2. Cf. G. Bagnani, *Arbiter of Elegance* (Toronto, 1954), pp. 80 ff., and see below pp. 209 ff.

3. See J. P. Sullivan, *The Satyricon of Petronius: A Literary Study* (London and Bloomington, Indiana, 1968), pp. 238 ff.

arguments may be singled out from the mass of more disputable
historical parallels and references.

We know from the evidence of certain glass cups and inscriptions
that Petraites (or Tetraites) was a famous gladiator of the time of Nero.
A gladiator Petraites is mentioned twice by Trimalchio (52.3 and 71.6):
he has Petraites' fights decorating cups in his possession, and he wants
them depicted on his tomb. Similarly, two other Imperial entertainers,
who can be dated fairly precisely, are both mentioned in the *Satyricon*:
Menecrates, a lyre-playing protegé of Nero's, and Apelles, a *tragoedus*
(tragic actor) contemporary with Caligula. The mention of these two
in the *Satyricon* fits precisely their actual chronological relationship.[1]

Such close coincidences as these, as well as the broad similarities
between the narrative of the *Satyricon* and the linguistic, historical and
economic background of the Roman world of the first century A.D.,
make the long-continued dispute about the dating of the work very
puzzling, until one recalls the strange but not yet entirely quashed
Baconian heresy in Shakespearian studies. Perhaps the identification
of Tacitus' Petronius and our author, like the attribution of the
Apocolocyntosis to the philosopher Seneca, seemed to some too good to
be true.[2] Unfortunately the attempts to date the *Satyricon* to periods
ranging from late in the reign of Augustus (Beck) to the reign of
Commodus (Marmorale), a time span of about two centuries (A.D. 10
to A.D. 192), suffer from two main defects: first, the need to postulate
lost literary works upon which the author of the *Satyricon* is dependent
for his imitations and parodies; second, the lack of a theory about the
artistic impulse and literary ambience of the author, whoever he was.
If, on the other hand, the Neronian dating is accepted, we have more
insight into the circumstances and motivation of the author of the
Satyricon.

1. The evidence for all this is laid out in H. T. Rowell, 'The Gladiator Petraites and the Date of
the *Satyricon*', *Transactions of the American Philological Association* 89 (1958), 14 ff.

2. A recent attempt to cast doubts on the identification may be found in *Petronii Arbitri Cena
Trimalchionis*, ed. M. S. Smith (Oxford, 1975), pp. 213 ff., who favours a somewhat earlier dating to
the principate of Tiberius or Caligula; see also P. A. George, 'Petronius and Lucan's *de Bello Civili*',
Classical Quarterly 24 (1974), 119 ff. The arguments for the Augustan and late second century dates
respectively may be found in C. Beck, *The Age of Petronius* (Cambridge, Mass., 1856) and E. V.
Marmorale, *La questione Petroniana* (Bari, 1948). R. E. Martin in 'Quelques remarques concernant
la date du *Satiricon*' in *Revue des Études Latines* 53 (1975), 182 ff., suggests that the work was written
in the Flavian era (A.D. 69-96). Whereas George and Smith reject allusions to Lucan, Martin accepts
them, but detects also echoes of Silius Italicus' *Punica*, which was being written in the eighties and
nineties of the first century.

According to Tacitus (*Annals* 14.16), in A.D. 59 Nero established a literary circle which went into session after dinner. It was made up of associates with some facility for verse, whose abilities had not yet attracted public attention. Here they would revise half-completed works or offer impromptu compositions for the Emperor's criticism and revision, since Nero was supposed to have a happy knack for such things, having been taught extempore composition by Seneca. There is evidence that membership of this circle led to political advancement.[1] M. Cocceius Nerva, the future Emperor (A.D. 96–8) belonged to it. Born in A.D. 35, he was only two years older than Nero, who hailed him as the Tibullus of his age and had a high respect for his critical powers (Martial 8.70; 8.26). Later he played a vigorous role in the suppression of the Pisonian conspiracy and was praetor in A.D. 66. Aulus Vitellius, another future Emperor (A.D. 68), also participated in Nero's literary activities; he presided at the *Neronia*, Nero's great literary and musical festival, and even after Nero's death arranged a recital from the *liber dominicus*, a collection of Neronian verse (Suetonius *Vitellius* 4; 11).

Silius Italicus, author of the *Punica*, was also close to Nero (Pliny *Letters* 37), becoming consul in A.D. 68; his contribution to the rampant literary activity at court was presumably the *Ilias Latina*, now thought to be his work. Fabricius Veiento, a satirist whose *Codicilli* attacked the senate and the priestly colleges, also rose to high honours and influence before his exile (Tacitus *Annals* 14.3). Perhaps even Titus, another future emperor (A.D. 79–81), displayed his well-known artistic gifts in the circle.

Others could be mentioned, although the most talented was obviously the poet Lucan, whose gifts, according to the Voss *Life*, promoted him to a premature quaestorship before his fatal break with the Emperor.

Into the circle, then, came T. Petronius Niger after his consulship in A.D. 62. He soon gained enormous influence over Nero, as his unofficial title of Arbiter of Elegance proves. His tastes, given Nero's enthusiasm for literature, must have been exercised in literary ways as well as in material refinements. His political power at court must have grown correspondingly; otherwise Tigellinus would not have grown jealous of him and encompassed his downfall. The *Satyricon*, so preoccupied with matters of taste, social and literary, and reflecting the growing hostility at court to the Annaean family, particularly to Seneca

---

1. See J. P. Sullivan, *Literature and Politics in the Age of Nero* (Ithaca, N. Y., 1985), pp. 19 ff.

and Lucan, was the perfect vehicle for Petronius' talents. There was also the additional advantage that the chosen form did not constitute a challenge to Nero's own literary work, which was essentially neo-Alexandrian poetry on such topics as the Sack of Troy, Attis, and Poppaea's amber hair.

The Extent of the Work and the Plot

There are indications in our MSS which, if they are to be trusted, indicate that the extant portions and some fragments of the *Satyricon* may belong to Books XIV, XV, and XVI of the whole; this would mean that the work was originally perhaps twenty books long (six or ten times its present length), if it was ever finished – a great but not impossible length for a work of this sort. As we have it now, the text is interpolated, corrupt and fragmentary. It is possible indeed that the market episode (c. 12 ff.) and the Quartilla episode (c. 16 ff.) are misplaced and belong to a slightly earlier part of the work (to Book XIV, if we could trust the interpolator of Fulgentius). But this has not yet been proved, and the abruptness of the transitions and the very odd sequence of meals in the earlier part of the work as we have it may be due simply to the loss of the connecting narrative. I have, therefore, left these episodes in the traditional place. I have followed the same practice with the occasional traces of a double tradition. It is tempting in the Quartilla episode to rearrange and amalgamate, as Gaselee did, the two entrances of the catamite or catamites, and elsewhere in the text to remove the brief summaries of the action which are found in our MSS as part of the actual narrative. But a translation is not the place to do this: this is an editor's work. I have therefore translated the whole text, including most of the interpolations once deleted by Müller, Fraenkel, and others, and excluding only certain obvious glosses.[1] After some consideration I have not interrupted the translation with summaries to bridge the gaps between the various fragments, nor have I relocated certain of the poems attributed to Petronius to those places in the main text where scholars have argued (quite plausibly) for their insertion. On the whole the plot is fairly clear in the important essentials,

---

1. For a discussion of the alleged interpolations, see J. P. Sullivan, 'Interpolations in Petronius', *Proceedings of the Cambridge Philological Society* (1976). For a list of my few omissions, see below, pp. 30 ff.

and the intelligent reader can easily work out what must have been happening.

A brief recapitulation of the earlier lost episodes as they can be reconstructed from allusions in the work may be worth giving. The plot seems to consist of the adventures of the narrator Encolpius: sometimes he plays a direct part and is closely involved; at other times he is merely a witness of certain events. Trimalchio's dinner-party is the best example of this. Such a loose plot obviously and deliberately allows for frequent digressions, e.g. discussions of literature, short Milesian tales like 'The Widow of Ephesus', parodies, and poems of varying length. Nevertheless what gives some tenuous continuity to Encolpius' adventures is the basic plot: the wrath of the ithyphallic deity, Priapus, against the inadequate hero. This comic motif (*gravis ira Priapi*) is patently based on the wrath of Poseidon against Odysseus in the *Odyssey*. This is not to suggest that the whole *Satyricon* was a close parody of the *Odyssey*, but merely that the unifying theme and certain subsidiary motifs were deliberately drawn from the *Odyssey*; the same may be said of several of the extant Greek novels.

So Encolpius at some point has offended Priapus (perhaps by impersonating him in some sexual ceremonies), and unfortunately, through various mishaps, he continues to offend this god. Shortly before the surviving portion of the work begins he and his two companions have witnessed and interrupted some secret Priapean rites conducted by the priestess Quartilla, perhaps near the long tunnel which links Naples and Puteoli, and still later in the work he kills a goose sacred to the god. Consequently the enmity of this powerful deity dogs him at intervals. Presumably for this reason he is still a poor exile, wandering from place to place, living by his wits. There are some indications that he first fell foul of Priapus in Massilia (Marseilles); he may have been exiled from that city (after a year's entertainment at public expense) to avert a plague. If the doubtful evidence can be trusted, he then took a hazardous journey by sea to Italy. He may have been in Rome for a while. Somewhere he was providentially rescued from the gladiatorial arena. His activities, it is clear, frequently cause him to run foul of the law and account for his constant travels and his low connections.

In Italy, Encolpius takes up with various companions, still living by theft and free hospitality. He seems to be moving down through Italy. At some point he is taken up by Lichas, a Tarentine ship owner, who is attracted by him. Encolpius, however, seduces his wife Hedyle,

commits some terrible outrage on Lichas himself in the portico of
Hercules at Baiae, the famous pleasure resort in South Italy, just above
Puteoli, the *Graeca urbs* in which the surviving portion of the story
opens. He also steals the robe and sacred rattle of the goddess Isis from
Lichas' ship. In the same area, and no doubt about the same time, he
falls in with the famous courtesan Tryphaena, who becomes his mistress.
But becoming jealous of her fondness for the young and handsome
Giton, whom he had at some point seduced and taken under his wing,
he procures her public disgrace and runs off with Giton. Jealousy is a
trait of Encolpius. Meeting Ascyltus, a young man very like himself,
Encolpius tries to keep his relationship with Giton secret from him.
The three of them are all involved in the murder of a certain Lycurgus,
whose villa they then rob. The proceeds of this they sew up in a ragged
tunic for safety, but during a temporary separation, perhaps while
stealing an expensive cloak from some country people, Encolpius loses
the cloak with the stolen money inside. Ascyltus plainly suspects his
companion's honesty. This sort of conflict, added to the jealousy over
Giton (not the last occasion on which Encolpius suffers from it),
eventually causes the break-up of the trio.

From the fragments, if they are connected with the novel, we might
deduce that the end of the work took place in Egypt and Encolpius
finally saw the end of his misfortunes and returned safely home to peace
and quiet.

It is not always easy to decide the order of the above events. As I
have said, it is not impossible that some of the earlier episodes in the
extant fragments are misplaced (e.g. the attempt to sell the stolen cloak).
If the present ordering in the MSS is accepted, then we find the trio
lodged in Puteoli and associating as men of culture with the teacher of
rhetoric Agamemnon, who has a school there. Encolpius is in the middle
of a discussion of the present system of rhetorical education with him,
when the work as we have it abruptly opens.

The Literary Qualities of the *Satyricon*

The dubious reputation of the *Satyricon* from quite early times and its
unfortunate association with literary *curiosa*, privately printed editions
and copies bound in black morocco, have militated against much serious
discussion of the work as literature until comparatively recently. Many
have recognized its value, but as one Frenchman said, '*On lit Pétrone,*

on ne cite pas.' The German scholar Niebuhr (1776–1831) summarized the accepted opinion when he remarked:

> The disgusting indecencies of which the remains of Petronius are full ... give him so bad a name, that he who confesses an intimate acquaintance with the fiction, and expresses gratification in it, exposes himself to a severe judgement, and affords a good opportunity for the display of sanctimonious hypocrisy.

A modern reader is unlikely to have much patience with such strictures, being reared on gamier fare than anything Petronius provides. In the words of Judge Woolsey on Joyce's *Ulysses*, the few sections to which exception might be taken are 'emetic' rather than 'aphrodisiac', and these are ingredients inseparable from Petronius' literary purposes. The final word on this aspect of the *Satyricon* was said by D. H. Lawrence in a letter to Lady Ottoline Morrell (dated 1 February 1916):

> He startled me at first, but I liked him. He is a gentleman when all is said and done ... Petronius is straight and above board. Whatever he does, he doesn't try to degrade and dirty the pure mind in him.[1]

There have been many characterizations of the *Satyricon* and for most of them there is some evidence in the work. It has been seen as an early picaresque novel like *Gil Blas*, *Guzman d'Alfarache* or even *Don Quixote*, the parody on knightly romances being matched by the parody on the *Odyssey* which runs through the *Satyricon*; alternatively, it has been interpreted as a homosexual parody on the conventional Greek romance about star-crossed, but faithful, lovers; it has been regarded simply as a connected collection of Milesian tales and comic sketches; it has been described as an elaborate satire on the basis of Epicurean morality against the violent and frustrating passions of greed, sex and anger; or, even more frequently, it has been taken as the first realistic novel in European literature.[2] The disconnected nature of the fragments, the loss of so much of the work, and the diversity of what remains, all make it hard to classify, even though there is something critically inadequate about throwing up one's hands and agreeing to

1. For other references to Petronius in modern literature, see Gareth Schmeling, 'T. S. Eliot and Petronius', *Comparative Literature Studies* 12 (1975) 393–410.

2. B. E. Perry, *The Ancient Romances* (Berkeley and Los Angeles, 1967), pp. 96 ff.; E. Courtney, 'Parody and Literary Allusion in Menippean Satire', *Philologus* 106 (1962) 86 ff.; G. Highet, *Collected Papers*, ed. R. Ball (New York, 1984), pp. 191–209; P. G. Walsh, *The Roman Novel* (Cambridge, 1970), pp. 4, 8 ff.; T. Haäg, *The Ancient Novel* (Oxford, 1983), pp. 168 ff.

regard it as something of a *beau monstre*, some unique portent like *Tristram Shandy*, *Finnegans Wake*, or Pound's *Cantos*, works that are at once a beginning and an end.

The best way to understand its nature is to consider it organically as a development of a literary tradition in the context of a certain milieu; it will be found to be, I believe, an explicable literary phenomenon whose features cease to surprise us and so cease to baffle our evaluation. In this way one may explain all the features which have led to one-sided characterizations of the work, while dispensing with those equally one-sided comparisons to single works of earlier or later literature which often serve to hide its exact nature.

Formally, the work belongs to the tradition of Menippean satire,[1] a moralistic and humorous *mélange* of prose and verse invented by Menippus of Gadara in the first half of the third century B.C. This was imitated and developed in Rome by M. Terentius Varro (116–27 B.C.) We know that it was an available form in Neronian times from the evidence of the extant *Apocolocyntosis* by Petronius' contemporary, the younger Seneca (see below, pp. 209 ff.), a serio-comic squib directed against the dead Emperor Claudius. Certainly a main characteristic of Menippean satire was the union of humour and philosophy (or whatever political, moral or aesthetic basis an author might substitute for this).

We cannot, however, say off-hand that Petronius' motive in writing his work was predominantly satirical in our sense, for he differs vastly from Persius, the other Neronian satirist who has survived. But what we can say with fair assurance is that, granted the continuance of a Roman tradition of Menippean satire, the very form and loose structure of Menippean satire might be attractive to the sort of genius and temperament we find in Petronius. It would require merely the enlargement of its potentialities to become an ideal vehicle of Petronius' literary abilities. As was said earlier, it would be highly unlikely that Nero's Arbiter of Elegance was not a literary arbiter as well as an arbiter of more tangible refinements. If this was so, Menippean satire was a perfect form for literary criticism, both directly and through parody, particularly as the fashion of writing books of criticism was not yet so firmly established as with us, and criticism was generally offered in satire form. It allowed also for the exercise of Petronius' admittedly

1. For a convenient and sound discussion of Menippean satire, see M. Coffey, *Roman Satire* (London, 1976), pp. 149 ff.

meagre verse talents, with the additional advantage that their attribution to fictional *personae* would not constitute any very high claims for their merit. The final and rather extraneous attraction of the form would be its suitability for the continuous recitals of which Nero's literary court circle was indubitably fond.

Yet for all its formal seductions, Menippean satire was still a branch of Roman satire, whose characteristic content had gradually become – despite its earlier broadness – a commentary on life and morals. It is clear from the evidence of Persius, and there is no reason to think the case different with Menippean satire, that Roman satire had developed into what we think of as true satire. The one difference there might be between Menippean and regular satire is the strong tradition of humour and fantasy, which is clearly indicated in the titles of Varro's lost works. This is particularly noticeable later in the Greek writings of Lucian and the Emperor Julian, both heavily influenced by Menippus. As a consequence, Petronius, who was a literary traditionalist, would be impelled – or attracted – by the exigencies of the form as he found it (for the degeneration of Menippean satire into a mere *mélange* of prose and verse came later, in Boethius for example) to take a large account, somehow or other, of this element as well as the more basic element of satire proper. This is perhaps a misleading way to put it, and it is not the way the artist works. We are talking here about the tension between the artist and the claims of his chosen form, claims which are imposed on the artist in one sense, but are voluntarily accepted by him for the artistic process. Even if the choice of Menippean satire was initially for its peripheral advantages (namely, looseness of structure, tolerance of digressions, opportunities for versification), an unlikely hypothesis with so impressive an artist as Petronius, his genius would then respond to the more essential nature of the form, even though his own literary excellence might develop or even change that nature into something other.

All this may seem oversubtle, but it is important to exclude the idea of Petronius' inventing a new genre which corresponds closely to the modern sprawling novel as practised by its more realistic and digressive practitioners, and, naturally, failing in its execution. The similarity to the novel is there, but it has other explanations.

If my view is correct, several important aspects of the *Satyricon* now find, directly or indirectly, their explanation. The digressions, such as the '*Carmen de Bello Civili*' (c. 119 ff.), although they fit so adventitiously

into the loose Menippean form, may be left aside: their *raison d'être* is
obvious enough. But the integral episodes of the work derive from satire
and were determined by Petronius' choice of genre. At least three
of them are paralleled in extant Roman satire, notably the '*Cena
Trimalchionis*', which has obvious affinities with Horace's '*Cena Nasidi-
eni*' (*Satires* 2.8), the episode at Croton, which intermittently satirizes
legacy hunters, a theme common to Horace and Juvenal (cf. Horace
Satires 2.5 and Juvenal *Satires* 1.37 ff., 55 ff.), and, finally, the satiric
description of women such as Circe, who prefer low-class lovers, a type
prominent in Juvenal's sixth satire and to be found also in Herondas
and elsewhere. No doubt other episodes, such as Encolpius' soliloquy
over the dead body of Lichas, might also have had literary ancestors –
a study of Varro's fragments and titles suggests further interesting
possibilities. Nor should one overlook the possibility of thematic
borrowings from the great Roman verse satire, Lucilius (d. 101 B.C.),
who is alluded to in c. 4 of Petronius.

If we leave satire proper, Encolpius' impotence has its parallel in
Ovid's mock-serious lament over his own fiasco in *Amores* 3.7, a subject
as appropriate to satire as to elegy, if not more so. Similarly we cannot
exclude the influence on Petronius' plot and incidents of the precursors
of our extant Greek romances; the earliest belongs to the late first
century A.D., but it can hardly be the first example of the genre. These
evidently had roots and parallels in various fictional narratives from
the Middle East.[1] Nor were these embryo novelists confined to the
sentimental plots of lovers separated and then, after many vicissitudes,
reunited. It would seem to be an accident of fortune or taste that our
surviving examples of the Greek novel are of this type. There is recent
evidence from papyrus of quite different plots, tone and treatment.[2]

It is important to remember that the Romans were unsophisticated
about literary cross-fertilization – Horace's discussion of Lucilius and
his predecessors in Attic comedy is proof enough of this. The main
themes of the work then seem predominantly satiric and the close
relation of humour or wit with moral satire, in ancient as well as modern
times, might seem to explain the nature of most of the *Satyricon*,
particularly if we add that ancient satirists often chose prurient and

---

1. See Graham Anderson, *Ancient Fiction: The Novel in the Graeco-Roman World* (London, 1984),
pp. 1 ff., although there the thesis is perhaps carried to extremes.
2. See P. Parsons, 'A Greek *Satyricon*?' *Bulletin of the Institute of Classical Studies* (London) 18
(1971) 53 ff.

disgusting targets for their humorous or ironic shafts, as did Jonathan Swift and some seventeenth-century writers such as Rochester and Dorset. But the truth is that Petronius, for all his satiric themes, does not strike us, on a careful reading, as a truly classical satirist. There is something oddly wrong in this classification, and the long debate over the nature of the work reinforces our doubts. For Petronius does not seem a serious moralist or even, like Juvenal, an adopter of a conventional *morale* from which to launch into his more vital and artistic preoccupations. He is completely disengaged from the moral situations he depicts and the episode at Croton is given an atmosphere of fantasy and humour rather than moral concern.

The '*Cena Trimalchionis*' offers the real clue to this difficulty. The theme is traditional, even if considerably deepened by experience and observation, but the standard adopted is clearly one of taste, as one might expect of its author, rather than any moral standard. But even this standard is constantly undercut by the deliberate satire on Encolpius, the mouthpiece of the satire. All his strictures on Trimalchio's vulgarity and pretentiousness lose their effect when Petronius makes his narrator expose himself time and again to the reader's contempt, however indulgent. As a partial consequence, although the sheer vitality of Petronius' creation must not be overlooked, Trimalchio more and more assumes the status of a great comic character rather than a mercilessly flayed object of satire. (Petronius' original *intentions* are naturally irrelevant – his initial aim may easily have been transcended.) Much the same may be said of Trimalchio's circle.

What has happened, I think, is this: Petronius' themes are at first dictated by the tradition of the genre he has chosen and his success or relative failure with them depends on their challenge to his imagination. Obviously the Trimalchio episode is more of a masterpiece than anything that happens elsewhere in Puteoli or at Croton. The challenge that he has been able to meet has been essentially a novelist's challenge, for we have seen that his artistic impulse is not really a satirist's impulse at all. His claim to be a satirist is no more than the fact that he has chosen traditional satiric topics where the air of disengagement is too obvious to be missed, and when he does approach satire from an implicit standard, it is a standard of taste which he constantly undercuts by irony. Encolpius is a failure both as a moral and an aesthetic repository, but at no point, except possibly in cc. 118 and 132 (both literary), does Petronius appear to offer his own views.

One important association of satire had obviously gone home to him, an association that was perhaps reinforced by a variety of circumstances, not all of them literary. Satire not only had a tradition of more or less conversational language (*sermoni propriora*, in Horace's phrase), but it also prided itself on its 'realism'. Of course Roman literature is always highly dependent on tradition and sometimes one might suspect that some of the 'realistic' topics which recur so often had become in fact stylized, if not fossilized – much as second-rate modern novels convert originally daring narrations of the sexual act into conventional and stylized descriptions. Still, the Roman satirists continued to decry stale mythological themes and proclaim that their form of art alone depicted reality (*quidquid agunt homines; hominem pagina nostra sapit; quodque facit populus;* etc.).

Naturally when one looks at the subjects of satire, one sees that this claim to represent reality is actually, in Mary McCarthy's phrase, 'a denigration of the real'. The satirist, like so many 'realistic' novelists, is presenting a partial view of reality and claiming that only the seamier, the more vulgar, side of life is truly real, the rest is the humbug of the canting moralist. Hence the predominance of sexual themes in the satirists, Petronius included: sex is the one subject at least for satire which outlives legacy-hunting, the ill-treatment of the Irish, and contemporary manifestations of bad taste.

In certain ages and milieux this view of life is more seductive than in others. Certain periods of high literary culture and material refinement seem affected by a *nostalgie de la boue* which may make itself felt both in life and in literature. Nero, we are told by Suetonius (*Nero* 26), used to wander at night in disguise into low taverns and get involved in disreputable escapades in Rome, and Petronius' interest in lower-class life, sordid sex and crime seems almost the literary counterpart of this. A comparison might be made with the 1890s in Europe where a high degree of literary sophistication went hand in hand with an interest in the more disreputable areas of life – Dorian Gray and Des Esseintes have the same peculiar contrasts of refinement and sordidness in their characters as Encolpius or Eumolpus.

Were this all, Petronius would find himself in the company of those satirists and novelists whose purblind view of reality makes them either inadequate commentators on life or highly partial visionaries saved from inadequacy only by their intensity and literary gifts. But Petronius, for all his acceptance of satiric themes and the satirist's view of life, is saved by his own irony and artistic ambivalence towards satire. He can accept the satiric themes, but he does not accept the moral premiss, either because of his Epicureanism or his own view of existence. The sordid becomes humorous; the sexual never becomes salacious or disgusting; the objects of his 'satire' become literary creations. If there is any commentary on existence, it is ultimately a novelist's commentary, almost a poet's, not the cruder and oversimplified commentary of the satirist. In Petronius we see the novelist taking over the satirist's task, while working with the satirist's themes – and it is not the so-called 'realistic' novelist who does what the satirist does even though he omits the more obvious moralizing, but rather the creative novelist who enlarges on life and reshapes it to his own artistic ends.

The proof is there in Trimalchio, although evidence may be found scattered throughout the work. The basic object of satire, the vulgar, uneducated but pretentious freedman, had no doubt a thousand counterparts in life, and Horace provided Petronius with an adequate model of satiric treatment in the somewhat similar character of Nasidienus. But the novelist's impulse in Petronius was greater than the satirist's and to build up the elaborate character of Trimalchio, Petronius drew on what he knew of life, including a considerable number of real persons. Trimalchio's fondness for the insipid rebus game (c. 56) he shares with the Emperor Augustus (cf. Suetonius, *Augustus* 75); his eccentricity about the importance of the digestive tract he shares with the Emperor Claudius (cf. Suetonius, *Claudius* 32); his morbid game of playing dead he has in common with at least two other Romans, Pacuvius and Turannius, both mentioned by Seneca (*Epistulae Morales* 12.8[1] and *De Brevitate Vitae* 20.3); and of course an important model was the freedman millionaire Calvisius Sabinus, described by Seneca (*Epistulae Morales* 27.5–8)[2]. Similarly, his astrological disquisition in c. 39 is not simply a piece of free invention, but a careful and witty compilation of current popular beliefs, just as the language and sentiments of Trimalchio's humbler friends seem convincing and plausible evidence of a careful study of their putative milieu. (It is worth comparing those passages in D. H. Lawrence's *Lady Chatterley's Lover*, where the housekeeper, Mrs Bolton, discusses affairs in the village with Clifford Chatterley.) All this amalgamation of direct observation and literary

1. See *Letters from a Stoic* XII (Harmondsworth, 1969).
2. See *Letters from a Stoic* XXVII (Harmondsworth, 1969).

hearsay (for we cannot deny realism to a novelist because his source is reportage or what he takes to be reportage) is, however, subordinated to the imaginative grasp which we feel at work in the presentation of that true novelistic creation, Trimalchio.

On the Text and Translation

The surviving text of Petronius is regrettably fragmented and mutilated. Edifying snippets were preserved in *florilegia*; sections, words and phrases are quoted by high-minded authors such as Fulgentius and John of Salisbury, or by metricians and grammarians. But the larger narrative comes down to us in three forms. The '*Cena Trimalchionis*', more or less intact, survives for posterity in a single MS, the *Traguriensis*. Now in Paris, it was written in 1423, but rediscovered only about 1652 in Trau (now Trogir in Jugoslavia); this is our sole witness to the *H*-tradition. The *L*-tradition is a collection of longer extracts from the work, which survives in several MSS, the most noted being a much-edited copy made by Joseph Scaliger in Leiden in 1571, the *Leidensis* (*l*). Finally we have the shorter excerpts (*O*), represented by three early MSS from the ninth and twelfth centuries (*B R P*) and a number of later MSS and early editions. These three sources and the *florilegia* overlap.[1] But the text that results from their amalgamation would be more unsatisfactory than it is were it not for the painstaking work of generations of scholars such as Scaliger, Pithoeus, Heinsius, Jacobs, Bücheler and Müller. An important task of the editor – and therefore of the translator – of Petronius is deciding on the plausibility of competing emendations.

In this revised translation I have generally followed the latest text, Konrad Müller's third edition in *Petronius Satyrica, Schelmengeschichte*, (Artemis Verlag, Munich, 1983). I record here my indebtedness in general to his work on the many difficulties presented by the MSS. I have ventured to disagree with his readings in a few places, sometimes because of the exigencies of any translator, who must find some sense

---

1. For a full and recent account, see K. Müller, *Petronius Satyrica, Schelmengeschichte* (Munich, 1983), pp. 381–448. For an admirably succinct account in English, see M. D. Reeve in L. D. Reynolds (ed.), *Texts and Transmission: A Survey of the Latin Classics* (Oxford, 1983), pp. 295 ff. For individual discussions of textual points and for earlier editions of the text see G. L. Schmeling and J. H. Stuckey, *A Bibliography of Petronius* (Leiden, 1977).

even where the truth is difficult to discern. The more significant differences and changes from Müller's text are listed below (p. 30).*

The Fragments attributed by editors to Petronius, with greater or lesser confidence, present further problems. Bücheler in his 1862 edition printed 53; Müller's latest edition has reduced these to 28, all of which have been directly connected, in one source or another, to Petronius. Whatever the number, some of these clearly need a context such as the *Satyricon* to make sense; others, however, might well be self-sufficient poems which may have come from some separate collection of Petronius' poetry. (Seneca's verse insertions in the *Apocolocyntosis* are firmly rooted in their setting, but we know that he published four books of poems apart from that.)

In any case, I have decided to err on the side of generosity and I have translated almost all of the short verse pieces which have the remotest claim, at least in some editors' thinking, to Petronian authorship.[1] Of the poems with some claim to authenticity, Poems XXXI–XXXII, XXVII, XXXIII–XLIV and XXVI are found in this order in a ninth century MS (Vossianus L. Q. 86). They are not attributed there to Petronius, but follow a number of epigrams specified as the work of Seneca. Two of this set of poems are quoted by Fulgentius as from Petronius (Fragments XVII and XXVIII) and, with XXVI, also quoted, are accepted as such by Müller. The rest, however, were also attributed to Petronius by Scaliger, who was impressed by their general resemblance to Petronius' style in the *Satyricon*. These offer a reasonable claim to inclusion.

Poems XLV–LVI were found in a lost MS once at Beauvais. The contents of this codex Bellacovensis were published in 1579 by Claude Binetus. XLV–LVI were attributed to Petronius in the MS, according to the editor; LV and LVI were not, although they impressed Binetus as Petronian in style. Six further poems which followed in the MS were given to Petronius by Baehrens (*Poetae Latini Minores* iv. 103–8), although neither style nor content indicates Petronian authorship. These are not translated here.

Another two poems (Fragments XXIX and XXX) are found in the ninth century in cod. Vossianus L. F. III under Petronius' name, and

---

1. Even the last little poem on Hermaphroditus, interesting but hardly Petronian, was included in Maurice Rat's edition of the *Satyricon* (Paris, 1934).

following the poems found in cc. 14 and 83 of the *Satyricon*. Stylistically, they have much in common with Petronius' other verse writings.[1]

For the convenience of the reader who may wish to consult the Latin, I have followed the sequence of the fragments as edited by Müller and then the order used by H. E. Butler in the Loeb Library, *Petronius, Seneca* (London & Cambridge, Mass., 1951, 1969).

The translation of such a highly original and artistic work as the *Satyricon*, written in a mixture of prose and verse, offers special problems also.[2] The amount of imitation and parody of other authors is considerable; the style moves from serious and elaborate discussion of literature to the humorous vernacular conversations of Trimalchio and his circle. And these are set within the basic narrative framework which is the generally terse, swift-moving Latinity of Encolpius. The complex problem of the prose style thus takes us to the very heart of the work.

Before discussing this major obstacle for the translator, it might be well to turn at once to the question of Petronius' verse insertions.

The verse of the *Satyricon* is of course dramatic *vers d'occasion* and, as such, subject to the exigencies of his plot. As a result, one cannot expect too much – nor does one get it. Petronius, on the evidence of the verse insertions and certain fragments, is not a great poet, despite the claims occasionally made for him. The few poems of merit sometimes included in the Fragments (e.g. LIII and LV in this translation) are not necessarily by Petronius. Some of the discredit must go to his somewhat reactionary critical principles in poetry. Petronius set himself against the mainstream of Latin verse, which was moving towards the wit of Martial and the pointed rhetoric of Juvenal, and is already well established in Latin literature by Nero's time in the works of Lucan. Whatever criticisms may be made of this, a mere traditionalism based on Virgil and Horace would be powerless to deflect or revolutionize contemporary poetic diction. Petronius' metrical virtuosity is, however, clear: he employs a variety of metres – choliambics, elegiacs, dactylic hexameters, hendecasyllables, etc. This, too, has to be taken into account by the translator, if only to the extent of trying to reproduce

1. For a general discussion of the MSS, see A. Wegner, 'The Sources of the Petronius Poems in the *Catalecta* of Scaliger', *Transactions of the American Philological Association* 64 (1933) 67 ff.

2. For a lengthier discussion of the problems and of other translations of Petronius in English, see J P Sullivan, 'On Translating Petronius', in D. R. Dudley (ed.), *Neronians and Flavians: Silver Latin* I (London, 1972), pp. 155 ff.

this *variety* of verse forms. Patently it is impossible to offer readable versions which reproduce these metres in English and so, like most translators, I have chosen whatever type of verse seemed suitable for the subject. It is, of course, an easy matter to ensure that the verse is bad where the Latin verse was intended to be bad. For the most part, I have attempted to be readable and therefore I have felt free to use modern methods of verse translation, notably *vers libre*, modern rhythm and diction, and pastiche. In various ways, like so many translators, I am indebted to Ezra Pound, and most notably to his *Homage to Sextus Propertius*, although this translation is in no way intended to be a 'creative translation' like that work. Pound's own epic, like Lucan's, is unfinished; and I have adopted the *Cantos* as my model for translating the long poem on the Civil War (c. 119 ff.). The original was meant to be a rehandling of the *Pharsalia* of Lucan, a sort of epic parody. There is no contemporary verse translation of Lucan to play host to the parasite, as the first three books of Lucan played host to Petronius' poem; in any case, the whole rationale of the exercise is too remote to us, so I have concentrated on making this strange fragment of an epic comprehensible to the modern reader by retaining the subject matter and making the style reminiscent at least of the style of the *Cantos*. With the poem on the Capture of Troy in c. 89, written in iambic *senarii* and reminiscent in other ways of the basic metre of Seneca's tragedies, I found the language too jejune to resort to Elizabethan iambic pentameters and so I tried to bring out its alliterative qualities by borrowing something from translations of Anglo-Saxon material, such as Pound's *The Seafarer*.

This opportunistic method of translation, however, will not serve for the prose sections. It would be gratifying if the translator, like Matthew Arnold with Homer, could simply point to a limited number of qualities in the original which he had tried to bring out in the translation. But this is difficult to do except sketchily: in the main, Petronius is deliberately and deceptively simple over large stretches of his work; there is, furthermore, a pervasive irony which leaves the reader often in some doubt as to the author's intentions at certain points (how serious, for example, is the opening discussion of contemporary rhetoric?). Above all, there is the constant auctorial sophistication which makes itself felt through the pretentious or unsuccessful sophistication which the narrator Encolpius tries to adopt. In few works do we have such a separation of the author and his narrative vehicle.

As I stated earlier, Petronius strikes us as peculiarly modern. As T. S. Eliot said of Donne:

> There are two ways in which we may find a poet [or writer] to be modern: he may have made a statement which is true everywhere and for all time ... or there may be an accidental relationship between his mind and our own.[1]

That 'accidental relationship' may only be partial, even if it accounts for the unexpected popularity in certain ages of a particular classic (as with the epigrammatist Martial in the Elizabethan and Jacobean periods). But there are certain indisputably Roman qualities of humour and fantasy, particularly in the episodes at Croton, which leave behind the cynical and sophisticated realism of the '*Cena Trimalchionis*', with which we feel completely at home.

These qualities are difficult to reproduce and, indeed, their interplay and local appearance in the work are sometimes hard to pin down exactly. I have tried in the preceding section to lay out my critical estimate of the work as a whole, but sometimes the particular intentions of a given section are problematic and it would be a dangerous optimism to force too blatant or crude an interpretation simply for the sake of brightness in translation. In Petronius above all the tone is of supreme importance, more important even than the range and flexibility of his style and subject matter, for it is through the tone that the objectivity and irony of the author make themselves apparent.

*Textual Changes:
2.7 *regula eloquentia* (Haase) for *eloquentiae regula* ... ; 2.8 *ad summam, quis postea* (Scriverius); 4.2 *propellunt* (*L*); 4.3 *artifici* (Müller) for *Attico*; 5.v.16 *vox Romana* (Sullivan) for *exonerata*; 6.1 *mutus* (Nisbet) for *motus*; 7.2 ⟨*subsequi coepi*⟩; 7.3 *inter vetulas* (Sullivan) for *inter titulos*; 9.9 *meridiana* (Walsh) for *de ruina*; 14.3 *quo cicer lupinosque* (Gronovius) for [*sicel*] ⟨*quo*⟩ *lupinos*[*que quibus*]; 14.5 *operto* (Wouweren) *capite quae* ... *steterat* for *aperto capite* [*quae* ... *steterat*]; 14.7 *nostram* [*scilicet*] *uno ore deridebant* (Ehlers) for *nostram scilicet de more ridebant*; 14.8 *repente* (Müller) for +*pene*+; 15.5 *constitutum* ⟨*diem*⟩ (Sullivan); 21.2 ⟨*cerasino*⟩ (Sullivan); 24.3 *num* (Rose) for *nostram*; 26.7 [*id* ... *cenae*] (Bücheler); 28.4 [*Trimalchione*] (Bücheler); 30.1 *multa iam* (Sullivan) for +*multaciam*+; 30.9 [*dextros*] (Fraenkel); 34.4 *habere* (Braswell) for *esse*; 35.4 ⟨*scorpionem*⟩ *marinum* (Sullivan); [*pisciculum*] (Gaselee); *oculatam* (Sullivan) for *oclopetam*; 37.7 *vides tantum auri* (Sullivan) for *t.a.v.*; 38.12 *liberti sceleratique*

(Sullivan) for *liberti scelerati, qui; aves ⟨aeno⟩ coctos* (Sullivan) *pisces lepores* (Reiske) for *aves ... cocos pistores*; 40.5 [qui altilia laceraverat] (Sullivan); 41.9 *invitare ⟨nos ipsi ad bibendum⟩ [convivarum sermones]* (Fuchs) for *invitare ... convivarum sermones*; 41.10 *pateram acinae* (Walsh) for + *pataracina* +; 42.2 [*cotidie*] (Rose); 42.4 ⟨*illae*⟩ (Ernout) for ⟨*muscae*⟩ (Heinsius); 44.5 *si simila siligine inferior esset* (Sullivan) for *similia sicilia interiores et*; 44.9 *assi* [*a dis*] (Gurlitt) for *assi a dis* (Burman); 48.7 ⟨*oculum*⟩ *pollice* (Sullivan) for *pollicem poricino*; 52.2 *mihi patronus meus* (*patav.*, Bücheler) for *patrono* ⟨*meo*⟩ *rex Minos*; 54.1 ⟨*in lectum*⟩ (Sullivan); 57.1 [*is ipse ... discumbebat*] (Fraenkel); 58.7 *nenias* (Scheffer) for *menias*; 61.2 *suavis* for *suavius* (*H*); 62.4 *stelas* (Reiske) ... *stellas* (*H*) for *stellas* (*H*) ... *stelas* (Bücheler); 62.9 *matutinas* (Heinsius) for + *matavitatau* +; 62.10 *in larem* (Sullivan) for *in larvam*; 62.14 *viderint qui de hoc aliae opinionis sint* (Sullivan) for *viderint alii quid de hoc exopinissent* (Bücheler); 66.7 [*catillum concacatum*] (Sullivan) *tum pax! pelamides* (Heinsius) for *pax Palamedes* (*H*); 67.7 *babaecalae* (Heinsius) for *barcalae* (*H*); 72.7 [⟨*et*⟩ *qui etiam pictum timueram canem*] (Müller); 73.5 [*quod Trimalchioni* ⟨*tem*⟩*perabatur*] (Sullivan); 74.13 *non meminit, sed de machina* (Bücheler) for *non meminit?* [*se*] *de machina*; 76.10 *libertos* for ⟨*per*⟩ *libertos*; 77.4 *casa adhuc* (*patav.*, Corbett) for + *cusuc* +; *sursum* (Sullivan) for *susum*; [*hospitium hospites* ⟨*C*⟩ *capit*] (Sullivan); 79.6 *tabernarius* [*Trimalchionis*] (Delz) for *tabellarius Trimalchionis*; 79.7 *ex vehiculis* (Sullivan) *rediens* (Müller) for + *vehiculis dives* +; *per eandem fenestram* (Sullivan) for + *per eandem ... terram* +; 83.4 [*etiam pictorum*] (Fraenkel); 83.5 [*fabulae quoque*] (Fraenkel); 87.1 [*id est ut pateretur satis fieri sibi*] (Haley); 88.7 *cultissima* (*R*) for + *consultissima* +; 89.1.31 *mari* (Tollius) for *minor*; 90.1 ⟨*quidam*⟩ (Sullivan); 94.10 *ante* ⟨*me*⟩ (Nodot); 99.5 *properandum* (*t^m*) for + *propudium* +; 100.6 [*subter constratum*] (Fraenkel); 100.7 [*exulem*] (Müller); 101.7 ⟨*nos*⟩ *naufragio imponimus* (Sullivan) for *naufragium imponimus*; 102.15 [*quod ... infigitur*] (Stephanie West); 104.4 *ut ... expiaret* (Nisbet) for *ut ... expiavit*; 111.2 [*Graeco more*] (Fraenkel); 114.3 *volturnus flabat* (Sullivan) for +... *ventus dabat* +; 114.3 (*vis maris*) *manifesta* (Sullivan) for *manifesta; 117.1 *divitationis* (Gruterus) for *divinationis*; 118.3 *inanitatem* (Sullivan) for *vanitatem*; *fabulas sententiarum tormento* (Sullivan) for *fabulosum sententiarum* + *tormentum* +; 119 l.9 *Ephyreiacum* (Heinsius) for *Ephyre* + *cum* +; l.11 *crustas* (Scaliger) for + *accusatius* +; l.79 *magistra* (Sullivan from *C L E* 255.3); ll.110, 113 (Bouchier) for 110, 115 (Suringar); ll.220–237 for ll.220, 223–237, 221–232 (Ehlers); 124.3 [*exaggerata verborum volubilitate*] (Stöcker); 125.1 *saepius* (Bücheler) for + *suis* +; 126.15 *curvaturam* (Fraenkel) for + *scripturam* +; 133.3 l.4 *septifluus* (*L*); 134 ⟨*peream*⟩ *nisi* (Sullivan) for ... *nisi*; 134.12 ll.11–16 (del. Wehle, def. Sullivan); 135.4 *clavum* ⟨*ligneum*⟩ ... *camella* [*lignea*] (Sullivan); 136.12 *pensationem* (Bücheler) for *pensionem*; 137.10 [*sine medulla*] *ventosas ... plenas* [*integro fructu*]; 135.8 l.17 *Battiadae vatis* (Pius) *miranda tradidit arte* (Müller) for + *Bachineas veteres mirando* +

tradidit aevo; 139.4 [*querellam*] (Fraenkel); 140.2 ⟨*coepit, cui soli posset*⟩ *credere* (Sullivan); 140.5 *pygica* (Sullivan) for *Aphrodisiaca* (Bücheler) or *pigiciaca* (MSS).

ACKNOWLEDGEMENTS

For this second edition I would like to express my general scholarly debts to Dr Konrad Müller, P. T. Eden and Gareth Schmeling; their help in various ways was invaluable. Allan Kershaw kindly read the proofs. Elizabeth Frech worked wonders in processing a complicated and much corrected original and saved me from many mechanical errors. To the late Betty Radice, once editor of this series, I am deeply indebted for her constant encouragement, advice and friendship.

THE SATYRICON

PUTEOLI

1. [*Encolpius*] . . . 'Our professors of rhetoric are hag-ridden in the same way, surely, when they shout "I got these wounds fighting for your freedom! This eye I lost for you. Give me a hand to lead me to my children. I am hamstrung, my legs can't support me." We could put up with even this stuff if it were a royal road to eloquence. But the only result of these pompous subjects and this empty thunder of platitudes, is that when young speakers first enter public life they think they have been landed on another planet. I'm sure the reason such young nitwits are produced in our schools is because they have no contact with anything of any use in everyday life. All they get is pirates standing on the beach, dangling manacles, tyrants writing orders for sons to cut off their fathers' heads, oracles advising the sacrifice of three or more virgins during a plague – a mass of cloying verbiage: every word, every move just so much poppycock.[1]

2. 'People fed on this kind of thing have as much chance of learning sense as dishwashers have of smelling clean. If you'll pardon my saying so, you are mainly responsible for ruining good speaking. Your smooth and empty sound effects provided a few laughs, and as a result you took the guts out of real oratory, and that was the end of it. Young men were not tied down to rhetorical exercises when it was Sophocles or Euripides who developed the proper language for them.[2] Academic pedants had not addled their wits when Pindar and the nine lyric poets shrank away from the Homeric style.[3] And apart from the poets I can cite, I certainly cannot see Plato or Demosthenes going in for this sort of training.[4] The elevated, what one might call the *pure* style, is not full of purple patches and bombast: it is lifted up by its intrinsic beauty. It is not so long since that long-winded spouting of yours travelled from Asia to Athens and its foul pestilential breath infected every youthful ambition.[5] Once the rules go, eloquence loses vigour and voice. In short, who since then has

equalled Thucydides or Hyperides in their reputation?[6] Why, not even poetry has shown a spark of life. All forms of literature have been faced with the same diet and lost their chance of a ripe old age. Even the great art of painting has met the same fate since the unscrupulous Egyptians invented short cuts for painters.'[7]

3. Agamemnon, after his own sweat in the classroom, did not allow me to hold forth in the colonnade for longer than himself.

'Young man,' he said, 'your opinions show extraordinary good taste and you have that extremely rare quality – a love for intellectual merit. So I shall not baffle you with any expertise. *Of course* teachers are making immoral concessions with these exercises – they *have* to humour the madmen. If the speeches they make do not win the approval of their young pupils, as Cicero says, "they will be the only ones in their schools".[8] When spongers in drama[9] are trying to get a dinner out of their rich friends, their main object is to find out what they would most like to hear. The only way they will get what they are after is by captivating their audience. It is the same with a tutor of rhetoric. Like a fisherman he has to bait his hook with what he knows the little fishes will rise for; otherwise he's left on the rocks without a hope of their biting.

4. 'What's the answer? It's the parents you should blame. They won't allow their children to be properly controlled. In the first place they sacrifice everything, even their hopes, to their ambition. Then in their over-eagerness they direct these immature intellects into public life. They will tell you that there is no mightier power than oratory and they dress up their boys as orators while they are still drawing their first breath. If only parents would not rush them through their studies! Then young men who are prepared to work would cultivate their minds with solid reading, mould their characters with sensible advice, and prune their words with a stylish pen. They would wait and listen before they tried themselves and they would realize that an adolescent taste is quite worthless. Then the noble art of oratory would have its true weight and dignity. Boys today are frivolous in school; young men are laughing-stocks in public life; and, the greatest shame of all, even when they are old they refuse to give up the mistakes they learnt earlier.

'But just to show you how I am not above a bit of low-level improvisation in the manner of Lucilius,[10] I'll throw you off a few lines expressing my feelings:

5.   'Ambition to fulfil the austere demands of Art,
            The mind moving to mighty themes,
            Demands discipline, simplicity –
            The heart like a mirror.
            Disdain the haughty seats of the mighty,
            Humiliating invitations to drunken dinners,
            The addictions, the low pleasures,
            The mental spark guttering out with the wine.
            Refuse theatre seats,
            Refuse to sell applause
            To the actor's empty mouthings.

            'Under smiling battlements of martial Athens,
            In Lacedaemonian colony,
            By the home of the Sirens even,
            No matter:
            Verse for your early education,
            Deep joyful draughts from Homeric springs
            Then full of the Socratic circle,
            Let your reins ride loose,
            Rattle the great sword of Demosthenes.
            Now our Roman squadrons swirl round you like a flood,
            Roman voices mixed with Greek music,
            Changing their savour.
            Then leave the forum behind
            And let your reading advance
            Till the power of Fortune
            Makes itself heard in History,
            Clearly and distinctly
                               in running cadences.
            War's epic sounds should feast your ears;
            Shudder at the mighty orotundities
            Of Cicero,
                     who never lost a cause.
            This is the right armour of genius –
            "Drink deep or taste not the Pierian spring."
            Only then pour out your heart.'[11]

6. As I was listening carefully to him, I did not notice Ascyltus
slipping away . . . and while I paced about silenced by this flood of ideas,
a huge crowd of students entered the colonnade. Apparently they had

been listening to an extempore declamation by whoever it was who had followed Agamemnon on the speaker's platform. While the young men were laughing at the points he made and picking to pieces the arrangement of the whole speech, I took the opportunity to slip away and started off hastily after Ascyltus. But I was not paying much attention to the way I went, and I had no idea where our lodging was.[12] Whichever direction I took, I came back to the same spot. Finally, worn out with running and dripping with sweat, I went up to an old woman selling fresh vegetables.

7. 'Excuse me, mother,' I began, 'I don't suppose you know where I'm staying, do you?'

She was amused by my naïve politeness.

'Why shouldn't I know?' she said. She got to her feet and set off in front of me. I thought she was uncanny, and followed her. And then, as we reached an out of the way place, the kind old lady threw back a patchwork curtain and said to me:

'This is where you must be staying.'

I was just telling her I did not recognize the place, when I caught sight of some naked old prostitutes and some customers furtively prowling up and down in the middle of them. Slowly, in fact too late, I realized I had been taken to a brothel. Cursing the old woman's tricks I covered my face and began hurrying right through the whore-house to the other side. At the very door who should bump into me but Ascyltus. Like me he was worn out and practically dead. It looked as though he had been brought there by the same little old woman. Greeting him with a smile, I asked what he was doing in this dreadful place.

8. He wiped away the sweat with his hands and said:

'If only you knew what has been happening to me!'

'What happened?' I said.

'I wandered through the whole town,' he began faintly, 'and I couldn't find where I'd left our lodgings. Then a respectable-looking gentleman came up and very kindly offered to show me the way. He went down various pitch-dark turnings and brought me to this place. Then he offered me money and began making improper suggestions. The woman had already got her money for the cubicle and he had his hand on me. If I'd not been stronger than he was, I should have been in a bad way.'

*

In fact, everyone all around seemed to have been drinking aphrodisiac . . . [13]

*

Our combined forces made short work of the nuisance.

*

9. As though through a fog I caught sight of Giton standing at the side of the street. I rushed to the spot . . .

*

I asked my little friend if he'd prepared anything for supper. At this the boy sat down on the bed and wiped away a stream of tears with his thumb. I was deeply shocked at the dear boy's state and urged him to tell me what had happened. Slowly and reluctantly – in fact I had to plead and threaten alternately – he told me:

'It was your dear friend, the fellow you go round with, anyway. Just a few minutes ago he ran into my room and began wanting to rape me. When I shouted for help, he took out his big knife and said: "If you're playing Lucretia, I'm your Tarquin." '[14]

When I heard this, I shook my fist in front of Ascyltus's face: 'What have you to say, you round-heeled tart! Your very breath stinks from your dirty ways!'

Ascyltus pretended to be horrified. Then he made an even braver show with his own fists and shouted far more loudly than I had: 'Shut up, you dirty gladiator! You could even perform for the noonday crowd. Shut up, you stab-in-the-dark! Even when you were at your best, you never managed to lay a decent woman. I was very close to you in the park, wasn't I? Just the way the boy is now in the hotel.'

'Didn't you slip away,' I said, 'when we were talking to the professor?'

10. 'Well, you fool, what did you expect me to do, when I was dying of hunger? I should have been listening to his rubbishy platitudes, I suppose! They're not worth a row of broken bottles – he'd be interpreting his dreams next! *You* are a hell of a sight worse – I didn't praise his poetry to cadge a dinner.' . . . So our mortifying quarrel collapsed in roars of laughter, and we turned peaceably to other things . . .

*

But his treachery stuck in my mind, so I said: 'Look, Ascyltus, I see it is impossible for us to get along together. I suggest we divide our belongings and try to make a living by ourselves. You've got an education and so have I. I don't want to interfere with your earnings, so I'll offer some other line. Otherwise every day hundreds of different things will set us at each other's throat, and get us talked about all over town.'

Ascyltus had no objection. He merely said: 'Look, at the moment we've accepted an invitation to dinner as teachers – don't let us waste the evening. Tomorrow, if this is the way you want it, I'll find myself lodgings and someone else to live with.'

'It's just wasting time,' I pointed out, 'why put off our pleasures?' My desires were responsible for the suddenness of this split. For some time now I had been wanting to be rid of my troublesome chaperon and be back on my old footing with dear little Giton.

*

11. I looked everywhere in the town before going back to our little room. At last I enjoyed his kisses without looking for excuses. I held the boy in my arms as though I'd never let him go. I had what I wanted and anyone would have envied me my luck. But we were still in the middle of this when Ascyltus came quietly to the door, forcibly shattered the bolts, and found me playing around with Giton. He filled the little room with laughter and applause. He rolled me out of the cloak I was lying in and said:

'What *were* you up to, my pious old friend? What's this? Are you just setting up house under the blanket?'

And he did not limit himself to words, but taking the strap from his bag he began to lay into me in earnest, punctuating it with insolent remarks like – 'So, that's your idea of fair shares, is it?'

*

12. It was getting dark when we came into the square.[15] We noticed a lot of things on sale, none of them of any great worth – in fact, the sort of things whose dubious origin is best concealed in the dim light of evening. As we ourselves had brought along the cloak we had stolen we decided to take advantage of this excellent opportunity by unfolding just the edge of it in a corner. Our hope was that the high-quality cloth would attract some chance buyer. It was not long before a countryman, who looked familiar to me, approached with a young woman companion and started examining the garment very closely. Ascyltus in turn shot a keen glance at the tunic dangling over the shoulders of the country customer. Suddenly he almost fainted and couldn't open his mouth. Even I lost some of my composure when I looked at the man. He appeared to be the very person who had found our tunic in the wilds. Clearly it was the same man. Ascyltus however was afraid to trust his

eyes in case he did something rash. So he began by moving closer like a customer, then he pulled the edge of it from his shoulders and ran his fingers carefully over it.

13. What a marvellous stroke of luck! The countryman's prying hands so far hadn't even tried the stitches. He was selling it like something a tramp had picked up and wanted to be rid of. As soon as Ascyltus realized our hoard was intact and the man selling it was a person of no account, he took me a little way out of the crowd and said: 'Do you know, dearie, the loot I was so cross about has returned to us. That's our tunic and it looks as if it's still stuffed with the money – it hasn't been touched. Now what are we going to do? How are we going to claim our property?'

I was delighted not only because I saw the loot but because I was now fortunately free of that loathsome suspicion. I opposed anything underhand: legal methods were clearly our best line of attack. If he would not hand someone else's property over to its rightful owner, then it would come to a court-order.

14. Ascyltus on the other hand was afraid of the law. 'Who knows us in this place?' he said. 'And who is going to believe what we say? I'm all for buying it now we have spotted it, even though it is our own. I would rather lay out a small sum to recover valuable property than go to court, where the outcome is very uncertain.

> 'What use are laws where money is king,
> Where poverty's helpless and can't win a thing?
> Even Cynics[16] who sneer are rarely averse
> To selling their scruples to fill up their purse.
> There's no justice at law – it's the bidding that counts
> And the job of the judge is to fix the amounts.'

However, apart from a solitary coin which we had intended to spend on chickpeas and lupines, we had no ready money. So in case the loot should slip from our fingers in the meantime, we decided to knock down the price of the cloak and take a small loss for the sake of the greater gain. As soon as we unwrapped our merchandise, the woman standing by the countryman with her head uncovered carefully examined the marks on it, grabbed the edge with both hands and screamed at the top of her voice: 'Stop the thieves!' As for us, we became panicky in case we looked at a loss, so we began hanging on to the torn and shabby tunic, and shouting just as indignantly that they had *our* property. But the two sides were in a very different position, and the dealers who had come milling round at the noise unanimously ridiculed our malicious charge. For they saw one side demanding back an extremely valuable cloak, while the other side was after a tattered old thing, which it would be a waste to use good patches on. Then Ascyltus suddenly managed to quieten their laughter and get himself heard:

15. 'Everyone obviously likes his own things best. Let them give us back our tunic and take back their cloak.' Although the countryman and the woman were in favour of this exchange, the night watchmen however had been summoned and they insisted that both articles should be deposited with them, so that a magistrate could look into the matter the next day. It was not merely the articles themselves that were at stake, but there was the quite different question that both parties were suspected of theft. It was agreed that persons to take charge of them should be appointed, and one of the dealers, a bald-headed man with a very knobbly forehead, who sometimes handled court cases too, had pounced on the cloak and was swearing that the exhibit would appear next day. Of course it was obvious what he was after: once the cloak was left with him it could be sat on by these thieves, and we would be too afraid of the legal proceedings to turn up at the appointed time. This was clearly what we wanted too, and by a piece of luck both sides got what they were after. The countryman, infuriated by our claim that this patched old thing was an exhibit, threw the tunic into Ascyltus' face. So much for our particular charge – the cloak was the only thing in dispute and we were told to hand it over into custody . . .

The prize was ours again, we thought, and we went hastily back to our lodgings. Once behind locked doors we began ridiculing the sharp wits of our accusers and the dealers equally – it was very smart of them to give us our money back.

> Anything on which I'm set
> Should be hard to get;
> A ready-made victory
> Never appeals to me.

*

16. But we had only just filled ourselves up with the supper Giton had kindly prepared, when there came a knock, bold enough to make the door rattle. We turned pale and asked who it was. 'Open up and you'll find out!' came the answer. As we were speaking, the bolt gave way of

its own accord and fell to the floor: the door was suddenly thrown open to admit the caller. It was a woman, however, with her head covered.

'Did you think you could make a fool out of me?' she said. 'I am Quartilla's personal maid and it was her religious service you burst into at the entrance to the grotto. And now she is on her way to the inn and she wants to talk to you. Don't get upset. She won't blame you or punish you for your mistake. She is really wondering what in heaven brought such charming young men to her part of the world.'

17. We had not yet said a word nor had we agreed one way or the other, when the lady herself entered with one young girl in attendance. She sat on my bed and cried for a long time. Not even this drew comment from us: in complete amazement we waited for this tearful show of grief to end. When the calculated storm of tears subsided, she uncovered her haughty head and wrung her hands till the joints cracked.

'What monstrous conduct is this?' she said. 'Where did you pick up such unimaginably criminal ways? Heaven knows, I'm deeply sorry for you. You see, it's absolutely forbidden – no one has ever seen it without being punished. Especially as our part of the world is so full of watchful powers that it's easier to run across a god than a man. And don't think I have come here for vengeance. I am more worried about your youth than my own injuries. Through sheer ignorance – I still believe this – you have committed an unforgivable sin. That very night I was full of unrest: I shivered with such a deadly chill I was afraid it was an attack of fever. And so I looked for a cure in my dreams and I was instructed to get hold of you and alleviate the onset of the attack by a subtle method which was revealed to me. But it is not the remedy I am so greatly concerned about; there is a deeper pain raging in my heart, which has brought me almost to death's door – I am afraid that in your youthful recklessness you will be driven to make public what you saw in the shrine of Priapus[17] and let out to all and sundry the workings of the divine mind. So I throw myself at your feet and I solemnly beg you not to make our nocturnal rites into a laughing-stock, and not to spread abroad the secrets of centuries – secrets which hardly three people know about.'

18. After this moving plea, she again burst into tears; shaking with great sobs, she pressed her face and bosom to my bed. I was torn between sympathy and fear. I told her not to be upset and not to worry on either score. No one would spread abroad her holy mysteries; and if

the god had revealed to her some further cure for her fever, then we were ready to assist the divine providence, no matter what the risk to us.

This promise made her more cheerful; she covered me with kisses, her tears turned to laughter, and she slowly smoothed the hair falling over my ears.

'I'll make a truce with you,' she said. 'I withdraw my charges. Though if you had not been amenable about this medicine I'm after, there was a mob waiting for tomorrow to avenge my injuries and vindicate my honour.

> 'Scorn only scoundrels; Pride makes its own laws:
> My passion is to go as I please.
> Even the wise man fights when offended,
> And the victor is merciful, when the fight's ended.'

Then she clapped her hands and suddenly burst into such a peal of laughter that she frightened us. The maid who had arrived before her did the same, and so did the little girl who had come in with her.

19. The whole place rang with their theatrical laughter, while we were still wondering why this sudden change of mood and looking now at each other, now at the women.[18]

*

'Therefore, I have given orders that not a living soul is to be allowed into this inn today, so I can get from you the remedy for my fever without any interruption.'

As Quartilla said this, Ascyltus looked stupefied for a moment. I personally went colder than winter in Gaul, and I couldn't get a word out. But our numbers banished any fears I felt of worse to come. After all, they were three weak women, if they wanted to try anything; on the other side, we, if nothing else, were of the male sex, but, in addition, we were certainly less hampered by clothes. In fact, I had already decided how we were to be matched, so that if it came to a fight, I would face Quartilla myself, Ascyltus the maid, and Giton the girl.

*

Then all our courage absolutely vanished. Our surprise was complete. Our eyes began to close at the prospect of certain death.

*

20. 'Please lady,' I said, 'if you have anything worse in store for us, get

it over quickly. Surely we have not committed such a great crime that we deserve to be tortured before we die.'

*

The maid, whose name was Psyche, carefully spread a blanket on the hard floor.

*

She tried to excite me, but the thing was cold with the chill of a thousand deaths.

*

Ascyltus had pulled his cloak over his head; obviously he had been warned it was dangerous to pry into other people's secrets.

*

The maid produced two thongs from her pocket and tied our hands and feet with them.

*

Our amusing conversation was just tailing off, when Ascyltus asked: 'Hey, don't I deserve a drink?' Summoned by my laughter, the maid clapped her hands and said: 'I did put it down near you, young man. But have you drunk all that medicine by yourself?' 'Really?' said Quartilla. 'Has Encolpius drunk all the aphrodisiac there was?'

*

Her sides shook with her charming laughter.

*

In the end even Giton joined in the joke, particularly when the little girl threw her arms round his neck and kissed him an incredible number of times without any struggle.

*

21. In our desperation we wanted to shout for help, but there was no one to come to our aid. Besides, whenever I wanted to call for assistance from outside, Psyche stuck a hairpin into my cheeks. Meanwhile the girl was stifling Ascyltus with a cosmetic brush which she had soaked in aphrodisiac.

Finally, up came a male prostitute, dressed in myrtle-green shaggy felt, which was tucked up under a cherry-red belt. He pulled the cheeks of our bottoms apart and banged us, then he slobbered vile, greasy kisses on us, until Quartilla, carrying a whalebone rod, with her skirts up round her, ordered an end to our torments.

*

Both of us swore a solemn oath that such a dreadful secret would die with us.

*

Some training attendants came in, who rubbed us with the appropriate oil and made us feel better. Somehow or other we threw off our weariness, put on dinner clothes again and were taken into the next room. There were three couches ready and every other refinement of gracious living magnificently laid out. We took our places as we were told, and beginning with some wonderful hors d'oeuvres we were then practically swimming in Falernian wine. After helping ourselves to a long series of dishes, we were beginning to fall asleep, when Quartilla said, 'Do you actually intend to go to sleep when you know the whole night has to be a vigil in honour of our guardian Priapus?'

*

22. Ascyltus, overcome by all he had gone through, was dropping off to sleep, so the maid he had rudely rejected took some soot and rubbed it all down his face and, without his feeling it in his drunken stupor, she painted his sides and shoulders with wine lees. I was also worn out, and I had already dropped into the lightest possible doze. In fact, the whole household, indoors and out, had done the same. Some were lying here and there round the feet of the guests, others were propped up against the walls, a number stayed in the doorway with their heads together. The lamps were running out of oil too, and were casting only a dim dying light, when two Syrians on the prowl entered the dining-room. They began quarrelling greedily among the silver and smashed a decanter they'd taken. Over went the table, silver and all, and a cup which was knocked off from quite a height cracked the maid's skull as she drooped over the couch. The blow made her scream and she gave the thieves away, as well as waking up some of the drunken guests. The would-be thieves, realizing they were trapped, dropped side by side next to a couch – you'd have thought it was pre-arranged – and began snoring as though they had been asleep for hours.

By now the butler likewise was awake and poured oil into the guttering lamps. The slaves, after rubbing their eyes a bit, had returned to their duties, and a girl with cymbals entered and the clash of brass woke everyone up.

23. The party began again and Quartilla called us back to drinking, the songs of the girl with the cymbals adding to the conviviality.

*

In comes a male prostitute, a low creature and just what you would expect in that house. Cracking his fingers with a groan, he blurted out some verses of this sort:

> 'Pansy boys, come out to play,
> You've been cropped the Delian way:
> Young or old, there's room for you
> And room for roaming fingers too!
> Hips and bottoms, waggle away,
> Pansy boys, come out to play.'

Once his lines were finished, he slobbered a filthy kiss on me. Then he even came on the couch and tried with all his strength to pull my clothes off. He kept working away fruitlessly at my crotch. Trickles of acacia-pomade ran down his sweaty forehead and there was so much powder in the wrinkles on his cheeks that he looked like a peeling wall in a thunderstorm.

24. I couldn't keep my tears back any longer, I was in the depths of misery.

'Please lady,' I said, 'surely you ordered me a night-cap.'[19] She clapped her hands daintily and said: 'Oh, you clever man. You're bubbling over with native wit. Well now, hadn't you discovered that a pansy could be a night-cap?'

Then in case my comrade-in-arms should get off too lightly, I said: 'Be fair. Is Ascyltus the only one at the table to have a holiday?'

'Really,' said Quartilla, 'let Ascyltus have a night-cap too.'

Thereupon the prostitute swapped horses and after making the changeover to my companion, pounded him with his buttocks and kisses.

Giton was standing there while all this went on and splitting his sides laughing. And Quartilla, catching sight of him, asked with great interest whose was the boy. I replied that he was my boy-friend.

'Then why hasn't he given me a kiss?' said Quartilla. And calling him to her, she pressed her lips to his. Then she slipped her hand into his clothes and felt his immature little tool. 'Tomorrow this will serve nicely as hors d'oeuvre to tempt my appetite,' she said. 'For the present, I don't want any ordinary stuffing after such a nice cod-piece.'

25. As she said this, Psyche came and laughingly whispered something in her ear:

'Yes, yes,' said Quartilla, 'thanks for reminding me. It's such an excellent opportunity, why shouldn't our little Pannychis lose her virginity?'

The girl was brought forward immediately – quite a pretty thing who appeared no more than seven years old. Everyone applauded and called for a wedding. I was quite taken aback by this and insisted that Giton, who was a very nice boy, was not up to this loose behaviour, nor was the girl old enough to take on the heavy duties of womanhood.

'Really?' said Quartilla. 'Is she any younger than I was when I had my first man? Juno's curse on me, if I can even remember being a virgin. When I was a child I played dirty games with boys of the same age, then as the years went by, I turned to bigger boys till I reached maturity. I even think this is the origin of the proverb – if you carry the calf, you can carry the bull.'

So in case my little friend should suffer worse treatment out of my sight, I got up to help with the ceremony.[20]

26. Psyche had already put a veil round the girl's head and old Nightcap was leading the way with a torch. The tipsy women, still clapping, had formed a long line and had fixed up a bridal chamber with draperies in the appropriate sacrilegious way. Then Quartilla, highly excited by all this playful obscenity, rose to her feet herself, seized Giton, and dragged him into the chamber.

It was obvious the boy had not struggled and even the girl had not been dismayed or scared by the mention of marriage. And so, when they were shut in and lying down, we sat round the chamber doorway, and Quartilla was one of the first to put an inquisitive eye to a crack she had naughtily opened, and spy on their childish play with prurient eagerness.[21] Her insistent hand pulled me down also to have a similar look, and since our faces were pressed together as we watched, whenever she could spare a moment, she would move her lips close to mine in passing and bruise me with sly kisses.

*

We threw ourselves on our beds and spent the rest of the night without fear.

DINNER WITH TRIMALCHIO

BOOK XV

26. The next day but one finally arrived [, and that meant the prospect of a free dinner]. But we were so knocked about that we wanted to run rather than rest. We were mournfully discussing how to avoid the approaching storm, when one of Agamemnon's slaves broke in on our frantic debate.

'Here,' said he, 'don't you know who's your host today? It's Trimalchio – he's terribly elegant . . . He has a clock in the dining-room and a trumpeter all dressed up to tell him how much longer he's got to live.'

This made us forget all our troubles. We dressed carefully and told Giton, who was very kindly acting as our servant, to attend us at the baths.

27. We did not take our clothes off but began wandering around, or rather exchanging jokes while circulating among the little groups. Suddenly we saw a bald old man in a reddish shirt, playing ball with some long-haired boys. It was not so much the boys that made us watch, although they alone were worth the trouble, but the old gentleman himself. He was taking his exercise in slippers and throwing a green ball around. But he didn't pick it up if it touched the ground; instead there was a slave holding a bagful, and he supplied them to the players. We noticed other novelties. Two eunuchs stood around at different points: one of them carried a silver pissing bottle, the other counted the balls, not those flying from hand to hand according to the rules, but those that fell to the ground. We were still admiring these elegant arrangements when Menelaus hurried up to us.

'This is the man you'll be dining with,' he said. 'In fact, you are now watching the beginning of the dinner.'

No sooner had Menelaus spoken than Trimalchio snapped his fingers. At the signal the eunuch brought up the pissing bottle for him, while he went on playing. With the weight off his bladder, he demanded water for his hands, splashed a few drops on his fingers and wiped them on a boy's head.

28. It would take too long to pick out isolated incidents. Anyway, we entered the baths where we began sweating at once and we went immediately into the cold water. Trimalchio had been smothered in perfume and was already being rubbed down, not with linen towels, but with bath-robes of the finest wool. As this was going on, three masseurs sat drinking Falernian in front of him. Through quarrelling they spilled most of it and Trimalchio said they were drinking his health.[1] Wrapped in thick scarlet felt he was put into a litter. Four couriers with lots of medals went in front, as well as a go-kart in which his favourite boy was riding – a wizened, bleary-eyed youngster, uglier than his master. As he was carried off, a musician with a tiny set of pipes took his place by Trimalchio's head and whispered a tune in his ear the whole way.

We followed on, choking with amazement by now, and arrived at the door with Agamemnon at our side. On the door-post a notice was fastened which read:

ANY SLAVE LEAVING THE HOUSE WITHOUT HIS MASTER'S
PERMISSION WILL RECEIVE ONE HUNDRED LASHES

Just at the entrance stood the hall-porter, dressed in a green uniform with a belt of cherry red. He was shelling peas into a silver basin. Over the doorway hung – of all things – a golden cage from which a spotted magpie greeted visitors.

29. As I was gaping at all this, I almost fell over backwards and broke a leg. There, on the left as one entered, not far from the porter's cubbyhole, was a huge dog with a chain round its neck. It was painted on the wall[2] and over it, in big capitals, was written:

BEWARE OF THE DOG

My colleagues laughed at me, but when I got my breath back I went on to examine the whole wall. There was a mural[3] of a slave market, price-tags and all. Then Trimalchio himself, holding a wand of Mercury and being led into Rome by Minerva. After this a picture of how he learned accounting and, finally, how he became a steward. The painstaking artist had drawn it all in great detail with descriptions underneath. Just where the colonnade ended Mercury hauled him up by the chin and rushed him to a high platform. Fortune with her horn of plenty and the three Fates spinning their golden threads were there in attendance.

I also noticed in the colonnade a company of runners practising with their trainer. In one corner was a large cabinet, which served as a shrine for some silver statues of the household deities with a marble figure of Venus and an impressive gold casket in which, they told me, the master's first beard was preserved.[4]

I began asking the porter what were the pictures they had in the middle.

'The Iliad, the Odyssey,' he said, 'and the gladiatorial show given by Laenas.'

30. Time did not allow us to look at many things there ... by now we had reached the dining-room, at the entrance to which sat a treasurer going over the accounts. There was one feature I particularly admired: on the door-posts were fixed rods and axes[5] tapering off at their lowest point into something like the bronze beak of a ship. On it was the inscription:

PRESENTED TO C. POMPEIUS TRIMALCHIO
PRIEST OF THE AUGUSTAN COLLEGE[6]
BY HIS STEWARD CINNAMUS

Beneath this same inscription a fixture with twin lamps dangled from the ceiling and two notices, one on each door-post. One of them, if my memory is correct, had written on it:

30 AND 31 DECEMBER
OUR GAIUS
IS OUT TO DINNER[7]

The other displayed representations of the moon's phases and the seven heavenly bodies. Lucky and unlucky days were marked with different coloured studs.[8]

Having had enough of these interesting things, we attempted to go in, but one of the slaves shouted: 'Right foot first!' Naturally we hesitated a moment in case one of us should cross the threshold the wrong way. But just as we were all stepping forward, a slave with his back bare flung himself at our feet and began pleading with us to get him off a flogging. He was in trouble for nothing very serious, he told us – the steward's clothes, hardly worth ten sesterces, had been stolen from him at the baths. Back went our feet, and we appealed to the steward, who was counting out gold pieces in the office, to let the man off.

He lifted his head haughtily: 'It is not so much the actual loss that annoys me,' he said, 'it's the wretch's carelessness. They were my dinner clothes he lost. A client had presented them to me on my birthday – genuine Tyrian purple, of course; however they had been laundered once. So what does it matter? He's all yours.'

31. We were very much obliged to him for this favour; and when we did enter the dining-room, that same slave whose cause we had pleaded ran up to us and, to our utter confusion, covered us with kisses and thanked us for our kindness.

'And what's more,' he said, 'you'll know right away who it is you have been so kind to. "The master's wine is the waiter's gift."'

Finally we took our places.[9] Boys from Alexandria poured iced water over our hands. Others followed them and attended to our feet, removing any hangnails with great skill. But they were not quiet even during this troublesome operation: they sang away at their work. I wanted to find out if the whole staff were singers, so I asked for a drink. In a flash a boy was there, singing in a shrill voice while he attended to me – and anyone else who asked for something did the same. It was more like a musical comedy than a respectable dinner party.

Some extremely elegant hors d'oeuvres were served at this point – by now everyone had taken his place with the exception of Trimalchio, for whom, strangely enough, the place at the top was reserved. The dishes for the first course[10] included an ass of Corinthian bronze with two panniers, white olives on one side and black on the other. Over the ass were two pieces of plate, with Trimalchio's name and the weight of the silver inscribed on the rims. There were some small iron frames shaped like bridges supporting dormice sprinkled with honey and poppy seed. There were steaming hot sausages too, on a silver gridiron with damsons and pomegranate seeds underneath.

32. We were in the middle of these elegant dishes when Trimalchio himself was carried in to the sound of music and set down on a pile of tightly stuffed cushions. The sight of him drew an astonished laugh from the guests.[11] His cropped head stuck out from a scarlet coat; his neck was well muffled up and he had put round it a napkin with a broad purple stripe and tassels dangling here and there. On the little finger of his left hand he wore a heavy gilt ring and a smaller one on the last joint

of the next finger. This I thought was solid gold, but actually it was studded with little iron stars. And to show off even more of his jewellery, he had his right arm bare and set off by a gold armlet and an ivory circlet fastened with a gleaming metal plate.

33. After picking his teeth with a silver toothpick, he began: 'My friends, I wasn't keen to come into the dining-room yet. But if I stayed away any more, I would have kept you back, so I've deprived myself of all my little pleasures for you. However, you'll allow me to finish my game.'

A boy was at his heels with a board of terebinth wood with glass squares, and I noticed the very last word in luxury – instead of white and black pieces he had gold and silver coins.[12] While he was swearing away like a trooper over his game and we were still on the hors d'oeuvres, a tray was brought in with a basket on it. There sat a wooden hen, its wings spread round it the way hens are when they are broody. Two slaves hurried up and as the orchestra played a tune they began searching through the straw and dug out peahens' eggs, which they distributed to the guests.

Trimalchio turned to look at this little scene and said: 'My friends, I gave orders for that bird to sit on some peahens' eggs. I hope to goodness they are not starting to hatch. However, let's try them and see if they are still soft.'

We took up our spoons (weighing at least half a pound each) and cracked the eggs, which were made of rich pastry. To tell the truth, I nearly threw away my share, as the chicken seemed already formed. But I heard a guest who was an old hand say: 'There should be something good here.' So I searched the shell with my fingers and found the plumpest little figpecker, all covered with yolk and seasoned with pepper.

34. At this point Trimalchio became tired of his game and demanded that all the previous dishes be brought to him. He gave permission in a loud voice for any of us to have another glass of mead if we wanted it. Suddenly there was a crash from the orchestra and a troop of waiters – still singing – snatched away the hors d'oeuvres. However in the confusion one of the side-dishes happened to fall and a slave picked it up from the floor. Trimalchio noticed this, had the boy's ears boxed and told him to throw it down again. A cleaner came in with a broom and began to sweep up the silver plate along with the rest of the rubbish. Two long-haired Ethiopians followed him, carrying small skin bags like

those used by the men who scatter the sand in the amphitheatre, and they poured wine over our hands – no one ever offered us water.

Our host was complimented on these elegant arrangements. 'Mars loves a fair fight,' he replied. 'That is why I gave orders for each guest to have his own table. At the same time these smelly slaves won't crowd so.'

Carefully sealed wine bottles were immediately brought, their necks labelled:

FALERNIAN

CONSUL OPIMIUS

ONE HUNDRED YEARS OLD[13]

While we were examining the labels, Trimalchio clapped his hands and said with a sigh:

'Wine has a longer life than us poor folks. So let's wet our whistles. Wine is life. I'm giving you real Opimian. I didn't put out such good stuff yesterday, though the company was much better class.'

Naturally we drank and missed no opportunity of admiring his elegant hospitality. In the middle of this a slave brought in a silver skeleton,[14] put together in such a way that its joints and backbone could be pulled out and twisted in all directions. After he had flung it about on the table once or twice, its flexible joints falling into various postures, Trimalchio recited:

> 'O woe, woe, man is only a dot:
> Hell drags us off and that is the lot;
> So let us live a little space,
> At least while we can feed our face.'

35. After our applause the next course was brought in. Actually it was not as grand as we expected, but it was so novel that everyone stared. It was a deep circular tray with the twelve signs of the Zodiac arranged round the edge. Over each of them the chef had placed some appropriate dainty suggested by the subject.[15] Over Aries the Ram, chickpeas; over Taurus the Bull, a beefsteak; over the Heavenly Twins, testicles and kidneys; over Cancer the Crab, a garland; over Leo the Lion, an African fig; over Virgo the Virgin, a young sow's udder; over Libra the Scales, a balance with a cheesecake in one pan and a pastry in the other; over Scorpio, a sea scorpion; over Sagittarius the Archer, a sea bream with eyespots; over Capricorn, a lobster; over Aquarius the

Water-Carrier, a goose; over Pisces the Fishes, two mullets. In the centre was a piece of grassy turf bearing a honeycomb. A young Egyptian slave carried around bread in a silver oven ... and in a sickening voice he mangled a song from the show *The Asafoetida Man*.

36. As we started rather reluctantly on this inferior fare, Trimalchio said:

'Let's eat, if you don't mind. This is the sauce of all order.' As he spoke, four dancers hurtled forward in time to the music and removed the upper part of the great dish, revealing underneath plump fowls, sows' udders, and a hare with wings fixed to his middle to look like Pegasus.[16] We also noticed four figures of Marsyas[17] with little skin bottles, which let a peppery fish-sauce go running over some fish, which seemed to be swimming in a little channel. We all joined in the servants' applause and amid some laughter we helped ourselves to these quite exquisite things.

Trimalchio was every bit as happy as we were with this sort of trick: 'Carve 'er!' he cried. Up came the man with the carving knife and, with his hands moving in time to the orchestra, he sliced up the victuals like a charioteer battling to the sound of organ music. And still Trimalchio went on saying insistently: 'Carve 'er, Carver!'

I suspected this repetition was connected with some witticism, and I went so far as to ask the man on my left what it meant. He had watched this sort of game quite often and said:

'You see the fellow doing the carving – he's called Carver. So whenever he says "Carver!" he's calling out his name and his orders.'

37. I couldn't face any more food. Instead I turned to this man to find out as much as I could. I began pestering him for gossip and information – who was the woman running round the place?

'Trimalchio's wife,' he told me, 'Fortunata is her name and she counts her money by the sackful. And before, before, what was she? You'll pardon me saying so, but you wouldn't of touched a bit of bread from her hand. Nowadays – and who knows how or why – she's in heaven, and she's absolutely everything to Trimalchio. In fact, if she tells him at high noon it's dark, he'll believe her. He doesn't know himself how much he's got, he's so loaded – but this bitch looks after everything; she's even in places you wouldn't think of. She's dry, sober and full of ideas – you see all that gold! – but she's got a rough tongue and she's a real magpie when she gets her feet up. If she likes you, she likes you – if she doesn't like you, she doesn't like you.

'The old boy himself now, he's got estates it'd take a kite to fly over – he's worth millions of millions.[18] There's more silver plate lying in his porter's cubbyhole than any other man owns altogether. As for his servants – boy, oh boy! I honestly don't think there's one in ten knows his own master. In fact he could knock any of these smart boys into a cocked hat.

38. 'And don't you think he buys anything, either. Everything is home-grown: wool, citrus, pepper. If you ask for hen's milk, you'll get it. In fact, there was a time when the wool he'd got wasn't good enough for him, so he brought some rams from Tarentum and banged them into his sheep. To get home-grown Attic honey, he ordered some bees from Athens – the Greek strain improved his own bees a bit at the same time.

'And here's something more – this last few days he wrote off for mushroom spores from India. Why, he hasn't a single mule that wasn't sired by a wild ass. You see all these cushions – every one of them has either purple or scarlet stuffing. There's happiness for you!

'But mind you, don't look down on the other freedmen here. They're dripping with the stuff. You see that man on the very bottom couch. At present he's got eight hundred thousand of his own. He started out with nothing. It's not long since he was humping wood on his own back. They say – I don't know myself, I've heard it – they say he stole a hobgoblin's cap and found its treasure. I don't begrudge anyone what God has given him. Besides, he can still feel his master's slap and wants to give himself a good time. For instance, the other day he put up a notice which said:

> GAIUS POMPEIUS DIOGENES
> IS MOVING TO HIS HOUSE AND
> WILL LET THE ROOM OVER
> HIS SHOP FROM 1 JULY

'Now that fellow in the freedman's place – look how well off he was once! I'm not blaming him – he had a million in his hands, but he slipped badly. I don't think he can call his hair his own. Yet I'd swear it wasn't his fault: there's not a better man alive. Some freedmen and crooks pocketed everything he had. One thing you can be sure of – you have partners and your pot never boils, and once things take a turn for the worse, friends get out from underneath. What a respectable business he had and look at him now! He was an undertaker. He used to eat like a king – boars roasted in their skins, elaborate pastry, braised game birds, as well as fish and hares. More wine was spilt under the table than another man keeps in his cellar. He wasn't a man, he was an absolute dream! When things were looking black, he didn't want his creditors to think he was bankrupt, so he put up notice of an auction like this:

'GAIUS JULIUS PROCULUS
AUCTION OF SURPLUS STOCK'

Trimalchio interrupted these pleasant reminiscences. The dish had already been removed and the convivial guests had begun to concentrate on the drink and general conversation. Leaning on his elbow, Trimalchio said:

39. 'Now you're supposed to be enjoying the wine. Fishes have to swim. I ask you, do you think I'm just content with that course you saw in the bottom of the dish? "Is this like the Ulysses you know?"[19] Well then, we've got to display some culture at our dinner. My patron – God rest his bones! – wanted me to hold up my head in any company. There's nothing new to me, as that there dish proves.[20] Look now, these here heavens, as there are twelve gods living in 'em, changes into that many shapes. First it becomes the Ram. So whoever is born under that sign has a lot of herds, a lot of wool, a hard head as well, a brassy front and a sharp horn. Most scholars are born under this sign, and most muttonheads as well.'

We applauded the wit of our astrologer and he went on:

'Then the whole heavens turns into the little old Bull. So bullheaded folk are born then, and cow-herds and those who find their own feed. Under the Heavenly Twins on the other hand – pairs-in-hand, yokes of oxen, people with big ballocks and people who do it both ways. I was born under the Crab, so I have a lot of legs to stand on and a lot of property on land and sea, because the Crab takes both in his stride. And that's why I put nothing over him earlier, so as not to upset my horoscope. Under Leo are born greedy and bossy people. Under the Virgin, effeminates, runaways and candidates for the chain-gang. Under the Scales, butchers, perfume-sellers and anyone who weighs things up. Under Scorpio poisoners and murderers. Under Sagittarius are born cross-eyed people who look at the vegetables and take the bacon. Under Capricorn, people in trouble who sprout horns through their

worries. Under the Water-Carrier, bartenders and jugheads. Under the
Fishes, fish-fryers and people who spout in public.

'So the starry sky turns round like a millstone, always bringing some
trouble, and men being born or dying.

'Now as for what you see in the middle, the piece of grass and on the
grass the honeycomb, I don't do anything without a reason – it's Mother
Earth in the middle, round like an egg, with all good things inside her
like a honeycomb.'

40. 'Oh, clever!' we all cried, raising our hands to the ceiling and
swearing that Hipparchus and Aratus[21] couldn't compete with *him*.

Then the servants came up and laid across the couches embroidered
coverlets showing nets, hunters carrying broad spears, and all the
paraphernalia of hunting. We were still wondering which way to look
when a tremendous clamour arose outside the dining-room, and –
surprise! – Spartan hounds began dashing everywhere, even round the
table. Behind them came a great dish and on it lay a wild boar of the
largest possible size, and, what is more, wearing a freedman's cap on
its head. From its tusks dangled two baskets woven from palm leaves,
one full of fresh Syrian dates, the other of dried Theban dates. Little
piglets made of cake were all round as though at its dugs, suggesting it
was a brood sow now being served. These were actually gifts to take
home. Surprisingly the man who took his place to cut up the boar was
not our old friend Carver but a huge bearded fellow, wearing leggings
and a damask hunting coat. He pulled out a hunting knife and made a
great stab at the boar's side and, as he struck, out flew a flock of thrushes.
But there were fowlers all ready with their limed reeds, who caught
them as soon as they began flying round the room.

Trimalchio gave orders for each guest to have his own bird, then
added: 'And have a look at the delicious acorns our pig in the wood has
been eating.'

Young slaves promptly went to the baskets and gave the guests their
share of the two kinds of date.

41. As this was going on, I kept quiet, turning over a lot of ideas as
to why the boar had come in with a freedman's cap on it. After working
through all sorts of wild fancies, I ventured to put to my experienced
neighbour the question I was racking my brains with. He of course
replied:

'Even the man waiting on you could explain this obvious point – it's
not puzzling at all, it's quite simple. The boar here was pressed into

service for the last course yesterday, but the guests let it go. So today it returns to the feast as a freedman.'

I damned my own stupidity and asked no more questions in case I looked like someone who had never dined in decent company.

As we were talking, a handsome youth with a garland of vine-leaves and ivy round his head, pretending to be Bacchus the Reveller, then Bacchus the Deliverer and Bacchus the Inspirer, carried grapes round in a basket, all the time giving us a recital of his master's lyrics in a high-pitched voice. At the sound, Trimalchio called out, 'Dionysus, now be Bacchus the Liberat...'

The lad pulled the freedman's cap off the boar and stuck it on his head. Then Trimalchio commented:

'Now you won't deny my claim to be the liberated sort.'[22] We applauded his joke and kissed the boy hard as he went round.

After this course Trimalchio got up and went to the toilet. Free of his domineering presence, we began to help ourselves to more drinks. Dama started off by calling for a cup of the grape.

'The day's nothin',' he said. 'It's night 'fore y'can turn around. So the best thing's get out of bed and go straight to dinner. Lovely cold weather we've had too. M'bath hardly thawed me out. Still, a hot drink's as good as an overcoat. I've been throwin' it back neat, and you can see I'm tight – the wine's gone to m'head.'

Seleucus took up the ball in the conversation:

42. 'Me now,' he said, 'I don't have a bath every day. It's like getting rubbed with fuller's earth, havin' a bath. The water bites into you, and your heart begins to melt. But when I've knocked back a hot glass of wine and honey, "Go fuck yourself," I say to the cold weather. Mind you, I couldn't have a bath – I was at a funeral today. Poor old Chrysanthus has just given up the ghost – nice man he was! It was only the other day he stopped me in the street. I still seem to hear his voice. Dear, dear! We're just so many walking bags of wind. We're worse than flies – at least they have got some strength in them, but we're no more than empty bubbles.

'And yet he had been on an extremely strict diet? For five days he didn't take a drop of water or a crumb of bread into his mouth. But he's gone to join the majority. The doctors finished him – well, hard luck, more like. After all, a doctor is just to put your mind at rest. Still, he got a good send-off – he had a bier, and all beautifully draped. His mourners – several of his slaves were left their freedom – did him proud, even though his widow was a bit mean with her tears. And yet he had been extremely good to her! But women as a sex are real vultures. It's no good doing them a favour, you might as well throw it down a well. An old passion is just an ulcer.'

43. He was being a bore and Phileros said loudly:

'Let's think of the living. He's got what he deserved. He lived an honest life and he died an honest death. What has he got to complain about? He started out in life with just a penny and he was ready to pick up less than that from a muck-heap, even if he had to use his teeth. So whatever he put a finger to swelled up like a honeycomb. I honestly think he left a solid hundred thousand and he had the lot in hard cash. But I'll be honest about it, since I'm a bit of a cynic: he had a foul mouth and too much lip. He wasn't a man, he was just trouble.

'Now his brother was a brave lad, a real friend to his friends, always ready with a helping hand or a decent meal.

'Chrysanthus had bad luck at first, but the first vintage set him on his feet. He fixed his own price when he sold the wine. And what properly kept his head above water was a legacy he came in for, when he pocketed more than was left to him. And the blockhead, when he had a quarrel with his brother, cut him out of his will in favour of some sod we've never heard of. You're leaving a lot behind when you leave your own flesh and blood. But he kept listening to his slaves and they really fixed him. It's never right to believe all you're told, especially for a businessman. But it's true he enjoyed himself while he lived. You got it, you keep it. He was certainly Fortune's favourite – lead turned to gold in his hand. Mind you, it's easy when everything runs smoothly.

'And how old do you think he was? Seventy or more! But he was hard as a horn and carried his age well. His hair was black as a raven's wing. I knew the man for ages and ages and he was still an old lecher. I honestly don't think he left the dog alone. What's more, he liked little boys – he could turn his hand to anything. Well, I don't blame him – after all, he couldn't take anything else with him.'

44. This was Phileros, then Ganymedes said:

'You're all talking about things that don't concern heaven or earth. Meanwhile, no one gives a damn the way we're hit by the corn situation. Honest to god, I couldn't get hold of a mouthful of bread today. And look how there's still no rain. It's been absolute starvation for a whole year now. To hell with the food officers! They're in with the bakers – "You be nice to me and I'll be nice to you." So the little man suffers, while those grinders of the poor never stop celebrating. Oh, if only we still had the sort of men I found here when I first arrived from Asia. Like lions they were. That was the life! Come one, come all! If plain flour was inferior to the very finest, they'd thrash those bogeymen till they thought God Almighty was after them.

'I remember Safinius – he used to live by the old arch then; I was a boy at the time. He wasn't a man, he was all pepper. He used to scorch the ground wherever he went. But he was dead straight – don't let him down and he wouldn't let you down. You'd be ready to play *morra*[23] with him in the dark. But on the city council, how he used to wade into some of them – no beating about the bush, straight from the shoulder! And when he was in court, his voice got louder and louder like a trumpet. He never sweated or spat – I think he'd been through the oven all right. And very affable he was when you met him, calling everyone by name just like one of us. Naturally at the time corn was dirt cheap. You could buy a penny loaf that two of you couldn't get through. Today – I've seen bigger bull's-eyes.

'Ah me! It's getting worse every day. This place is going down like a calf's tail. But why do we have a third-rate food officer who wouldn't lose a penny to save our lives? He sits at home laughing and rakes in more money a day than anyone else's whole fortune. I happen to know he's just made a thousand in gold. But if we had any balls at all, he wouldn't be feeling so pleased with himself. People today are lions at home and foxes outside.

'Take me. I've already sold the rags off my back for food and if this shortage continues I'll be selling my bit of a house. What's going to happen to this place if neither god nor man will help us? As I hope to go home tonight, I'm sure all this is heaven's doing.

'Nobody believes in heaven, see, nobody fasts, nobody gives a damn for the Almighty. No, people only bow their heads to count their money. In the old days high-class ladies used to climb up the hill barefoot, their hair loose and their hearts pure, and ask God for rain. And he'd send it down in bucketfuls right away – it was then or never – and everyone went home like drowned rats. Since we've given up religion the gods nowadays keep their feet wrapped up in wool. The fields just lie . . .'

45. 'Please, please,' broke in Echion the rag-merchant, 'be a bit more cheerful. "First it's one thing, then another," as the yokel said when he lost his spotted pig. What we haven't got today, we'll have tomorrow. That's the way life goes. Believe me, you couldn't name a better country,

if it had the people. As things are, I admit, it's having a hard time, but it isn't the only place. We mustn't be soft. The sky don't get no nearer wherever you are. If you were somewhere else, you'd be talking about the pigs walking round ready-roasted back here.

'And another thing, we'll be having a holiday with a three-day show that's the best ever – and not just a hack troupe of gladiators but freedmen for the most part. My old friend Titus has a big heart and a hot head. Maybe this, maybe that, but something at all events. I'm a close friend of his and he's no way wishy-washy. He'll give us cold steel, no quarter and the slaughterhouse right in the middle where all the stands can see it. And he's got the wherewithal – he was left thirty million when his poor father died. Even if he spent four hundred thousand, his pocket won't feel it and he'll go down in history. He's got some real desperadoes already, and a woman who fights in a chariot, and Glyco's steward who was caught having fun with his mistress. You'll see quite a quarrel in the crowd between jealous husbands and romantic lovers. But that half-pint Glyco threw his steward to the lions, which is just giving himself away. How is it the servant's fault when he's forced into it? It's that old pisspot who really deserves to be tossed by a bull. But if you can't beat the ass you beat the saddle. But how did Glyco imagine that poisonous daughter of Hermogenes would ever turn out well? The old man could cut the claws off a flying kite, and a snake don't hatch old rope. Glyco – well, Glyco's got his. He's branded for as long as he lives and only the grave will get rid of it. But everyone pays for their sins.

'But I can almost smell the dinner Mammaea is going to give us – two denarii apiece for me and the family. If he really does it, he'll make off with all Norbanus's votes, I tell you he'll win at a canter. After all, what good has Norbanus done us? He put on some half-pint gladiators, so done in already that they'd have dropped if you blew at them. I've seen beast fighters[24] give a better performance. As for the horsemen killed, he got them off a lamp – they ran round like cocks in a backyard. One was just a cart-horse, the other couldn't stand up, and the reserve was just one corpse instead of another – he was practically hamstrung. One boy did have a bit of spirit – he was in Thracian armour,[25] and even he didn't show any initiative. In fact, they were all flogged afterwards, there were so many shouts of "Give 'em what for!" from the crowd. Pure cowards, that's all.

' "Well, I've put on a show for you," he says. "And I'm clapping you," says I. "Reckon it up – I'm giving more than I got. So we're quits."'

46. 'Hey, Agamemnon! I suppose you're saying "What is that bore going on and on about?" It's because a good talker like you don't talk. You're a cut above us, and so you laugh at what us poor people say. We all know you're off your head with all that reading. But never mind! Will I get you some day to come down to my place in the country and have a look at our little cottage? We'll find something to eat – a chicken; some eggs. It'll be nice, even though the weather this year has ruined everything. Anyway, we'll find enough to fill our bellies.

'And by now my little lad is growing up to be a student of yours. He can divide by four already. If he stays well, you'll have him ready to do anything for you. In his spare time, he won't take his head out of his exercise book. He's clever and there's good stuff in him, even if he is crazy about birds. Only yesterday I killed his three goldfinches and told him a weasel ate them. But he's found some other silly hobbies, and he's having a fine time painting. Still, he's already well ahead with his Greek, and he's starting to take to his Latin, though his tutor is too pleased with himself and unreliable. He's well-educated but doesn't want to work. There is another one too, not so trained but he is conscientious – he teaches the boy more than he knows himself. In fact, he even makes a habit of coming around on holidays, and whatever you give him, he's happy.

'Anyway, I've just bought the boy some law books, as I want him to pick up some legal training for home use. There's a living in that sort of thing. He's done enough dabbling in poetry and such like. If he objects, I've decided he'll learn a trade – barber, auctioneer, or at least a barrister – something he can't lose till he dies. Well, yesterday I gave it to him straight: "Believe me, my lad, any studying you do will be for your own good. You see Phileros the lawyer – if he hadn't studied, he'd be starving today. It's not so long since he was humping round stuff to sell on his back. Now he can even look Norbanus in the face. An education is an investment, and a proper profession never goes dead on you."'

47. This was the sort of chatter flying round when Trimalchio came in, dabbed his forehead and washed his hands in perfume. There was a very short pause, then he said:

'Excuse me, dear people, my inside has not been answering the call for several days now. The doctors are puzzled. But some pomegranate rind and resin in vinegar has done me good. But I hope now it will be back on its good behaviour. Otherwise my stomach rumbles like a bull. So if any of you wants to go out, there's no need for him to be embarrassed. None of us was born solid. I think there's nothing so tormenting as holding yourself in. This is the one thing even God Almighty can't object to. Yes, laugh, Fortunata, but you generally keep me up all night with this sort of thing.

'Anyway, I don't object to people doing what suits them even in the middle of dinner – and the doctors forbid you to hold yourself in. Even if it's a longer business, everything is there just outside – water, bowls, and all the other little comforts. Believe me, if the wind goes to your brain it starts flooding your whole body too. I've known a lot of people die from this because they wouldn't be honest with themselves.'

We thanked him for being so generous and considerate and promptly proceeded to bury our amusement in our glasses. Up to this point we'd not realized we were only half-way up the hill, as you might say.

The orchestra played, the tables were cleared, and then three white pigs were brought into the dining-room, all decked out in muzzles and bells. The first, the master of ceremonies announced, was two years old, the second three, and the third six. I was under the impression that some acrobats were on their way in and the pigs were going to do some tricks, the way they do in street shows. But Trimalchio dispelled this impression by asking:

'Which of these would you like for the next course? Any clodhopper can do you a barnyard cock or a stew and trifles like that, but my cooks are used to boiling whole calves.'

He immediately sent for the chef and without waiting for us to choose he told him to kill the oldest pig.

He then said to the man in a loud voice:

'Which division are you from?'

When he replied he was from number forty, Trimalchio asked:

'Were you bought or were you born here?'

'Neither,' said the chef, 'I was left to you in Pansa's will.'

'Well, then,' said Trimalchio, 'see you serve it up carefully – otherwise I'll have you thrown into the messengers' division.'

So the chef, duly reminded of his master's magnificence, went back to his kitchen, the next course leading the way.

48. Trimalchio looked round at us with a gentle smile: 'If you don't like the wine, I'll have it changed. It is up to you to do it justice. I don't

buy it, thank heaven. In fact, whatever wine really tickles your palate this evening, it comes from an estate of mine which as yet I haven't seen. It's said to join my estates at Tarracina and Tarentum.[26] What I'd like to do now is add Sicily to my little bit of land, so that when I want to go to Africa, I could sail there without leaving my own property.

'But tell me, Agamemnon, what was your debate about today? Even though I don't go in for the law, still I've picked up enough education for home consumption. And don't you think I turn my nose up at studying, because I have two libraries, one Greek, one Latin. So tell us, just as a favour, what was the topic of your debate?'

Agamemnon was just beginning, 'A poor man and a rich man were enemies...' when Trimalchio said: 'What's a poor man?' 'Oh, witty!' said Agamemnon, and then told us about some fictitious case or other. Like lightning Trimalchio said: 'If this happened, it's not a fictitious case – if it didn't happen, then it's nothing at all.'

We greeted this witticism and several more like it with the greatest enthusiasm.

'Tell me, my dear Agamemnon,' continued Trimalchio, 'do you remember the twelve labours of Hercules and the story of Ulysses – how the Cyclops tore out his eye with his thumb.[27] I used to read about them in Homer, when I was a boy. In fact, I actually saw with my own eyes the Sybil at Cumae[28] dangling in a bottle, and when the children asked her in Greek: "What do you want, Sybil?" she used to answer: "I want to die." '

49. He was still droning on when a server carrying the massive pig was put on the table. We started to express our amazement at this speed and swear that not even an ordinary rooster could be cooked so quickly, the more so as the pig seemed far larger than it had appeared before. Trimalchio looked closer and closer at it, and then shouted:

'What's this? Isn't this pig gutted? I'm damn certain it isn't. Call the chef in here, go on, call him!'

The downcast chef stood by the table and said he'd forgotten it.

'What, you forgot!' shouted Trimalchio. 'You'd think he'd only left out the pepper and cumin. Strip him!'

In a second the chef was stripped and standing miserably between two guards. But everyone began pleading for him:

'It does tend to happen,' they said, 'do let him off, please. If he does it any more, none of us will stand up for him again.'

Personally, given my tough and ruthless temperament, I couldn't contain myself. I leaned over and whispered in Agamemnon's ear:

'This has surely got to be the worst slave in the world. Could anyone forget to clean a pig? I damn well wouldn't let him off if he forgot to clean a fish.'

But not Trimalchio. His face relaxed into a smile.

'Well,' he said, 'since you have such a bad memory, gut it in front of us.'

The chef recovered his shirt, took up a knife and with a nervous hand cut open the pig's belly left and right. Suddenly, as the slits widened with the pressure, out poured sausages and blood-puddings.

50. The staff applauded this trick and gave a concerted cheer – 'Hurray for Gaius!' The chef of course was rewarded with a drink and a silver crown, and was also given a drinking cup on a tray of Corinthian bronze. Seeing Agamemnon staring hard at this cup, Trimalchio remarked:

'I'm the only person in the world with genuine Corinthian.'

I was expecting him with his usual conceit to claim that all his plate came from Corinth. But he was not as bad as that.

'Perhaps you're wondering,' he went on, 'how I'm the only one with genuine Corinthian dishes. The simple reason is that the manufacturer I buy from is named Corinth – but what can be Corinthian, if you don't have a Corinth to get it from?

'You mustn't take me for a fool: I know very well where Corinthian metalwork first came from. When Troy was captured that crafty snake Hannibal piled all the bronze, silver and gold statues into one heap and set them on fire, and they were all melted to a bronze alloy. The metalworkers took this solid mass and made plates, dishes, and statuettes out of it. That is how Corinthian plate was born, not really one thing or another, but everything in one.[29] You won't mind my saying so, but I prefer glass – that's got no taste at all. If only it didn't break, I'd prefer it to gold, but it's cheap stuff the way it is.

51. 'Mind you, there was a craftsman once who made a glass bowl that didn't break. So he got an audience with the Emperor,[30] taking his present with him ... Then he made Caesar hand it back to him and dropped it on the floor. The Emperor couldn't have been more shaken. The man picked the bowl off the ground – it had been dinted like a bronze dish – took a hammer from his pocket and easily got the bowl

as good as new. After this performance he thought he'd be in high heaven, especially when the Emperor said to him:

'"Is there anyone else who knows this process for making glass?"

'But now see what happens. When the man said no, the Emperor had his head cut off, the reason being that if it was made public, gold would have been as cheap as muck.

52. 'Now I'm very keen on silver. I have some three-gallon bumpers more or less... how Cassandra killed her sons,[31] and the boys are lying there dead – very lifelike. I have a bowl my patron left to me with Daedalus shutting Niobe in the Trojan Horse. What's more, I have the fights of Hermeros and Petraites on some cups – all good and heavy. No, I wouldn't sell my know-how at any price.'

While he was talking, a young slave dropped a cup. Trimalchio looked in his direction.

'Get out and hang yourself,' he said, 'you're utterly useless.' Immediately the boy's lips trembled and he begged Trimalchio's pardon.

'What are you asking me for?' snapped his master, 'as though I was the trouble! I'm just asking you not to let yourself be such a useless fool.'

In the end however, as a favour to us, he let him off and the boy ran round the table to celebrate... and shouted, 'Out with the water – in with the wine!'

We all showed our appreciation of his amusing wit – especially Agamemnon, who knew how to angle for further invitations. But our admiration went to Trimalchio's head. He drank with even greater cheerfulness and was very nearly drunk by now.

'Doesn't anyone want my dear Fortunata to dance?' he said. 'Honestly, no one dances the *Cordax*[32] better.'

Then he stuck his hands up over his forehead and gave us a personal imitation of the actor Syrus, while all the staff sang in chorus:

'Madeia, Perimadeia.'

In fact, he would have taken the floor, if Fortunata had not whispered in his ear. She must have told him, I suppose, that such low fooling did not suit his dignity. But you never saw anyone so changeable – one minute he would be frightened of Fortunata and the next minute he would be back in character again.

53. What really interrupted his coarse insistence on dancing was his

accountant, who sounded as though he was reading out a copy of the Gazette:

'26 July: Births on the estate at Cumae: male 30, female 40. Wheat threshed and stored: 500,000 pecks. Oxen broken in: 500.

'On the same date: the slave Mithridates crucified[33] for insulting the guardian spirit of our dear Gaius.

'On the same date: Deposits to the strong-room (no further investment possible): 10,000,000 sesterces.

'On the same date: a fire broke out on the estate at Pompeii beginning at the house of Nasta the bailiff.'

'What!' said Trimalchio. 'When was an estate bought for me at Pompeii?'

'Last year,' said the accountant, 'so it hasn't yet come on the books.'

Trimalchio flared up:

'If any land is bought for me and I don't hear of it within six months, I refuse to have it entered on the books.'

The official edicts were read out and the wills of certain gamekeepers. In specific codicils they said they were leaving Trimalchio nothing. Then the names of some bailiffs; the divorce of a freedwoman, the wife of a watchman, on the grounds of adultery with a bath-attendant; the demotion of a hall-porter to a job at Baiae; the prosecution of a steward; and the result of an action between some bedroom attendants.

Finally the acrobats arrived. One was a silly idiot who stood there holding a ladder and made his boy climb up the rungs, give us a song and dance at the top, then jump through blazing hoops, and hold up a large wine-jar with his teeth.

Only Trimalchio was impressed by all this: art wasn't appreciated, he considered, but if there were two things in the world he really liked to watch, they were acrobats and horn-players. All the other shows were not worth a damn.

'As a matter of fact,' he said, 'once I even bought some comic-actors, but I preferred them putting on Atellan farces,[34] and I told my conductor to keep his songs Latin.'

54. Just as he was saying this, the boy tumbled down on Trimalchio's couch. Everyone screamed, the guests as well as the servants – not because they were worried over such an awful person (they would happily have watched his neck being broken) but because it would have been a poor ending to the party if they had to offer their condolences for a comparative stranger. Trimalchio himself groaned heavily and

leaned over his arm as though it were hurt. Doctors raced to the scene, but practically the first one there was Fortunata, hair flying and cup in hand, telling the world what a poor unfortunate thing she was. As for the boy who had fallen, he was already crawling round our feet, begging for mercy. I had a very uneasy feeling that his pleadings might be the prelude to some funny surprise ending, as I still remembered the chef who had forgotten to gut his pig. So I began looking round the dining-room for some machine to appear out of the wall, especially after a servant was beaten for using white instead of purple wool to bandage his master's bruised arm.

Nor were my suspicions far out, because instead of punishment, there came an official announcement from Trimalchio that the boy was free, so that no one could say that such a great figure had been injured by a slave.

55. We all applauded his action and started a desultory conversation about how uncertain life was.

'Well,' says Trimalchio, 'an occasion like this mustn't pass without a suitable record.' He immediately called for his notebook, and without much mental exertion he came out with:

> 'What comes next you never know,
> Lady Luck runs the show,
>   So pass the Falernian, lad.'

This epigram brought the conversation round to poetry and for quite a time the first place among poets was given to Mopsus of Thrace[35] until Trimalchio said:

'Tell me, professor, how would you compare Cicero and Publilius? I think Cicero was the better orator, but Publilius the better man. Now could there be anything finer than this:

> 'Down luxury's maw, Mars' walls now wilt.
> Your palate pens peacocks in plumage of gilt:
> These Babylon birds are plumped under lock
> With the guinea hen and the capon cock.
> That long-legged paragon, winged castanet,
> Summer's lingering lease and winter's regret –
> Even the stork, poor wandering guest,
> Is put in your pot and makes that his nest.
> Why are Indian pearls so dear in your sight?
> So your sluttish wife, draped in the diver's delight,

May open her legs on her lover's divan?
What use are green emeralds, glass ruin of man,
Or carbuncles from Carthage with fire in their flint?
Unless to let goodness gleam out in their glint.
Is it right for a bride to be clad in a cloud
Or wearing a wisp show off bare to the crowd?

56. 'Well now, whose profession do we think is most difficult after literature? I think doctors and bankers. A doctor has to know what people have in their insides and what causes a fever – even though I do hate them terribly the way they put me on a diet of duck. A banker has to spot the brass under the silver. Well, among dumb animals the hardest worked are cattle and sheep. It's thanks to cattle we have bread to eat, and it's thanks to sheep and their wool that we're well dressed. It's a low trick the way we eat mutton and wear woollens. Bees, now, I think are heavenly creatures – they spew honey, though people suppose they get it from heaven. But at the same time they sting, because where there's sweet you'll find bitter there too.'

He was still putting the philosophers out of work when tickets were brought round in a cup and the boy whose job it was read out the presents.[36] '*Rich man's prison* – a silver jug. *Pillow* – a piece of neck came up. *Old man's wit and a sour stick* – dry salt biscuits came up and an apple on a stick. *Lick and spit* got a whip and a knife. *Flies and a fly-trap* was raisins and Attic honey. *Dinner-clothes and city-suit* got a slice of meat and a notebook. *Head and foot* produced a hare and a slipper. *Lights and letters* got a lamprey and some peas.' We laughed for ages. There were hundreds of things like this but they've slipped my mind now.

57. Ascyltus, with his usual lack of restraint, found everything extremely funny, lifting up his hands and laughing till the tears came. Eventually one of Trimalchio's freedman friends flared up at him.

'You with the sheep's eyes,' he said, 'what's so funny? Isn't our host elegant enough for you? You're better off, I suppose, and used to a bigger dinner. Holy guardian here preserve me! If I was sitting by him, I'd stop his bleating! A fine pippin he is to be laughing at other people! Some fly-by-night from god knows where – not worth his own piss. In fact, if I pissed round him, he wouldn't know where to turn.

'By god, it takes a lot to make me boil, but if you're too soft, worms like this only come to the top. Look at him laughing! What's he got to laugh at? Did his father pay cash for him? You're a Roman knight, are you? Well, my father was a king.

' "*Why are you only a freedman?*" did you say? Because I put myself into slavery. I wanted to be a Roman citizen, not a subject with taxes to pay.[37] And today, I hope no one can laugh at the way I live. I'm a man among men, and I walk with my head up. I don't owe anybody a penny – there's never been a court-order out for me. No one's said "*Pay up*" to me in the street.'

'I've bought a bit of land and some tiny pieces of plate. I've twenty bellies to feed, as well as a dog. I bought my old woman's freedom so nobody could wipe his dirty hands on *her* hair. Four thousand I paid for myself. I was elected to the Augustan College and it cost me nothing. I hope when I die I won't have to blush in my coffin.

'But you now, you're such a busybody you don't look behind you. You see a louse on somebody else, but not the fleas on your own back. You're the only one who finds us funny. Look at the professor now – he's an older man than you and we get along with him. But you're still wet from your mother's milk and not up to your ABC yet. Just a crackpot – you're like a piece of wash-leather in soak, softer but no better! You're grander than us – well, have two dinners and two suppers! I'd rather have my good name than any amount of money. When all's said and done, who's ever asked me for money twice? For forty years I slaved but nobody ever knew if I was a slave or a free man. I came to this colony when I was a lad with long hair – the town hall hadn't been built then. But I worked hard to please my master – there was a real gentleman, with more in his little finger-nail than there is in your whole body. And I had people in the house who tried to trip me up one way or another, but still – thanks be to his guardian spirit! – I kept my head above water. These are the prizes in life: being born free is as easy as all get-out. Now what are you gawping at, like a goat in a vetch-field?'

58. At this remark, Giton, who was waiting on me, could not suppress his laughter and let out a filthy guffaw, which did not pass unnoticed by Ascyltus' opponent. He turned his abuse on the boy.

'So!' he said. 'You're amused too, are you, you curly-headed onion? A merry Saturnalia to you! Is it December, I'd like to know?[38] When did *you* pay your liberation tax?[39] ... Look, he doesn't know what to do, the gallow's bird, the crow's meat.

'God's curse on you, and your master too, for not keeping you under control! As sure as I get my bellyful, it's only because of Trimalchio that I don't take it out of you here and now. He's a freedman like myself. We're doing all right, but those good-for-nothings, well – . It's easy to see, like master, like man. I can hardly hold myself back, and I'm not naturally hot-headed – but once I start, I don't give a penny for my own mother.

'All right! I'll see you when we get outside, you rat, you excrescence. I'll knock your master into a cocked hat before I'm an inch taller or shorter. And I won't let you off either, by heaven, even if you scream down God Almighty. Your cheap curls and your no-good master won't be much use to you then – I'll see to that. I'll get my teeth into you all right. Either I'm much mistaken about myself or you won't be laughing at us behind your golden beard. Athena's curse on you and the man who first made you such a forward brat.

'I didn't learn no geometry or criticism and such silly rubbish, but I can read the letters on a notice board and I can do my percentages in metal, weights, and money. In fact, if you like, we'll have a bet. Come on, here's my cash. Now you'll see how your father wasted his money, even though you do know how to make a speech.

'Try this:

> 'Something we all have.
> Long I come, broad I come. What am I?

'I'll give you it: something we all have that runs and doesn't move from its place: something we all have that grows and gets smaller.[40]

'You're running round in circles, you've had enough, like the mouse in the pisspot. So either keep quiet or keep out of the way of your betters – they don't even know you're alive – unless you think I care about your box-wood rings that you swiped from your girl-friend! Lord make me lucky! Let's go into town and borrow some money. You'll soon see they trust this iron one.

'Pah! a drownded fox makes a nice sight, I must say. As I hope to make my pile and die so famous that people swear by my dead body, I'll hound you to death. And he's a nice thing too, the one who taught you all these tricks – a muttonhead, not a master. We learned different. Our teacher used to say: "Are your things in order? Go straight home. No looking around. And be polite to your elders." Nowadays it's all an absolute muck-heap. They turn out nobody worth a penny. I'm like you see me and I thank god for the way I was learnt.'

59. Ascyltus began to answer this abuse, but Trimalchio, highly amused by his friend's fluency, said:

'No slanging matches! Let's all have a nice time. And you, Hermeros, leave the young fellow alone. His blood's a bit hot – you should know better. In things like this, the one who gives in always comes off best. Besides, when you were just a chicken, it was cock-a-doodle too, and you had no more brains yourself. So let's start enjoying ourselves again, that'll be better, and let's watch the recitations from Homer.'

In came the troupe immediately and banged their shields with their spears. Trimalchio sat up on his cushion and while the reciters spouted their Greek lines at one another in their usual impudent way, he read aloud in Latin in a sing-song voice. After a while, he got silence and asked:

'Do you know which scene they were acting? Diomede and Ganymede were the two brothers. Their sister was Helen. Agamemnon carried her off and offered a hind to Diana in her place. So now Homer is describing how the Trojans and Tarentines fought each other. Agamemnon, of course, won and married off his daughter Iphigenia to Achilles. This drove Ajax insane, and in a moment or two he'll explain how it ended.'[41]

As Trimalchio said this, the reciters gave a loud shout, the servants made a lane, and a calf was brought in on a two-hundred pound plate: it was boiled whole and wearing a helmet. Following it came Ajax, slashing at the calf with a drawn sword like a madman. After rhythmically cutting and slicing, he collected the pieces on the point and shared them among the surprised guests.

60. But we were not given long to admire these elegant turns, for all of a sudden, the coffered ceiling began rumbling and the whole dining-room shook. I leapt to my feet in panic, as I was afraid some acrobat was coming down through the roof. The other guests also looked up to see what strange visitation this announced. Would you believe it – the panels opened and suddenly an enormous hoop was let down, with gold crowns and alabaster jars of toilet cream hanging from it. While we were being told to accept these as presents, I looked at the table … Already there was a tray of cakes in position, the centre of which was occupied by a Priapus made of pastry, holding the usual things in his very adequate lap – all kinds of apples and grapes.

Greedily enough, we stretched out our hands to this display, and in a flash a fresh series of jokes restored the general gaiety. Every single cake and every single apple needed only the slightest touch for a cloud of saffron to start pouring out and the irritating vapour to come right in our faces.

Naturally we thought the fish must have some religious significance to be smothered in such an odour of sanctity, so we raised ourselves to a sitting position and cried:

'God save Augustus, the Father of his People!'

All the same, even after this show of respect, some of the guests were snatching the apples – especially me, because I didn't think I was pushing a generous enough share into Giton's pocket.

While all this was going on, three boys in brief white tunics came in. Two of them set down on the table the household deities,[42] which had amulets round their necks; the other, carrying round a bowl of wine, kept shouting: 'God save all here!' . . .

Our host said that one of the gods was called Cobbler, the second Luck, and the third Lucre. There was also a golden image of Trimalchio himself, and as all the others were pressing their lips to it we felt too embarrassed not to do the same.

61. After we had all wished each other health and happiness, Trimalchio looked at Niceros and said:

'You used to be better company at a party. You're keeping very quiet nowadays: you don't say a word – I don't know why. Do me a favour to please me. Tell us about that adventure you had.'

Niceros was delighted by his friend's affable request and said:

'May I never make another penny if I'm not jumping for joy to see you in such form. Well, just for fun – though I'm worried about those schoolteachers there in case they laugh at me. That's up to them. I'll tell it all the same. Anyway, what do I care who laughs at me. It's better to be laughed at than laughed down.'

'*When thus he spake,*' he began this story:

'When I was still a slave, we were living down a narrow street – Gavilla owns the house now – and there as heaven would have it, I fell in love with the wife of Terentius the innkeeper.

'You all used to know Melissa from Tarentum, an absolute peach to look at. But honest to god, it wasn't her body or just sex that made me care for her, it was more because she had such a nice nature. If I asked her for anything, it was never refused. If I had a penny or halfpenny, I gave it to her to look after and she never let me down.

'One day her husband died out at the villa. So I did my best by hook or by crook to get to her. After all, you know, a friend in need is a friend indeed.

62. 'Luckily the master had gone off to Capua to look after some odds and ends. I seized my chance and I talked a guest of ours into walking with me as far as the fifth milestone. He was a soldier as it happened, and as brave as hell. About cock-crow we shag off, and the moon was shining like noontime. We get to where the tombs are and my chap starts making for the grave-stones, while I, singing away, keep going and start counting the stars. Then just as I looked back at my mate, he stripped off and laid all his clothes by the side of the road. My heart was in my mouth, I stood there like a corpse. Anyway, he pissed a ring round his clothes and suddenly turned into a wolf. Don't think I'm joking, I wouldn't tell a lie about this for a fortune. However, as I began to say, after he turned into a wolf, he started howling and rushed off into the woods.

'At first I didn't know where I was, then I went up to collect his clothes – but they'd turned to stone. If ever a man was dead with fright, it was me. But I pulled out my sword, and I fairly slaughtered the early morning shadows till I arrived at my girl's villa.

'I got into the house and I practically gasped my last, the sweat was pouring down my crotch, my eyes were blank and staring – I could hardly get over it. It came as a surprise to my poor Melissa to find I'd walked over so late.

' "If you'd come a bit earlier," she said, "at least you could've helped us. A wolf got into the grounds and tore into all the livestock – it was like a bloody shambles. But he didn't have the last laugh, even though he got away. Our slave here put a spear right through his neck."

'I couldn't close my eyes again after I heard this. But when it was broad daylight I rushed off home like the innkeeper after the robbery. And when I came to the spot where his clothes had turned to stone, I found nothing but bloodstains. However, when I got home, my soldier friend was lying in bed like a great ox with the doctor seeing to his neck. I realized he was a werewolf and afterwards I couldn't have taken a bite of bread in his company, not if you killed me for it. If some people think differently about this, that's up to them. But me – if I'm telling a lie may all your guardian spirits damn me!'

63. Everyone was struck with amazement.

'I wouldn't disbelieve a word,' said Trimalchio. 'Honestly, the way my hair stood on end – because I know Niceros doesn't go in for jokes. He's really reliable and never exaggerates.

'Now I'll tell you a horrible story myself. A real donkey on the roof! When I was still in long hair (you see, I led a very soft life from my boyhood) the master's pet slave died. He was a pearl, honest to god, a beautiful boy, and one of the best. Well, his poor mother was crying over him and the rest of us were deep in depression, when the witches suddenly started howling – you'd think it was a dog after a hare.

'At that time we had a Cappadocian chap, tall and a very brave old thing, quite the strong man – he could lift an angry ox. This fellow rushed outside with a drawn sword, first wrapping his left hand up very carefully, and he stabbed one of the women right through the middle, just about here – may no harm come to where I'm touching! We heard a groan but – naturally I'm not lying – we didn't see the things themselves. Our big fellow, however, once he was back inside, threw himself on his bed. His whole body was black and blue, as though he'd been whipped. The evil hand, you see, had been put on him.

'We closed the door and went back to what we had to do, but as the mother puts her arms round her son's body, she touches it and finds it's only a handful of straw. It had no heart, no inside, no anything. Of course the witches had already stolen the boy and put a straw baby in its place.

'I put it to you, you can't get away from it – there are such things as women with special powers and midnight hags that can turn everything upside down. But that great tall fellow of ours never got his colour back after what happened. In fact, not many days later, he went crazy and died.'

64. Equally thrilled and convinced, we kissed the table and asked the midnight hags to stay at home till we got back from dinner.

By this time, to tell the truth, there seemed to be more lights burning and the whole dining-room seemed different,[43] when Trimalchio said:

'What about you, Plocamus, haven't you a story to entertain us with. You used to have a fine voice for giving recitations with a nice swing and putting songs over – ah me, the good old days are gone.'

'Well,' said Plocamus, 'my galloping days finished after I got gout. Besides, when I was really young I nearly got consumption through singing. How about my dancing? How about my recitations? How about my barber's shop act? When was there anybody so good apart from Apelles himself?'[44]

Putting his hand to his mouth he let out some sort of obscene whistle which he afterwards insisted was Greek.

Trimalchio, after giving us his own imitation of a fanfare of trumpets, looked round for his little pet, whom he called Croesus. The boy, however, a bleary-eyed creature with absolutely filthy teeth, was busy wrapping a green cloth round a disgustingly fat black puppy. He put half a loaf on the couch and was cramming it down the animal's throat while it kept vomiting it back. This business reminded Trimalchio to send out for Scylax, 'protector of the house and the household'.

A hound of enormous size was immediately led in on a chain. A kick from the hall-porter reminded him to lie down and he stretched himself out in front of the table. Trimalchio threw him a piece of white bread, remarking:

'Nobody in the house is more devoted to me.'

The boy, however, annoyed by such a lavish tribute to Scylax, put his own little pup on the floor and encouraged her to hurry up and start a fight. Scylax, naturally following his canine instincts, filled the dining-room with a most unpleasant barking and almost tore Croesus' Pearl to pieces. Nor was the trouble limited to the dog-fight. A lampstand was upset on the table as well and not only smashed all the glass but spilled hot oil over some of the guests.

Not wanting to seem disturbed by the damage, Trimalchio gave the boy a kiss and told him to climb on his back. The lad climbed on his mount without hesitation, and slapping his shoulder blades with the flat of his hand, shouted amid roars of laughter:

'Big mouth, big mouth, how many fingers have I got up?'

So Trimalchio was calmed down for a while and gave instructions for a huge bowl of drink to be mixed and served to all the servants, who were sitting by our feet. He added the condition:

'If anyone won't take it, pour it over his head. Day's the time for business, now's the time for fun.'

65. This display of kindness was followed by some savouries, the very recollection of which really and truly makes me sick. Instead of thrushes, a fat capon was brought round for each of us, as well as goose-eggs in pastry hoods. Trimalchio surpassed himself to make us eat them; he described them as boneless chickens. In the middle of all this, a lictor knocked at the double doors and a drunken guest entered wearing white, followed by a large crowd of people. I was terrified by this lordly apparition and thought it was the chief magistrate arriving.

So I tried to rise and get my bare feet on the floor. Agamemnon laughed at this panic and said:

'Get hold of yourself, you silly fool. This is Habinnas – Augustan College and monumental mason.'

Relieved by this information I resumed my position and watched Habinnas' entry with huge admiration. Being already drunk, he had his hands on his wife's shoulders; loaded with several garlands, oil pouring down his forehead and into his eyes, he settled himself into the praetor's place of honour[45] and immediately demanded some wine and hot water. Trimalchio, delighted by these high spirits, demanded a larger cup for himself and asked how he had enjoyed it all.

'The only thing we missed,' replied Habinnas, 'was yourself – the apple of my eye was here. Still, it was damn good. Scissa was giving a ninth-day dinner[46] in honour of a poor slave of hers she'd freed on his death-bed. And I think she'll have a pretty penny to pay with the five per cent liberation tax, because they reckon he was worth fifty thousand. Still, it was pleasant enough, even if we did have to pour half our drinks over his wretched bones.'

66. 'Well,' said Trimalchio, 'what did you have for dinner?'

'I'll tell you if I can – I've such a good memory that I often forget my own name. For the first course we had a pig crowned with sausages and served with blood-puddings and very nicely done giblets, and of course beetroot and pure wholemeal bread – which I prefer to white myself: it's very strengthening and I don't regret it when I do my business. The next course was cold tart and a concoction of first-class Spanish wine poured over hot honey. I didn't eat anything at all of the actual tart, but I got stuck into the honey. Scattered round were chickpeas, lupines, a choice of nuts and an apple apiece – though I took two. And look, I've got them tied up in a napkin, because if I don't take something in the way of a present to my little slave, I'll have a row on my hands.

'Oh yes, my good lady reminds me. We had a hunk of bear-meat set before us, which Scintilla was foolish enough to try, and she practically spewed up her guts; but I ate more than a pound of it, as it tasted like real wild-boar. And I say if bears can eat us poor people, it's all the more reason why us poor people should eat bears.

'To finish up with, we had some cheese basted with new wine, snails all round, chitterlings, plates of liver, eggs in pastry hoods, turnips, mustard, and then, wait a minute, little tunny fish! There were pickled cumin seeds too, passed round in a bowl, and some people were that bad-mannered they took three handfuls. You see, we sent the ham away.

67. 'But tell me something, Gaius, now I ask – why isn't Fortunata at the table?'

'You know her,' replied Trimalchio, 'unless she's put the silver away and shared out the left-overs among the slaves, she won't put a drop of water to her mouth.'

'All the same,' retorted Habinnas, 'unless she sits down, I'm shagging off.'

And he was starting to get up, when at a given signal all the servants shouted *'Fortunata'* four or more times. So in she came with her skirt tucked up under a yellow sash to show her cerise petticoat underneath, as well as her twisted anklets and gold-embroidered slippers. Wiping her hands on a handkerchief which she carried round her neck, she took her place on the couch where Habinnas' wife was reclining. She kissed her. 'Is it really you?' she said, clapping her hands together.

It soon got to the point where Fortunata took the bracelets from her great fat arms and showed them to the admiring Scintilla. In the end she even undid her anklets and her gold hair net, which she said was pure gold. Trimalchio noticed this and had it all brought to him and commented:

'A woman's chains, you see. This is the way us poor fools get robbed. She must have six and a half pounds on her. Still, I've got a bracelet myself, made up from one-tenth per cent to Mercury[47] – and it weighs not an ounce less than ten pounds.'

Finally, for fear he looked like a liar, he even had some scales brought in and had them passed round to test the weight.

Scintilla was no better. From round her neck she took a little gold locket, which she called her 'lucky box'. From it she extracted two earrings and in her turn gave them to Fortunata to look at.

'A present from my good husband,' she said, 'and no one has a finer set.'

'Hey!' said Habinnas. 'You cleaned me out to buy you a glass bean. Honestly, if I had a daughter, I'd cut her little ears off. If there weren't any women, everything would be dirt cheap. As it is, we've got to drink cold water and piss it out hot.'

Meanwhile, the women giggled tipsily between themselves and kissed each other drunkenly, one crying up her merits as a housewife, the other crying about her husband's demerits and boy-friends. While they had their heads together like this, Habinnas rose stealthily and taking Fortunata's feet, flung them up over the couch.[48]

'Oh, oh!' she shrieked, as her underskirt wandered up over her knees. So she settled herself in Scintilla's lap and hid her burning red face in her handkerchief.

68. Then came an interval, after which Trimalchio called for dessert. Slaves removed all the tables and brought in others. They scattered sawdust tinted with saffron and vermilion, and something I had never seen before – powdered mica. Trimalchio said at once:

'I could make you just settle for this. There's dessert for you! The first tables've deserted.[49] However, if you people have anything nice, bring it on!'

Meanwhile a slave from Alexandria, who was taking round the hot water, started imitating a nightingale, only for Trimalchio to shout: 'Change your tune!'

More entertainment! A slave sitting by Habinnas' feet, prompted, I suppose, by his master, suddenly burst out in a sing-song voice:

'Meantime Aeneas was in mid-ocean with his fleet.'[50]

No more cutting sound ever pierced my eardrums. Apart from his barbarous meandering up and down the scale, he mixed in Atellan verses,[51] so that Virgil actually grated on me for the first time in my life. When he did finally stop through exhaustion, Habinnas said:

'He's never had any real training. I just had him taught by sending him along to peddlers on the street corner. He's no one to equal him if he wants to imitate mule-drivers or hawkers. He's terribly clever, really. He's a cobbler, a cook, a confectioner – a man that can turn his hand to anything. But he's got two faults; if he didn't have them, he'd be one in a million – he's circumcised and he snores. I don't mind him being cross-eyed – so is Venus. That's why he's never quiet and his eyes are hardly ever still. I got him for three hundred denarii.'

69. Scintilla interrupted him: 'Of course, you're not telling them all the tricks that wretch gets up to. He's a pimp – but I'll make sure he gets branded for it.'

Trimalchio laughed: 'I know a Cappadocian[52] when I see one. He's not slow in looking after himself and, by heaven, I admire him for it. You can't take it with you.

'Now, Scintilla, don't be jealous. Believe me, we know all about you women too. As sure as I stand here, I used to bang the mistress so much that even the old boy suspected; so he sent me off to look after his farms. But I'd better save my breath to cool my porridge.'

As though he'd been complimented the wretched slave took out an earthenware lamp from his pocket and for more than half an hour gave imitations of trumpet-players, while Habinnas hummed an accompaniment, pressing down his lower lip with his hand. Finally coming right into the middle, he did a flute-player with some broken reeds, then he dressed up in a greatcoat and whip and did the Life of the Muleteer, till Habinnas called him over, kissed him, and gave him a drink:

'Better and better, Massa!' he said. 'I'll give you a pair of boots.'

There would have been no end to all these trials if an extra course had not arrived – pastry thrushes stuffed with raisins and nuts. After them came quinces with thorns stuck in them to look like sea-urchins. All this would have been all right, but there was a far more horrible dish that made us prefer even dying of hunger. When it was put on the table, looking to us like a fat goose surrounded by fish and all sorts of game, Trimalchio said:

'Whatever you see here, friends, is made from one kind of stuff.'

I, of course, being very cautious by nature, spotted immediately what it was and glancing at Agamemnon, I said:

'I'll be surprised if it isn't all made of wax, or any rate mud. I've seen that sort of imitation food produced at the Saturnalia in Rome.'

70. I hadn't quite finished what I was saying when Trimalchio said:

'As sure as I hope to expand – my investments of course, not my waist-line – my chef made it all from pork. There couldn't be a more valuable man to have. Say the word and he'll produce a fish out of a sow's belly, a pigeon out of the lard, a turtle dove out of the ham, and fowl out of the knuckle. So he's been given a nice name I thought of myself – he's called Daedalus.[53] And seeing he's a clever lad, I brought him some carvers of Styrian steel as a present from Rome.'

He immediately had them brought in and gazed at them with admiration. He even allowed us to test the point on our cheeks.

All of a sudden in came two slaves, apparently having had a quarrel at the well; at any rate they still had water jugs on their shoulders. But while Trimalchio was giving his decision about their respective cases, neither of them paid any attention to his verdict: instead they broke each other's jugs with their sticks. Staggered by their drunken insolence, we couldn't take our eyes away from the fight till we noticed oysters and scallops sliding out of the jugs, which a boy collected and carried round on a dish. The ingenious chef was equal to these elegant refinements – he brought in snails on a silver gridiron, singing all the time in a high grating voice.

I blush to say what happened next. Boys with their hair down their backs came round with perfumed cream in a silver bowl and rubbed it on our feet[54] as we lay there, but first they wrapped our legs and ankles in wreaths of flowers. Some of the same stuff was dropped into the decanter and the lamp.

Fortunata was now wanting to dance,[55] and Scintilla was doing more clapping than talking, when Trimalchio said:

'Philargyrus – even though you are such a terrible fan of the Greens[56] – you have my permission to join us. And tell your dear Menophila to sit down as well.'

Need I say more? We were almost thrown out of our places, so completely did the household fill the dining-room. I even noticed that the chef, the one who had produced the goose out of pork, was actually given a place above me, and he was reeking of pickles and sauce. And he wasn't satisfied with just having a place, but he had to start straight off on an imitation of the tragedian Ephesus,[57] and then challenge his master to bet against the Greens winning at the next races.

71. Trimalchio became expansive after this argument.

'My dear people,' he said, 'slaves are human beings too. They drink the same milk as anybody else, even though luck's been agin 'em. Still, if nothing happens to me, they'll have their taste of freedom soon. In fact, I'm setting them all free in my will. I'm giving Philargyrus a farm, what's more, and the woman he lives with. As for Cario, I'm leaving him a block of flats, his five per cent manumission tax, and a bed with all the trimmings. I'm making Fortunata my heir, and I want all my friends to look after her.

'The reason I'm telling everyone all this is so my household will love me now as much as if I was dead.'

Everyone began thanking his lordship for his kindness, when he became very serious and had a copy of his will brought in. Amid the sobs of his household he read out the whole thing from beginning to end.

Then looking at Habinnas, he said:

'What have you to say, my dear old friend? Are you building my monument the way I told you? I particularly want you to keep a place at the foot of my statue and put a picture of my pup there, as well as paintings of wreaths, scent-bottles, and all the contests of Petraites, and thanks to you I'll be able to live on after I'm dead. And another thing! See that it's a hundred feet facing the road and two hundred back into the field. I want all the various sorts of fruit round my ashes and lots and lots of vines. After all, it's a big mistake to have nice houses just for when you're alive and not worry about the one we have to live in for much longer. And that's why I want this written up before anything else:

THIS MONUMENT DOES NOT GO TO THE HEIR

'But I'll make sure in my will that I don't get done down once I'm dead. I'll put one of my freedmen in charge of my tomb to look after it and not let people run up and shit on my monument. I'd like you to put some ships there too, sailing under full canvas, and me sitting on a high platform in my robes of office, wearing five gold rings[58] and pouring out a bagful of money for the people. You know I gave them all a dinner and two denarii apiece. Let's have in a banqueting hall as well, if you think it's a good idea, and show the whole town having a good time. Put up a statue of Fortunata on my right, holding a dove, and have her leading her little dog tied to her belt – and my little lad as well, and big wine-jars tightly sealed up so the wine won't spill. And perhaps you could carve me a broken one and a boy crying over it. A clock in the middle, so that anybody who looks at the time, like it or not, has got to read my name. As for the inscription now, take a good look and see if this seems suitable enough:

'HERE SLEEPS
GAIUS POMPEIUS TRIMALCHIO
MAECENATIANUS[59]
ELECTED TO THE AUGUSTAN COLLEGE IN HIS ABSENCE
HE COULD HAVE BEEN ON EVERY BOARD IN ROME
BUT HE REFUSED
GOD-FEARING BRAVE AND TRUE
A SELF-MADE MAN
HE LEFT AN ESTATE OF 30,000,000
AND HE NEVER HEARD A PHILOSOPHER
FAREWELL
AND YOU FARE WELL, TRIMALCHIO'

72. As he finished Trimalchio burst into tears. Fortunata was in tears,

Habinnas was in tears, in the end the whole household filled the dining-room with their wailing, like people at a funeral. In fact, I'd even begun crying myself, when Trimalchio said:

'Well, since we know we've got to die, why don't we live a little. I want to see you enjoying yourselves. Let's jump into a bath – you won't be sorry, damn me! It's as hot as a furnace.'

'Hear! Hear!' said Habinnas. 'Turning one day into two – nothing I like better.' He got up in his bare feet and began to follow Trimalchio on his merry way.

I looked at Ascyltus. 'What do you think?' I said. 'Now me, if I see a bath, I'll die on the spot.'

'Let's say yes,' he suggested, 'and while they're going for their bath, we can slip out in the crowd.'

This seemed a good idea, so Giton led us through the portico till we reached the door, where the hound chained there greeted us with such a noise that Ascyltus actually fell into the fishpond. Not only that, as I was drunk too, when I tried to help the struggling Ascyltus I was dragged into the same watery trap. However, the hall-porter saved us and by his intervention pacified the dog and dragged us trembling to dry land. Giton had already bought off the beast in a most ingenious way. He had scattered whatever he had got from us at dinner in front of the barking hound, and distracted by the food, it had choked down its fury.

Nevertheless, when, shivering and wet, we asked the hall-porter to let us out through the front door, he said: 'You're wrong if you think you can leave through the door you came in. No guest has ever been let out through the same door. They come in one way and go out another.'

73. What could we do after this piece of bad luck, shut up in this modern labyrinth and now beginning to regret that bath? We asked him to please show us the way to the bath-hall, and, throwing off our clothes, which Giton began drying at the door, we went in. There stood Trimalchio, and not even there could we get away from his filthy ostentation. He told us there was nothing better than a private bath, and that there had once been a bakery on that very spot. Then he sat down as though tired, and being tempted by the acoustics of the bath, with his drunken mouth gaping at the ceiling, he began murdering some songs by Menecrates[60] – or so we were told by those who understood his words.

The rest of the guests ran round the edge hand in hand, roaring away with a tremendous noise. Some were trying to pick up rings from the floor with their hands tied behind their backs, or were kneeling and trying to bend their necks backwards and touch the tips of their big toes. We left them to their games and sat down in the hot tub, which was being heated to Trimalchio's liking.

Well, after shaking off our drunken stupor, we were taken to another dining-room where Fortunata had laid out an elegant spread ... In fact, I noticed some bronze fishermen on the lamps as well as tables of solid silver, with gold inlaid pottery spread around and wine pouring from a leather wine-flask before our very eyes.

'Today, my friends,' said Trimalchio, 'my little slave had his first shave: he's a careful fellow — no offence meant! — who watches the pennies. So let's whet our throttles and not stop eating till daylight.'

74. Just as he was speaking, a cock crowed. Upset by this, Trimalchio ordered some wine to be poured out under the table and even had the lamps sprinkled with it undiluted. He actually changed his ring to his right hand.[61]

'That trumpeter,' he said, 'didn't give the signal without good reason. There should be a fire next or else somebody will be dying in the neighbourhood – God spare us! So whoever gets me that bringer of bad news, there's a tip for him.'

Before the words were out of his mouth, a cock was brought in and Trimalchio ordered it to be put in the pan and cooked. It was cut up by that very skilful chef and it was thrown into the pot. While Daedalus drew the scalding liquid, Fortunata ground pepper in a box-wood grinder.

After this dish Trimalchio looked at the servants and said:

'Why haven't you had dinner yet? Off you go and let some others come on duty.'

Up came another squad and as the first set called out: 'Good night, Gaius!' the new arrivals shouted: 'Good evening, Gaius!'

This led to the first incident that damped the general high spirits. Not a bad-looking boy entered with the newcomers and Trimalchio jumped at him and began kissing him at some length. Fortunata, asserting her just and legal rights, began hurling insults at Trimalchio, calling him a low scum and a disgrace, who couldn't control his beastly desires. 'You dirty dog!' she finally added.

Trimalchio took offence at this abuse and flung his glass into Fortunata's face. She screamed as though she'd lost an eye and put her trembling hands across her face. Scintilla was terrified too and hugged the quaking woman to her breast. An obliging slave pressed a little jug of cold water to her cheek, while Fortunata rested her head on it and began weeping. Trimalchio on the other hand said:

'Well, well, forgotten her flute-girl days, has she? She doesn't remember, but she was bought and sold, and I took her away from it all and made her as good as the next. Yet she puffs herself up like a frog and doesn't even spit for luck. Like wood, not woman. But those as are born over a shop don't dream of a house. May I never have a day's good luck again, if I don't teach that Cassandra[62] in clogs some manners!

'There was I, not worth twopence, and I could have had ten million. And you know I'm not lying about it. Agatho, who runs the perfume shop, he took me on one side just recently and said: "You don't want to let your family die out, you know!" But me, trying to do the right thing and not wanting to look changeable, I cut my own throat.

'All right! I'll make you want to dig me up with your bare nails. Just so you'll know on the spot what you've done for yourself – Habinnas! I don't want you to put her statue on my tomb, so at least when I'm dead I won't have any more squabbles. And another thing! Just to show I can get my own back – when I'm dead I don't want her to kiss me.'

75. After this thunderbolt, Habinnas began asking him to calm down: 'There's none of us does no wrong,' he said, 'we're human beings, not gods!' Scintilla said the same, calling him Gaius, and she began asking him, in the name of his guardian spirit, to give in.

Trimalchio held back his tears no longer. 'I ask you, Habinnas,' he said, 'as you hope to enjoy your bit of savings – if I did anything wrong, spit in my face. I kissed this very careful little fellow, not for his pretty looks, but because he's careful with money – he says his ten times table, he reads a book at sight, he's got himself some Thracian kit out of his daily allowance, and he's bought himself an easy chair and two cups out of his own pocket. Doesn't he deserve to be the apple of my eye? But Fortunata won't have it.

'Is that the way you feel, high heels? I'll give you a piece of advice: don't let your good luck turn your head, you kite, and don't make me show my teeth, my little darling – otherwise you'll feel my temper. You know me: once I've decided on something, it's fixed with a twelve-inch nail.

'But to come back to earth – I want you to enjoy yourselves, my dear people. After all, I was once like you are, but being the right sort I got where I am. It's the old headpiece that makes a man, the rest is all rubbish. "Buy right – sell right!" – that's me! Different people will give you a different line. I'm just on top of the world, I'm that lucky.

'But you, you snoring thing, are you still moaning? I'll give you something to moan about in a minute.

'However, as I'd started to say, it was my shrewd way with money that made me my fortune. I came from Asia as big as this candlestick. In fact, every day I used to measure myself against it, and to get some whiskers round my beak quicker, I used to oil my lips from the lamp. Still, for fourteen years I was the old boy's fancy. And there's nothing wrong if the boss wants it. But I did all right by the old girl too. You know what I mean – I don't say anything because I'm not the boasting sort.

76. 'Well, as heaven will have it, I became boss in the house, and the old boy, look, was mine, heart and soul. That's about it – he made me co-heir with the Emperor[63] and I got a senator's fortune.[64] But nobody gets enough, never. I wanted to go into business. Not to make a long story of it, I built five ships, I loaded them with wine – it was absolute gold at the time – and I sent them to Rome. You'd have thought I ordered it – every single ship was wrecked. That's fact, not fable! In one single day Neptune swallowed up thirty million. Do you think I gave up? This loss, I swear, just whetted my appetite – it was as if nothing had happened. I built more boats, bigger and better and luckier, so nobody could say I wasn't a man of courage. You know, the greater the ship, the greater the confidence. I loaded them again – with wine, bacon, beans, perfumes and slaves. At this point Fortunata did the decent thing, because she sold off all her gold trinkets, all her clothes, and put ten thousand in gold pieces in my hand. This was the yeast my fortune needed to rise. What heaven wants soon happens. In one voyage I carved out a round ten million. I immediately bought back all my old master's estates. I build a house, I invest in slaves and haulage. Whatever I touched grew like a honeycomb. Once I had more than the whole country, then down tools! I retired from business and began advancing loans to freedmen.

'Actually I was tired of trading on my own account, but it was an astrologer who convinced me. He happened to come to our colony, a sort of Greek, Serapa by name, and he could have told heaven itself what to do. He even told me things I'd forgotten. He went through everything for me from A to Z. He knew me inside out – the only thing he didn't tell me was what I ate for dinner the day before. You'd have thought he'd never left my side.

77. 'Wasn't there that thing, Habinnas? – I think you were there: "You got your lady wife out of those *certain circumstances*. You are not lucky in your friends. Nobody thanks you enough for your trouble. You have large estates. You are nursing a viper in your bosom."

'And he said – though I shouldn't tell you – I have thirty years, four months, and two days to live. What's more, I shall soon receive a legacy. My horoscope tells me this. If I'm allowed to join my estates to Apulia,[65] I'll have lived enough.

'Meantime, under the protection of Mercury, I built this house. As you know, it was still a shack, now it's a shrine. It has four dining-rooms,[66] twenty bedrooms, two marble colonnades, a row of box-rooms up above, a bedroom where I sleep myself, a nest for this viper, and a really good lodge for the porter. In fact, when Scaurus[67] came here, he didn't want to stay anywhere else, even though he's got his father's guest house down by the sea. And there are a lot of other things I'll show you in a second.

'Believe me: have a penny, and you're worth a penny. You got something, you'll be thought something. Like your old friend – first a frog, now a king.

'Meantime, Stichus, bring out the shroud and the things I want to be buried in. Bring some cosmetic cream, too, and a sample from that jar of wine I want my bones washed in.'

78. Stichus did not delay over it, but brought both his white shroud and his purple-edged toga into the dining-room ... Trimalchio told us to examine them and see if they were made of good wool. Then he said with a smile:

'Now you, Stichus, see no mice or moths get at those – otherwise I'll burn you alive. I want to be buried in style, so the whole town will pray for my rest.'

He opened a bottle of nard on the spot, rubbed some on all of us and said:

'I hope this'll be as nice when I'm dead as when I'm alive.' He now ordered wine to be poured into a big decanter and he said:

'I want you to think you've been invited to my wake.'

The thing was becoming absolutely sickening, when Trimalchio, showing the effects of his disgusting drunkenness, had a fresh entertainment brought into the dining-room, some cornet players. Propped up on a lot of cushions, he stretched out along the edge of the couch and said: 'Pretend I'm dead and say something nice.'

The cornet players struck up a dead march. One man in particular, the slave of his undertaker (who was one of the most respectable persons present), blew so loudly that he roused the neighbourhood. As a result, the fire brigade in charge of the nearby area, thinking Trimalchio's house was on fire, suddenly broke down the front door and began kicking up their usual sort of din with their water and axes.

Seizing this perfect chance, we gave Agamemnon the slip and escaped as rapidly as if there really were a fire . . .

EUMOLPUS

79. There was no torch available to show us the way, and as it was half-way through the night, the silence gave us little hope of meeting anyone with a light. Add to this too much wine and our ignorance of the place, which would have been a problem even in daylight. So after we had dragged our bleeding feet over all the sharp stones and jutting pieces of broken crockery for nearly a full hour, we were rescued by Giton's ingenuity. Afraid of losing his way even in daytime, the lad had shrewdly marked all the pillars and posts with chalk, and the bright marks, gleaming through even the thickest darkness, showed us the way. Yet we had to sweat just as much once we arrived at the inn. The old woman, after soaking herself so long with her guests, wouldn't have felt it if you'd put a fire under her, and we should probably have had to spend the night on the doorstep if the landlord, returning from the coaches, had not turned up. He naturally didn't make a noise very long but just broke the inn-door down and finally let us in through the same way.

> Ye gods and goddesses! O what a night!
> How soft the bed! We clung so warm and tight,
> Our lips exchanged our souls in mingled breath.
> Farewell, all worldly cares! O welcome, death!

I congratulated myself too soon. For once the wine had made me relax my drunken hands; Ascyltus, utterly unscrupulous, took the boy away from me in the night and transferred him to his bed. And rolled up coolly with someone else's boy-friend (was Giton conscious of the assault or was he pretending?) he fell asleep wrapped in an embrace he had no right to, lost to all sense of justice.

When I awoke and ran my hands over the empty joyless bed ... if you can trust what a lover says, I wondered whether to run my sword through both of them and continue their sleep into death. Following a safer policy, I roused Giton with my fists, but looking at Ascyltus with a savage expression I said:

'You have wrecked all mutual confidence and friendship with your criminal ways, so pack up right away and find somewhere else to practise your filthy habits.'

He made no opposition but once we had shared the loot equally, he said:

'Right, now let's split the boy too.'

80. I thought this was a parting joke. But he drew his sword with a murderous hand, saying:

'You are not going to enjoy this prize you are sitting on alone. I must have my share even if I cut it off with this sword to avenge myself.'

I did the same and wrapping my cloak round my arm, dropped into a fighting crouch. In the middle of this heartbreaking lunacy the poor boy held on to our knees in tears and begged us not to let the inn see another pair of Theban brothers[1] or to sully the sanctity of our beautiful friendship with each other's blood.

'If there must be bloodshed at any price,' he cried, 'look, I offer you my throat, get your hands on it, press your points home. I'm the one to die, because I broke up a sworn friendship.'

We put up our steel after this plea. Ascyltus was the first to speak:

'I'll put an end to this quarrel. Let the boy himself go with the one he wants, so that he at least may have the liberty of choosing his lover.'

Imagining our long intimacy had come to mean as much as ties of blood, I had no fears. On the contrary, I jumped headlong at the offer and gave the decision to the judge. There was no hesitation, not the slightest appearance of it. The last syllable was scarcely out of my mouth when he got up and chose Ascyltus as his lover. Thunderstruck by this verdict, just as I was, I fell on the bed. I would have laid violent hands on myself like an executioner, if I hadn't begrudged my rival that victory. Ascyltus left proudly with his prize and abandoned his comrade-in-arms, his dearest friend a little while ago, his companion even in misfortune; he abandoned him in all his misery in a place full of strangers.

> Friendship's a word and friends know its value –
> The counters slide merrily all through the game –
> Your friends broadly smiling, while fortune was by you:
> Their backs even broader when trouble came.

*

[The mime has begun
And the father is there,
And here is the son
And the millionaire.
Then closes the page,
When played is their part,
On the laughter upstage
And the masks of their art –
Then their true faces appear.][2]

81. I soon dried my tears but being afraid that, in addition to all my other troubles, Menelaus the assistant lecturer might find me alone in my lodgings, I collected my bags and sadly rented a quiet place along the seafront. I holed up there for three days, constantly aware of my loneliness and humiliation; I would beat my breast, already sore with sobbing, and again and again I'd cry out loud through all the groans that racked me:

'Why couldn't that earthquake have swallowed me up? Or the sea, such a menace even to innocent people? Did I escape the law, did I outwit the arena, did I kill my host, only to end up, despite my claims to be a daring criminal, just lying here, a beggar and an exile, abandoned in a lodging-house in a Greek town? And who brought this loneliness upon me? An adolescent wallowing in every possible filth, who even on his own admission had been rightly run out of town, free – for sex, freeborn – for sex, whose youth you'd buy with a ticket, who had been hired as a girl even by someone who thought he was a male. As for the other one! Putting on women's clothes the day he became a man, talked into effeminacy by his mother, doing only woman's work in the slave pen, and after he couldn't meet his debts and had to change his sexual ground, he abandoned the claims of an old friendship and – in the name of decency! – sold out everything like a whore on the strength of a one-night stand. Now the loving pair lie clutching each other whole nights on end and perhaps when they are worn out by their love-play, they laugh at my loneliness. But they won't get away with it. As sure as I'm a man and not a slave, I'll right my wrongs with their guilty blood.'

82. With these words I fastened my sword to my side and, not to let bodily weakness endanger my mission, I restored my strength with a heavy meal. Then I rushed out into the street and went round all the arcades like a madman. But while I was thinking of nothing but blood and destruction, my face like thunder and full of rage (I was dropping

my hand continually to my dedicated hilt), a soldier noticed me, a con man or a thug.

'Hey there, friend,' he said, 'what's your regiment and who's your company commander?'

Although I lied boldly about my commander and my regiment, he said:

'Well, tell me something. Do the soldiers in your army walk about in slippers?'

As my face and my very trembling betrayed the lie, he told me to give up my weapons and keep out of trouble. I'd been robbed and, worse, my revenge had been nipped in the bud. I walked back towards my lodgings and gradually, as my boldness decreased, I began to feel grateful for the thug's audacity.

*

> Craving the water around, apples above his head,
>   Poor Tantalus can neither drink nor eat.[3]
> This is the rich man's image: in plenty dogged by dread
>   To drink dry-mouthed, to choke and starve on meat.

*

One should not rely a great deal on one's plans as fate has a way of her own.

*

83. I went into an art gallery, which had a wonderful variety of paintings. For instance, I even saw work by Zeuxis[4] still unaffected by the ravages of time. And I examined, not without a certain thrill, some sketches by Protogenes,[5] so lifelike they were a challenge to nature herself. I practically worshipped that masterpiece of Apelles[6] that they call The Goddess on One Knee. The lines of the paintings were so subtle and clear-cut that you could see them as expressing the subjects' very souls. Here the eagle, way up high, was carrying off the Idaean youth[7] to heaven, there a dazzling white Hylas repulsed the lascivious Naiad. Apollo cursed his murderous hands and decorated his unstrung lyre with a new flower. Surrounded by the faces of these lovers, I burst out as though I were alone:

'So love affects gods, too. Jupiter didn't find anything to love in heaven, but at least when going to sin on earth he injured no one. The nymph that snatched Hylas away would have controlled her passion if she had thought Hercules would come to restrain her. Apollo called back the boy's soul into a flower – all of them enjoyed embraces free from rivalry. But I took to my heart a crueller friend than Lycurgus.'[8]

All of a sudden, however, as I was arguing with the wind, a white-haired old man entered the gallery. His face was lined and seemed to have in it a promise of something impressive. But his clothes were shabby and this made it clear that he belonged to the class of intellectuals so hated generally by the rich. He therefore came and stood by my side . . .

'I am a poet,' he said, 'and a poet of no mean ability, I like to think, at least if poetry prizes are to be trusted when favouritism confers them even on mediocrity. "Why," you ask, "are you so badly dressed then?" For this one reason – concern for the intellect never made anyone rich.

> 'The trader trusts the sea: his goods are sold;
> The soldier from campaigns wears belted gold;
> Cheap flatterers sprawl drunk in purple shirts;
> Seducers courting newly married flirts
> Are rich from playing their seductive parts.
> Only a poet is a tattered thing,
> Cold scarecrow, mute and endlessly sighing
> For the lonely, lost and now deserted arts.

84. 'No doubt about it. If a man sets his face against every temptation and starts off on the straight and narrow, he's immediately hated because of his different ways. No one can approve of conduct different from his own. And secondly, those who are interested in piling up money don't want anything else in life regarded as better than what they have themselves. So lovers of literature are sneered at by whatever means possible to show that they too are inferior to wealth.'

*

'I suspect somehow that poverty is the twin sister of talent.'

*

'I'd like to think that the man who hounds me in my hard life were honest enough to be conciliated. As it is, he's hardened in crime and cleverer than the very pimps.'

*

85. [*Eumolpus*] 'When I was taken out to Asia on the paid staff of a treasury official, I accepted some hospitality in Pergamum.[9] I was very pleased to accept this invitation not only because of the elegance of the quarters but also because my host had a very good-looking son, and I

thought up a way to prevent his father becoming suspicious of me. Whenever any mention was made at the table of taking advantage of pretty boys, I flared up so violently and I was so stern about my ears being offended by obscene talk that the mother especially regarded me as a real old-world philosopher. From then on I escorted the young lad to the gymnasium, I organized his studies, I taught him and gave him good advice. After all, we didn't want any greedy seducer admitted to the house.

*

'One holiday, when the celebrations had given him time to play, we were lounging in the dining-room, since the long day's enjoyment had made us too lazy to go to bed. About midnight, I realized the boy was awake. So in a very nervous whisper I breathed a prayer.

'"Dear Venus," I said, "if I can kiss this boy without his knowing it, I'll give him a pair of doves tomorrow."

'Hearing the price of my pleasure, the boy started snoring, and I therefore went to work on the faker and kissed him several times. Content with this beginning, I rose early next morning and brought him the choice pair of doves he was expecting and fulfilled my vow.

86. 'Next night, given the same opportunity, I altered my prayer.

'"If I can run my hands all over him," I said, "without his feeling anything, I'll give him two really savage fighting cocks for his patience."

'At this offer the boy moved over to me of his own accord. I think he was getting afraid I might fall asleep. Naturally I dispelled his worries and his whole body became a whirlpool in which I lost myself, although I stopped short of the ultimate pleasure. Then when day came, I brought the delighted boy what I'd promised.

'The third night gave me similar licence, and I got up, and close to his ear, as he tossed restlessly, I said:

' "O eternal gods, if I can get the full satisfaction of my desires from him in his sleep, for this happiness tomorrow I shall give the boy the finest Macedonian thoroughbred – but with this proviso, only if he feels nothing."

'The lad had never slept so soundly before. First I filled my hands with his milk-white breasts, then I clung to his lips, and finally I reduced all my longings to one climax.

'In the morning he sat in his room and waited for me to follow my usual practice. Of course, you know how much easier it is to buy doves and cocks than a thoroughbred, and besides, I was nervous in case such an extravagant gift should make my kindness suspect. So after walking round for a few hours, I returned to my host's house and gave the boy nothing more than a kiss. He looked round, as he threw his arms about my neck, and said:

'"Please, sir, where's my thoroughbred?"

*

87. 'This offence had lost me the headway I had made, nevertheless I returned to my old freedom. A few days later when a similar chance left us in the same position, hearing the father snoring, I began asking the boy to become friends with me again, and I said all the other things that a strong physical urge dictates. But clearly annoyed, he only said:

'"Just go to sleep or I'll tell father."

'Nothing is too hard to get if you're prepared to be wicked. Even while he was saying, "I'll wake father," I slipped into the bed and without much of a fight from him I took my pleasure by force. Actually he was not displeased that I'd been so naughty, and after complaining for a long time that he'd been tricked and that he'd been laughed at and talked about among his schoolfriends because he had boasted to them of my wealth, he said finally:

'"But you'll see I'm not like you. Do it again, if you wish."

'Well, I was back in the boy's favour with all his hard feelings gone, and after taking advantage of his kindness, I fell asleep. The boy, however, being fully mature and of an age very much able to take it, was not content with the repeat performance. He woke me up from my sleep saying:

'"Don't you want anything?"

'Of course it wasn't a tiresome job yet, so somehow, ground between the panting and sweating, he got what he wanted and I fell back asleep, exhausted with passion. Less than an hour later he began poking me with his hand and saying,

'"Why aren't we getting on with it?"

'Being woken up so often, I really flared up. I gave him his own back: '"Just you go to sleep or I'll tell your father."'

*

88. Cheered by this conversation, I began to ask my mentor ... about the age of the pictures and the subject of some of the obscure ones, at the same time pressing him for reasons for the present decadence, when the loveliest of the arts were dying out, not least painting, which had vanished without the slightest trace. His reply was:

'Financial greed has caused this change. In former days when sheer merit was still sufficient, the liberal arts flourished and there was great competition to bring to light anything of benefit to posterity. Democritus, for instance, distilled all forms of vegetable life and spent his days in scientific experiments to discover the properties of minerals and plants.[10] Eudoxus[11] grew old on the top of one of the highest mountains to further his knowledge of astronomy, and Chrysippus purged his brain three times with hellebore to allow himself to continue his investigations.

'To turn to the plastic arts, Lysippus[12] was so preoccupied with the lines of one statue that he died of poverty, and Myron, who almost captured the souls of men and animals in his bronzes, left no heir. But we, besotted with drink and whoring, daren't study even arts with a tradition. Attacking the past instead, we acquire and pass on only vices. What has happened to dialectic?[13] Astronomy? Or the road most cultivated to wisdom? Who has ever gone into a temple and prayed to become eloquent – or to approach the fountainhead of philosophy? People do not even ask for a sound mind or body, but before they touch the threshold one man immediately promises an offering if he can arrange the funeral of a rich relation, another if he can dig up some treasure, another if he can come into a safe thirty million. Even the senate, the standard of rectitude and goodness, habitually promises the Capitol a thousand pounds of gold, and to remove anyone's doubts about financial greed, tries to influence even Jove with money.

'So don't be surprised that painting is on the decline, when a lump of gold seems more beautiful to everybody, gods and men, than anything those crazy little Greeks, Apelles and Phidias[14], ever made.

89. 'But I notice you can't pull yourself away from that painting of the Fall of Troy.[15] Well, I'll try and interpret its subject in verse:

'The tenth harvest, tenth year of the Troy-siege,
The Phrygians forlorn, doubt-fraught and frightened,
Calchas the soothsayer downcast,
A dark daunting upon him.
The Delian doled out his destinies   5
And tall trees toppled on Ida,
Their boles borne from the mountain;
Trunks trimmed, massed for its making,
For hewing the horse, shaping the fell shape.

A cave is uncovered, a cavern to capture the foe-camp.   10
Into it, taut from the ten-year taking,
Their valour is hidden, deep in the gods' vail;
Doughty Danaans dwell in the depths of it.
  The thousand-fold fleet we felt was in full flight,
    Your fields, O my fatherland, freed from the fighting.   15
Words so declared on horse side,
Sinon, steady in death's sight, said it,
And our hearts ever steady for our destruction.

Uncaged, careless of combat, the crowd came,
Praising and prayerful. Cheeks washed with weeping,   20
Joy in the faint heart, tears yet trickling –
Terror retracts them.
      Priest of the sea god,
Loud Laocoön, locks lank, hails the assemblage,
His flung spear wounding the wide womb: 25
Fate slows his sinews; blade-point rebounding
Makes us trust; more truth in the treachery.
Yet again Laocoön, hardening his halt hands,
Aims at the sheer side his double axe-stroke.
Hear cry of captives, lo, at their murmuring   30
The oak-bulk breathes of foreigners' faintness –
The captured captains move to Troy's capture,
With fresh frauds reviving the fighting.

Other prodigies press us and portents.
Where tall Tenedos breaks back the billows,   35
Swollen the straits surge up with sea-surf,
And the waters, broken, wince back, breaking the sea-calm.
As in the nightwatch oars sound from far-off,
Of fleets faring through sea foam, sea face
Groaning of grazes from fir-keels coursing.   40
Back stare we.
Waves speed snakes, sinuously doubling, rockwards;
As tall ships, their breasts scatter spindrift;
Tails tolling thunder, head fringes, foam-freed,
Shine as their eyes shine. Thundery skin-sheen   45
Shines on the water, as waves hiss and tremble.
Men stand mindless. Laocoön's loved ones,
In sacred ribbons and Phrygian tiring, his twin sons,
Are suddenly twined in the twinkling snake-coils.

They lock little fingers into the snake-jaws,   50
Each for the other, neither from self-love –
Brother for brother, their love is requited,
Death a deliverance from mutual mourning.
Added then unto their doom is the old one,
Hopeless as helper.   55
The serpents, sated from slaying,
Beset him, bear to the earth his body,
He lies mid the altars, priest now a victim,
Making the ground groan.
What is sacred is soiled, Troy, doomed to destruction,   60
Destroys first its godhead.

Full moon aloft had lifted its white glow,
Leading the lesser lights with radiant torchbrand:
The sons of Priam were sleeping and wine-soaked –
"Undo the bolts, ye Danaans, bring out your brave ones!"   65
Chieftains acquitting themselves in combat,
As in Thessalian hills a horse out of halter
Shakes its neck and its mane, for the onrush.
Swords now unsheathed, brandishing bucklers,
They fly to the fray, dealing death to the drunken,   70
Sent in their sleep to the death-sleep;
Here brands are brought from the altars
To turn against Troy town the worship of Trojans.'

90. Some of the people walking about in the colonnades interrupted Eumolpus' recitation with a shower of stones. Being familiar with this sort of appreciation of his genius, he covered his head and fled from the sanctuary. I was nervous myself in case they should call me a poet too. So I followed his fleeing figure and arrived at the seafront. As soon as we were out of range and could stop, I said:

'Listen, what's wrong with you? You've been with me for less than two hours and you've spoken more often like a poet than a human being. I'm not surprised people chase you with stones. I'm going to fill my pockets with rocks and whenever you start taking wings, I'll let some blood from your head.'

His face changed and he said:

'My lad, today is not the first time I've tested the air like that. In fact I've never gone into a theatre to give a recitation without getting this sort of unexpected reception from the spectators. But I don't want to quarrel with you as well, so I'll keep off the stuff for the whole day.'

'Right,' I said, 'if you swear off this madness for today, we'll dine together.'

*

I gave the landlord of my little place the task of preparing a simple meal.

*

91. I saw Giton leaning against the wall with towels and scrapers,[16] and looking depressed and confused. You could tell he didn't like his menial position. To confirm my observation . . . He turned towards me, his face softening with pleasure:

'Don't be hard on me, my dear. Where there are no weapons around, I speak freely. Take me away from this bloody criminal and punish me as savagely as you like for what I've been regretting. I feel so bad about everything, it will be a sufficient consolation to die because you wanted me to.'

I told him to stop complaining in case someone should guess our plans, and abandoning Eumolpus, who was reciting a poem in the main bath, I dragged Giton through a dark and sordid exit and flew hastily to my lodgings. Then, with the doors barred, I rushed to take him in my arms and press my cheeks to his tearful face. For a long time neither of us recovered his voice. The boy's lovely breast heaved with a succession of sighs.

'Oh, this shouldn't happen,' I said, 'for me to love you, though I was deserted, and for there to be no scar on my heart from that great wound. What have you to say after giving yourself to another lover? Did I deserve this treatment?'

When he realized he was still loved, he raised his eyebrows . . .

'I left the decision about our love to no other judge but you. But I won't complain of anything any more, I won't remember anything any more, if you prove your regrets by behaving honourably.'

As I poured all this out with sobs and tears, he wiped my face with a cloak and said:

'Encolpius, please, I appeal to your memory to be honest. Did I desert you or did you betray me? I admit this and I'm not ashamed of it – when I saw two armed men, I went to the stronger.'

I kissed that wise little breast and threw my arms round his neck, and to let him fully realize that I was reconciled and I was renewing our friendship as sincerely as ever, I hugged him to my heart.

92. It was well into the night and the woman had taken care of our orders for dinner, when Eumolpus hammered on the door.

'How many of you are there?' I asked, and meanwhile began peeping carefully through a chink in the door to see if Ascyltus had come with him. Then seeing my guest by himself, I let him in immediately. As he threw himself on the bed and saw Giton in full view fixing the table, he nodded his head, saying:

'There's a pretty Ganymede. It should be a nice day.'

Such a studied opening did not make me happy and I was afraid I had joined up with someone just like Ascyltus. Eumolpus pressed on, and when the boy gave him a drink, he said:

'I prefer you to the whole bathful of them,' and after greedily emptying the glass, he said he had never had such a disagreeable time and he explained:

'You know, I was almost beaten up even while I was taking my bath, just because I tried to recite a poem to the people sitting round my tub. After I'd been thrown out of the bath, I began going round every nook and cranny and calling out "Encolpius" in a loud voice. And somewhere else a naked young man, who had lost his clothes, was demanding someone called Giton with equally indignant shouts. And while the boys just ridiculed me for a lunatic with the most impudent imitations, a huge crowd surrounded him with applause and the most awestruck admiration. You see, he had such enormous sexual organs that you'd think the man was just an attachment to his penis. What a man for the job! I think he starts yesterday and finishes tomorrow. So he found help in no time. Someone or other, a Roman knight and notorious for his tastes, the loungers said, covered him with his own clothes as he went wandering round and took him off home – to enjoy such a piece of luck on his own, I suppose. Whereas I wouldn't have got even my own clothes back from the sneaky attendant there if I hadn't produced someone who knew me. A polished wick is much more profitable than a polished wit.'

While Eumolpus was telling us this, my expression kept changing all the time, now through amusement at my rival's misfortunes, now through annoyance at his successes. But all the same, I said nothing and passed the food, pretending the story had no personal interest for me.

＊

93. 'What's legitimate we hold cheap; our wayward hearts love our offences.[17]

> 'Pheasants snared in Colchis, in Africa game-birds,
> These are the rarities that have to be chased;
> White goose and duckling,
> Gaudy in their gay plumes,
> Are left to the populace, not to our taste.

> Parrot-wrasse from far shores, haul from Syrtes,
> Bought at the price of some great shipwreck,
> These are for the table –
> Mullet's indigestible –
> Don't ask the cost: you can pay by cheque.

> Wives are out of fashion. Better get a girl-friend –
> A little more expensive but really very nice.
> Rose leaves are out of date,
> Cinnamon's the thing now.
> Anything hard to get is well worth the price.'

'Is this how you keep your promise,' I said, 'not to produce any verse today? As a favour, at least let *us* off – we never threw stones at you. Because if anyone drinking in the same house we're in smells the suggestion of a poet, he'll rouse the whole neighbourhood and finish us all off for the same reason. Have some thought for us and remember the art gallery or the public baths.'

Giton, being a very gentle boy, remonstrated with me for this way of speaking, and said it wasn't right for me to abuse someone older than myself, while forgetting my obligations and letting my insults spoil the meal I had provided in all kindness. And there was a lot of other moderate and courteous things he said, which came very well from his pretty lips.

*

94. [*Eumolpus to Giton*] 'What a lucky mother,' said he, 'to have such a child! Bravo! Your good looks and your good sense make a rare mixture. Don't think you've wasted all that breath: you've found someone who loves you. I'll fill poems with your praises. I'll follow you as your teacher and guardian, even when you don't ask me to. And Encolpius is not losing, he's in love with someone else.'

That soldier who took away my sword was a piece of luck for

Eumolpus too. Otherwise I would have cooled the spleen I'd felt against Ascyltus in Eumolpus' blood. Giton was not unaware of this. He went out of the room on the pretext of getting some water and by his prudent withdrawal damped my anger. Then a few moments later, as my fury rekindled, I said:

'Eumolpus, I prefer you even speaking in verse to the sort of thoughts you are having. Now I'm a hot-tempered man and you are a lecherous one. You can see how these temperaments don't go together. So you have to regard me as a madman and give in to my insanity – now get out quick!'

Confused by this outburst, Eumolpus did not ask the reason for my anger, but going straight out over the threshold, suddenly slammed the door of the room, and, as I was expecting nothing of the sort, shut me in; he swiftly removed the key and ran off to look for Giton.

Shut up inside like that, I decided to finish everything by hanging myself. I had already put the bed frame against the wall, tied a belt to it, and was inserting my neck in the noose when the door was unlocked and Eumolpus came in with Giton and in a race against death brought me back to life. In his grief Giton, unlike Eumolpus, went mad with rage; he raised a great outcry and pushing me with both hands precipitated me on top of the bed.

'You're wrong, Encolpius,' he said, 'if you think by any possible chance you can die before me. I tried first: I looked for a sword in Ascyltus' rooms. If I had not found you, I was going to throw myself to my death. To make you realize death isn't far away if you look for it, see in your turn what you wanted me to see.'

With this he snatched a razor from Eumolpus' hired servant and slashing his throat once and then twice, collapsed at our feet.

Thunderstruck, I let out a cry and following his collapsing body to the floor, I looked for a way to die with the same instrument. But Giton showed not the slightest suspicion of a wound nor could I feel any pain myself. It was a practice razor and blunted for the purpose: to give apprentices the courage a barber needs, it had a sheath fitted round it. This was the reason why the servant had not panicked at his snatching the razor and why Eumolpus had not intervened in this fake death scene.

95. While this love drama was being played out, the landlord came in with the rest of our little dinner and at the sight of the disgraceful sprawling heap on the floor, he shouted:

'Hey, are you people drunk or runaway slaves? Or both? Who turned that bed up? What's the meaning of all this criminal behaviour? But of course – you were going to do a moonlight flit to avoid paying your room rent. But you're not getting away with it. Because I'll have you know the place doesn't belong to some widow but to Marcus Mannicius.'

Eumolpus yelled back: 'Are you threatening us?' and at the same time he hit the man hard in the face with the flat of his hand. Reckless from so much drinking with the guests, the fellow hurled an earthenware pot at Eumolpus' head, split his forehead in mid-shout, and flung himself out of the room. Eumolpus was not standing for this insult; he snatched up a wooden candlestick, followed him as he made off and avenged his pride with a tremendous shower of blows. The whole household came rallying round, as well as a crowd of drunken guests. I, however, took this opportunity for my revenge by shutting Eumolpus out. Having put paid to the bastard, I was of course without a rival and I went on to put the room and the evening to their full use.

Meanwhile the kitchen staff and the people who lived in the building were beating up Eumolpus now that he couldn't get inside   one was aiming for his eyes with a spit covered with sizzling tripes, while another went through his battle-drill with a butcher's hook. One old woman in particular, a bleary old hag, dressed in the filthiest clothes and wearing odd wooden clogs, came dragging along an enormous dog on a chain and set him on Eumolpus. But he defended himself from all these threats with his candlestick.

96. We were watching everything through a hole left in the door when the handle had been pulled off a little while ago, and I was cheering every blow that reached Eumolpus. Giton, however, with his usual compassion pressed me to open the door and rescue him. As my resentment was still with me, I didn't restrain myself but smashed him on the head with a sharp bended knuckle for his pains. He sat down on the bed in tears while I applied each eye alternately to the hole and feasted my eyes on the sight of Eumolpus in trouble   this was rich food indeed! I was recommending him to a good lawyer when the manager of the lodging house, Bargates by name, who had been disturbed at his dinner, was carried into the centre of the brawl by two porters – he had bad feet, it seems. After coming out with a long and furious diatribe in a foreign accent about drunken sots and runaway slaves, he then looked at Eumolpus and said:

'It was you, was it, you wonderful poet? Now why don't these no-good slaves get off quick and stop fighting? ...'

'The woman I'm living with is acting high and mighty with me. So be a friend and write some nasty verses about her so she'll know her place.'

*

97. While Eumolpus was talking privately to Bargates, a town crier entered the hotel accompanied by a policeman and quite a number of other people. Waving a torch that gave out more smoke than light, he made the following announcement:

'LOST, A SHORT WHILE AGO IN THE BATHS, A BOY AGED ABOUT SIXTEEN. HE IS CURLY-HAIRED, SOFT-SKINNED, GOOD-LOOKING, AND GOES BY THE NAME OF GITON. THERE IS A REWARD OF ONE THOUSAND SESTERCES FOR ANYONE WHO WILL BRING HIM BACK OR GIVE ANY INFORMATION OF HIS WHEREABOUTS.'

Not far from the announcer stood Ascyltus, wearing a multi-coloured shirt and displaying the description and the reward on a silver plate.

I ordered Giton to get immediately under the bed and tie his hands and feet to the webbing that held the mattress on the frame – the way Ulysses had once clung to the ram – and so stay out of the hands of the searchers.

Giton was not slow to obey and in a moment he inserted his hands in the fastenings and beat Ulysses at his own tricks. To avoid leaving any room for suspicion, I filled the bed with clothes and made up the traces of a man about my size.

Meanwhile Ascyltus, after going round all the occupied rooms, came to mine and became more hopeful because he found the doors more carefully bolted. The policeman, however, inserting an axe where the doors joined, loosened the bolts from their hold.

I fell at Ascyltus' knees and, appealing to the memory of our friendship and our companionship in misfortune, I begged him at least to let me see my little friend. In fact, to lend some sincerity to my hypocritical appeals, I said:

'I know you've come to kill me, Ascyltus. Why else have you brought an axe? Well, vent your rage on me. Look, I'm showing you my neck, spill the blood you really came for under the pretence of a search.'

Ascyltus rejected the injustice of the charge and assured me he was only looking for the runaway who belonged to him and didn't want to kill a helpless man, least of all a man he regarded as a very dear friend even after that fateful quarrel.

98. The policeman on the other hand did not take things so easily. Snatching a rod from the innkeeper he pushed it under the bed and even tried all the cracks in the wall. Giton pulled himself away from the poking, and holding his breath in a great panic, pressed his mouth to the very bedbugs . . .

But as the broken door could keep no one out of the room, Eumolpus burst in excitedly:

'I've got the thousand sesterces,' he said. 'I'm going after the advertiser now – he's only just leaving. I'm fully justified in betraying you; I'll explain that Giton is in your possession.'

He was determined about this even as I clasped his knees and begged him not to kill two dying men.

'You would be quite right to be flaming mad,' I added, 'if you could bring forward your prisoner. The boy just got away among the crowd and I haven't a suspicion where he's going to. For pity's sake, Eumolpus, bring the lad back – even hand him over to Ascyltus.'

While I was persuading him till he almost believed this, Giton, through holding his breath to bursting point, sneezed three times in rapid succession, so hard that the bed shook. At the noise Eumolpus said: 'God bless you, Giton!'

When the mattress was pulled back too, he saw our Ulysses, and even a hungry Cyclops would have had pity on him. Turning to me, he said:

'What's this, you thief? You didn't have the courage to tell me the truth even when you were caught. Why, if the god in charge of human destinies hadn't forced a sign from the lad as he hung there, I'd have been wandering round the bar-rooms like a fool.'

*

Giton, far more conciliatory than I, first of all bound up the cut on his forehead with cobwebs soaked in oil; then he replaced his tattered clothes with his own little cloak, and embracing the now mollified poet and pressing kisses on him like poultices, said to him:

'My dear, dear father, we are all completely in your hands. If you love your little Giton, now is the time to save him. I wish some terrible fire would burn me up, just me, or some freezing sea would cover me. I'm the object of all these crimes, I'm the cause. If I were to die, it would reconcile the people at each other's throats.'

*

99. [*Eumolpus*] 'Always and everywhere I have lived as though each day were my last and would never return.'

*

With tears flowing from my eyes, I begged him to become my friend again too: the madness of jealousy was not in a lover's control. Nevertheless I would take great care never to say or do anything again that could offend him. Only let him, as befitted a poet and scholar, smooth away without a scar all the rancour festering in his heart.

'The snows cling longer in rough and uncultivated regions, but where the ground has come under the plough, the light frost vanishes from its bright expanse even while you are speaking. It's the same way with anger in human breasts: it chokes an untutored heart, but slips away from a cultivated mind.'

'What you say is true,' said Eumolpus, 'and to prove it, look, I'll even kiss you and put an end to our quarrel. Well now, I hope everything will be all right. Get your things together and follow me, or if you prefer, you lead the way.'

He was still talking when the door was pushed and creaked open, and a rough-bearded sailor stood in the doorway.

'You're late, Eumolpus,' he said. 'You'd think you didn't know we have to hurry.'

We all got up without delay, and Eumolpus ordered his servant, who had been asleep for some time, to start moving with his baggage. Giton and I got together what we had for the journey; I sent up a prayer to the stars and passed aboard.

*

100. 'It's annoying that our new acquaintance likes the boy. But aren't the best things in life free to all? The sun shines on everyone. The moon, accompanied by countless stars, leads even the beasts to pasture. What can you think of lovelier than water? But it flows for the whole world. Is love alone then to be something furtive rather than something to be gloried in? Exactly, that's just it – I don't want any of the good things of life unless people are envious of them. One man, and old at that, will be no trouble: even if he wished to try something, he'll give himself away through panting.'

I put forward these considerations with something less than confidence and managed to overcome my inward disagreement. Then, with my head buried in my tunic, I began pretending to sleep.

But suddenly as though fortune were determined to take all the heart out of me, a voice on deck could be heard complaining:

'So he made a fool of me, did he?'

It was a male voice that sounded to my ears like an old friend and sent me into palpitations. Then a woman, apparently cut to the quick and equally indignant, blazed out with even greater vehemence:

'If only some god would put Giton into my hands, what a welcome I'd have for the wanderer!'

Both of us were so shaken by these unexpected sounds that the blood drained from our faces. Myself in particular, as though caught up in some distressing nightmare, found my voice only after a long interval and with trembling hands I pulled at Eumolpus' cloak, just as he was falling off to sleep.

'For heaven's sake, sir, can you tell us whose ship this is and who are aboard?'

He was annoyed at being awakened.

'Was this the reason why you wanted us to occupy the most secluded place on the ship, so that you could stop us sleeping? Anyway, suppose I told you that Lichas of Tarentum was the owner of this boat and that he was taking Tryphaena to Tarentum into exile, what does it matter?'

101. Thunderstruck by this, I broke out trembling and, baring my throat, I said:

'Fate has utterly defeated me at last.'

Giton indeed fainted across my chest and went on lying there. When the sweat broke out and revived us, I gripped Eumolpus by the knees.

'Show some pity for us,' I said, 'we're as good as dead. In the name of our common education, lend us a helping hand. Our last hour has come and unless you prevent it, it can only be a blessing.'

Overwhelmed by this wrongful accusation, Eumolpus swore by all the gods and goddesses that he neither knew what had happened nor had he planned any deliberate treachery – with the most straightforward of intentions and in all good faith he had brought his friends to the boat he'd long before planned to take.

'Anyway,' he said, 'what is the trap here? Who is the Hannibal sailing with us? It's just Lichas of Tarentum, a very respectable man, who is not only the owner of this boat which he's in command of, but also of a number of farms and a trading company. He's carrying a commercial cargo to market. This is your Cyclops and pirate-captain, and we owe our passage to him. And as well as this man, there's Tryphaena, the loveliest woman in the world, who travels from place to place in the service of pleasure.'

'These are the people we're running away from,' said Giton and went on to explain briefly to the frightened Eumolpus the reasons for their hatred and the seriousness of the danger.

Confused and not knowing what to do, Eumolpus suggested we each put forward our ideas:

'You have to imagine we've got into the Cyclops' cave. Some way of escape has to be found, short of involving ourselves in a shipwreck and extricating ourselves from every possible risk.'

'No,' said Giton, 'better get the pilot to take the ship back into some port – not for nothing, obviously – and tell him your brother is not a good sailor and is in the final stages. You can cover up the deception by looking worried and shedding some tears, so the pilot will be touched and do what you want.'

Eumolpus argued that this wasn't possible. 'You see,' he said, 'large ships make their way into well-curved harbours, and it is not likely that my brother could have fallen ill so quickly. And another thing, perhaps Lichas will want to look at the sufferer out of a feeling of duty. You can see how very useful that would be to us, deliberately summoning the captain to the very ones running away from him. But suppose the ship could be diverted from its long voyage and suppose Lichas did not go round the sick-beds no matter what, how could we leave the ship without being seen by everyone? With heads covered or bare? Covered? Then everyone would want to give a hand to the invalids. Bare? Then that would be simply advertising ourselves.'

102. I interposed: 'Why don't we rely on really bold measures, slip down a rope, get into the ship's boat, cut the painter and leave the rest to fortune? Not that I'm calling on Eumolpus to share this risk. I'm happy if luck's on our side as we go down.'

'Not a bad plan,' said Eumolpus, 'if it would work. But everyone will notice you leave, especially the pilot, who stays on watch all night and also observes the movement of the stars. Now you might trick him somehow, even with his eyes open, if you were taking your leave by another part of the ship. As it is, you have to slide down by the stern, by the very steering gear where the painter hangs down. Besides, I'm surprised, Encolpius, that it hasn't occurred to you that one sailor stays in the boat on continuous day and night watch and you couldn't get rid of him without killing him or throwing him overboard by brute force.

For this you must ask yourselves how brave you are. As for my coming with you, I shirk no danger that offers any hope of safety. I presume that not even you would want to risk your lives for nothing as though they were trifles. See whether you like this idea: I'll drop you into two leather bags, tie them up with straps and put you among my clothes, leaving the tops a little way open of course, so you can get air and food. Then I'll raise the alarm that my two slaves have thrown themselves in the sea during the night through fear of worse punishment. Then on arrival in port, I'll carry you off like luggage without any suspicion.'

'Oh, really,' I said, 'you'd tie us up as though we were solid right through and our bellies didn't give us any trouble, or as though we didn't even sneeze or snore? Or just because this type of trick did work nicely once? But suppose we could stand being tied up for one day. What happens if either a calm or bad weather holds us up longer? What would we do? Clothes tied up too long get ruined by creases and papers tied together lose their shape. We're young and not used to hard work; will we stand up to being tied and covered like statues?

'Some safe way still has to be found. You look at my idea. Eumolpus as a literary man surely has some ink. So let's use this as a dye and change our colour – hair right down to fingernails. Disguised as Ethiopian slaves, we can wait on you quite happily without any chance of being tortured and at the same time we can trick our enemies by our change of colour.'

Giton added: 'Why not circumcise us too, so we look like Jews, and bore holes in our ears to imitate Arabs, and whiten our faces so Gauls would take us as fellow-countrymen. As though this colouring by itself could change our shapes. A lot of details have to be consistent to keep up the deception! Suppose a face could stay stained for some time. Suppose no drops of water produce spots on our skins and our clothes don't cling to the ink. Well then, can we also puff out our lips into that hideous swollen look? Can we change our hair with a curling-iron? Can we cut our foreheads with scars? Can we open our legs till they're bandy? Can we touch the ground with our ankles? Can we produce foreign-looking beards? Artificial dye stains your body, it doesn't change it. Listen to my coward's way out – let's tie our heads in our clothes and throw ourselves to the bottom.'

103. 'Gods and men forbid,' Eumolpus exclaimed, 'that you should end your lives in so ugly a fashion. Better do what I tell you. My hired man, as you know from the razor, is a barber. Let him shave the hair

off both of you right away, not just your heads but your eyebrows too. I'll follow up by marking your foreheads with an artistic inscription, so you'll appear to have been punished with branding. The letters will simultaneously lull the suspicions of the people looking for you and hide your faces under cover of the punishment marks.'

No time was lost working the trick. We went stealthily to the side of the ship and presented our heads and eyebrows to the barber to be shaved. Eumolpus covered both our foreheads with the huge letters and with a liberal hand extended the notorious inscription for runaway slaves over the whole of our faces.

As it happened, one of the passengers, who was leaning against the side of the ship and emptying his sick stomach, noticed in the moonlight the barber bent over his unseasonable office. Swearing at the bad omen which was reminiscent of a last offering in a shipwreck, he flung himself back to his berth. Pretending to ignore the seasick man and his curse, we returned to our melancholy procedures and, wrapped in silence, spent the remaining hours of the night sleeping fitfully.

*

104. [*Lichas*] 'I dreamt Priapus said to me: "Since you are looking for him, I want you to know that Encolpius has been brought aboard your boat through my agency."'[18]

Tryphaena shuddered and said:

'You would think we'd slept in the one bed. I dreamt that the statue of Neptune that I'd noticed in the great temple at Baiae said: – "You will find Giton on Lichas' ship."'

'You should realize from this,' said Eumolpus, 'how godlike a man Epicurus[19] was. He condemned this sort of nonsense in a very humorous way.' ...[20]

But Lichas, to play safe with Tryphaena's dream, said: 'Who's going to stop us searching the boat? That way we'll avoid any appearance of condemning the workings of the divine mind.' ... The man who had noticed our furtive and worried behaviour in the dark (Hesus was his name) suddenly shouted:

'Then those are the ones who were having a shave in the dark – and that's a terrible thing to do, by god! I'm told no mortal soul should cut his nails or hair on a ship unless the wind and the sea are at odds.'[21]

105. Lichas, shocked by this report, started blazing:

'Is it true that someone cut his hair on the ship, and in the dead of night at that? Bring the culprits out here immediately, so I'll know whose heads should roll to purify the ship.'

'I gave the orders,' said Eumolpus. 'And as I was going to be on the same ship I didn't intend any bad omen for myself, but since they had long shaggy hair, in case I appeared to be making a prison out of the ship, I gave orders for the condemned men to be cleaned up. Another reason was to allow the marks of the letters to be entirely visible to the eyes of readers and not hidden by their covering of hair. Among other things they spent my money on a whore the two of them kept, and I dragged them from her last night soaked in wine and scent. In fact they still smell of what was left of my inheritance.' . . .

So to appease the guardian spirit of the ship, it was decided to give each of us forty lashes. So there was no delay. The furious sailors laid into us with ropes and tried to placate the ship's guardian with our worthless blood. I personally absorbed three lashes with Spartan disdain. But Giton after one blow cried out so loudly that Tryphaena's ears could hear nothing but that well-known voice. And it was not merely the mistress who was thrown into confusion; her maids too, pulled by the familiar tones, rushed to the victim. Giton with his marvellous body had already made the sailors drop their whips and his silent appeal had even begun working on their savage hearts before the maids cried out in chorus:

'It's Giton, Giton! Keep your cruel hands off him. It's Giton, lady. Help him!'

Tryphaena lent an already believing ear to their cries and flew quickly to the boy's side. Lichas, who knew me best, as though he too had vocal testimony, ran to me and without considering my hands or face, but immediately stretching out an investigating hand to my private parts, he said:

'How are you, Encolpius?'

Will anyone now be surprised that Ulysses' nurse after twenty years found a scar sufficient identification[22] when this shrewd man so cleverly went straight to the one thing that identified the runaway, despite the total confusion of the lines we use for physical identification?

Tryphaena began to cry, taking the punishment for real – for she believed that the marks really had been branded on our foreheads – and in a rather subdued manner she began to ask what prison had got hold of us in our travels, and whose hands had been cruel enough to carry out this punishment, making it clear, however, that some of the maltreatment had been richly deserved by us for running away and for hating a situation where we were so well off ...

106. Highly irritated, Lichas leapt forward:

'You simple-minded woman! As though burns from the iron had absorbed the letters. I wish they *had* branded themselves with the inscription. We would have had this consolation at the very least. As it is we have been the victims of a pure farce and made ridiculous by a mere outline.'

Tryphaena was prepared to be merciful, seeing she had not lost her pleasures forever, but Lichas, still remembering his wife's seduction and the affronts he had received in the colonnade of Hercules,[23] exclaimed with a violently contorted face:

'You've realized, I suppose, Tryphaena, that heaven takes some interest in human affairs. It brought the culprits unawares to our ship and warned us of what they'd done in a pair of corroborating dreams. So think, what possibility is there of pardoning men that the god himself has handed over for punishment? As for me, I'm not a cruel man, but I'm afraid I'd suffer whatever penalty I remitted.'

Swayed by so superstitious an argument, Tryphaena said she would not interfere with the punishment; on the contrary, she was even in favour of such richly deserved reprisals. She had suffered no less serious an injury than Lichas – her reputation as a decent woman had been impugned at a public meeting.

*

107. [*Eumolpus*] 'They chose me for this task, I suppose, because I'm well known and they asked me to reconcile them to their own one-time dearest friends.[24] Unless perhaps you think the young men fell into this trap accidentally, even though the first thing every traveller asks is into whose care he is committing himself. So let your hearts be softened now reparations have been made and allow these free citizens to go where they are bound without interference. Slave owners who are brutal and unrelenting actually hinder the satisfaction of their sadistic impulses if conscience is ever likely to bring runaways back. And we don't kill enemies who are handed over to us. What more are you after? What more do you want? Lying before your eyes, begging for mercy, are two young men, respectable, honest and what is more important than either of these things, once bound in friendship to you. For god's sake, if they had run off with your money or had betrayed your trust, yet you might still be well satisfied by these punishment marks you see. Look, you can

trace the brand of slavery on their foreheads and their respectable faces have voluntarily undergone a penalty that puts them outside society.'

Lichas interrupted this plea for mercy and said:

'Don't confuse the issue, but deal with each item. And first of all, if they came of their own accord, why did they cut all the hair from their heads? Anyone who disguises his face is planning deception, not satisfaction. And another thing, if they were trying to ingratiate themselves through an intermediary, why did you do everything you could to keep your protégés out of sight? It is obvious from this that the culprits fell into the trap through sheer chance and you looked for a way to baffle our revenge. As for the odium you are bringing on our heads by shouting about their respectability and honesty, watch you don't damage your case through over-confidence. What should the injured parties do when the guilty come running to be punished? They were our friends, of course! Then they deserve all the greater punishment. A man who attacks strangers is called a criminal, a man who attacks friends, a monster.'

Eumolpus refuted this unjust attack.

'I see,' he said, 'that the greatest objection to these poor young men is the fact that they cut off their hair during the night. According to this argument, they apparently came on the ship by accident, not deliberately. Now I'd like you to hear an account as frank as the matter was simple. Before they embarked, they wanted to rid their heads of a troublesome and superfluous burden, but the unexpectedly favourable wind caused them to delay carrying out their intention. However they didn't think it mattered when they began doing what they had wanted to do, because they didn't know about sailors' superstitions and the code of the sea.'

To this Lichas said:

'What use was it in their helpless position to shave their heads? Unless perhaps bald men tend to be more pitiful objects? In any case what use is it looking for the truth from an interpreter?

'What have you to say, you criminal? Did a salamander burn your eyebrows off? What god did you dedicate your hair to? Speak up, you poisonous creature!'

108.   I simply gaped, terrified by the thought of being punished, and I could find nothing to say, the case was so open and shut. I was such a confused and ugly object – for besides the disgrace of my shorn head, my eyebrows were as bare as my forehead – that didn't seem right

for me to say or do anything. But once a dripping sponge had been wiped over my tearful face, and the wetted ink, streaming over it, reduced all my features to a dark cloud, anger turned to hatred ...

Eumolpus however said he would not allow anyone to outrage respectable people contrary to all moral and legal principles, and he not only verbally but bodily interposed himself between us and their threatening temper.

His travelling servant was there to help him in his intervention as well as one or two very feeble passengers – giving moral support in the dispute rather than any physical aid. And I was not asking anything for myself, but holding my fists before Tryphaena's eyes I said loudly in firm clear tones that I would resort to what force I had, if that criminal woman, the only one who deserved a thrashing on the whole ship, did not leave Giton alone. At my boldness Lichas blazed up into further anger: he was indignant with me for forgetting my own situation to shout so loudly for someone else. Tryphaena, blazing at the insult, was in just as much of a rage and she forced the whole ship's company to take sides. On our side Eumolpus' man armed himself and distributed his razors amongst us. On their side Tryphaena's entourage put up their bare fists and even the maids, yelling away, did not abandon the front line. There was only the navigator, who threatened to give up steering the ship if this madness brought on by the lust of the dregs of society did not stop. But the crazy struggle continued raging none the less, they fighting for revenge, we for our lives.

A good many went down on both sides without any fatalities. Even more retreated from the battlefield bleeding from their wounds. And yet no one's anger abated. Then Giton, like the hero he was, held his menacing razor over his genitals and threatened to cut off the cause of all our misery. Tryphaena averted this extreme action by an unambiguous pardon. Several times I myself put the barber's razor to my throat with no more intention of killing myself than Giton had of carrying out his threat. But he played his tragic role more boldly because he knew he had the razor he'd already cut his throat with.

Both lines stood there in position. So when it was obvious that it was going to be no ordinary battle, the navigator managed with difficulty to persuade Tryphaena to accept the role of ambassador and make a truce. The requisite promises were solemnly offered and accepted. Tryphaena then extended an olive-branch plucked from the ship's figurehead and boldly began the negotiations.

'What madness,' she cries, 'makes peace become war?
What guilt is on our hands? No hero from Troy
Elopes on this ship, no Paris with the betrothed
Of Menelaus tricked. No maddened Medea
Makes of her brother's blood a weapon.[25]
Rejected love is the driving force.
Ah me! Who takes to arms and calls for death
Amid these waves?
            Is one death not enough?
Surpass not the sea – send no fresh floods
To swell the savage waves.'

109. As the woman poured all this out in shrill distressed tones, the lines hesitated a moment and our hands dropped peaceably – the fight was over. Eumolpus took command and made full use of this change of heart. Prefacing it with a violent attack on Lichas, he wrote out and signed a treaty, the formula of which was:

'You, Tryphaena, sincerely undertake not to complain of any past injury done to you by Giton or to bring up, avenge, or by any other method attempt to pursue any action committed before today. You undertake not to impose any service on the boy against his will, whether it be an embrace, kiss, or sexual intercourse, unless for each service you pay one hundred denarii in cash.

'Secondly: you, Lichas, sincerely undertake not to persecute Encolpius with insulting words or looks or make any inquiries as to where he sleeps at night. Otherwise you are to pay two hundred denarii in cash for each separate offence.'

Once the treaty was concluded on these terms, we put away our weapons and, to avoid any lingering resentment after the ceremony, we agreed to put the past behind us with an exchange of kisses. Amid the general encouragement our hatred simmered down and a picnic was brought out on the battlefield, which restored everyone's high spirits. The whole ship rang with the songs and as a sudden calm had interrupted the voyage, we had one man trying to harpoon the fish as they jumped out of the water and another trying to drag the struggling catch aboard with baited fishhooks. And surprise, sea-birds had even perched along the yard and a clever bird-catcher got at them with reeds woven together. They stuck to the limed twigs and were brought down into his hands. The air took hold of the floating plumes and the light spray whirled the feathers over the sea.

Lichas was beginning to be friendly to me again. Tryphaena was splashing Giton with the dregs of her drink, when Eumolpus, being well into his cups, got the idea of throwing out some quips about bald heads and brandmarks, until, exhausting his weak witticisms, he went back to his poetry and began reciting a little elegy on hair:

> 'Your hair has fallen out – your only good feature;
> A cruel storm has stripped the foliage of spring.
> Each temple misses its natural shade
> And a bare expanse grins under worn stubble.
> Oh, the gods, the gods cheat us!
> Our Youth's first glories are Youth's first forfeits.

*

> Poor boy,
> One moment your hair
> Was shining gold
> And you were more beautiful
> Than Phoebus or his sister
> Now you are shinier
> Than a bronze
> Or the round cap
> Of a mushroom after rain.
> You run nervously
> From the laughter of ladies.
> Death's sooner than you think,
> You must believe –
> See now, Death has begun at the top.'

110. He was ready to give us more of the same, I think, or worse, but Tryphaena's maid takes Giton down to the lower half of the ship and dresses the boy's head in one of her mistress's curly wigs. In fact, she even produces eyebrows from a box and, by cunningly following the outlines of the missing features, entirely restored his appearance.

Tryphaena recognized the real Giton and, moved to tears, gave the boy this time a really sincere kiss.

For myself, although I was delighted to see the boy restored to his pristine glory, I began covering my face more than ever. I realized how bizarre my deformity was – not even Lichas thought me worth talking to. But the same girl got me out of my depression by taking me to one side and fixing me up with an equally handsome head of hair. In fact, my face was brighter and more attractive, because mine was a yellow wig.

*

However, Eumolpus, our champion in time of trouble and the author of the present harmony, to prevent the general merriment lapsing into silence without a few stories, began a succession of gibes about feminine fickleness – how easily they fell in love, how quickly they forgot even their children. There was no woman so pure that she could not be driven crazy by some stranger's physical attractions. He wasn't thinking of old tragedies or famous historical names but of something that happened within his own living memory, and he would tell us about it if we wanted to hear it. So when everyone's eyes and ears were turned to him, he began the following story.

111. 'There was once a lady of Ephesus[26] so famous for her fidelity to her husband that she even attracted women from neighbouring countries to come just to see her. So when she buried her husband, she was not satisfied with following him to his grave with the usual uncombed hair or beating her breast in front of the crowd, but she even accompanied the dead man into the tomb, and when the corpse was placed in the underground vault, she began watching over it from then on, weeping day and night. Neither her parents nor her relations could induce her to stop torturing herself and seeking death by starvation. Finally the magistrates were repulsed and left her, and this extraordinary example to womankind, mourned by everyone, was now spending her fifth day without food. A devoted servant sat with the ailing woman, added her tears to the lady's grief, and refilled the lamp in the tomb whenever it began to go out. Naturally there was only one subject of conversation in the whole town: every class of people admitted there had never been such a shining example of true fidelity and love.

'In the meantime the governor of the province ordered the crucifixion of some thieves to be carried out near the humble abode where the wife was crying over the corpse of the lately deceased. Next night the soldier who was guarding the crosses to prevent anyone removing one of the bodies for burial noticed a light shining clearly among the tombs and, hearing the sounds of someone mourning, he was eager to know – a general human failing – who it was and what was going on. Naturally he went down into the vault and, seeing a beautiful woman, at first stood rooted to the spot as though terrified by some strange sight or a vision from hell. When he observed the dead man's body and noted the woman's tears and scratched face, surmising rightly that here was a woman who could not bear her intense longing for the dead man, he brought her his bit of supper and began pleading with the weeping woman not to prolong her hopeless grief and break her heart with useless lamentation. The same end, the same resting-place awaited everyone, he told her – along with all the other things that restore grief-stricken minds to sanity. But in spite of the stranger's consoling words, the woman only tore at her breast more violently and draped her mangled hair over the body of the dead man. The soldier still refused to withdraw; instead, using the same arguments, he tried to press food on her servant until the girl, seduced by the smell of the wine, first gave in herself, stretched out her hand to his tempting charity, and then, refreshed by the food and drink, began to lay siege to her mistress's resolution.

'"What good is it," she said to her, "for you to drop dead of starvation, or bury yourself alive or breathe your last innocent breath before fate demands it?

Believe you that ashes or the buried ghosts can know?[27]

Won't you come back to life? Won't you give up your womanly error and enjoy the comforts of life as long as you can? That very corpse lying there should be your encouragement to live."

'No one is ever reluctant to listen when pressed to eat or stay alive. Parched from taking nothing day after day, the woman allowed her resolution to be sapped and filled herself with food no less avidly than the girl who had given in first.

112. 'But you know what temptations follow on a full stomach. The inducements the soldier had used to persuade the lady into a desire to live became part also of an attempt on her virtue. For all her chastity the man appealed to her: he was neither unpleasing nor ill-spoken, she thought. Moreover, her maid spoke on his behalf and quoted the line:

Would you fight even a pleasing passion?[28]

'Need I say more? The woman couldn't refuse even this gratification of the flesh and the triumphant soldier talked her into both. They then slept together, not just the night they first performed the ceremony but the next night too, and then a third. The doors of the vault were of course closed, so if a friend or a stranger came to the tomb, he thought that the blameless widow had expired over her husband's body.

'Actually the soldier, delighted with the lady's beauty and the whole secret liaison, had bought whatever luxuries he could afford and carried them to the tomb on the very first night. As a result, the parents of one of the crucified men, seeing the watch had been relaxed, took down the hanging body in the dark and gave it the final rites. The soldier, tricked while he lay enjoying himself and seeing next day one of the crosses without a corpse, in terror of punishment, explained to the woman what had happened. He would not wait for the judge's verdict, he said – his own sword would carry out sentence for his dereliction of duty. Only let her provide a place for him in death and let the tomb be the last resting-place for both her lover and her husband. The woman's pity was equal to her fidelity:

'"Heaven forbid," she said, "that I should see simultaneously two funerals, for the two men I hold dearest. I'd rather hang the dead than kill the living."

'Suiting the deed to the word, she told him to take the body of her husband from the coffin and fix it to the empty cross. The soldier followed the sensible woman's plan, and next day people wondered how on earth the dead man had managed to get up on the cross.'

113. The sailors greeted the story with roars of laughter; Tryphaena blushed rather and laid her cheek affectionately on Giton's neck. Lichas however was not amused. Shaking his head angrily, he said:

'If his commander-in-chief had been an honourable man, he should have put the husband's body back in the tomb and nailed the woman to the cross.'

No doubt he had remembered Hedyle and the robbery on his ship before the lecherous elopement. But the terms of the treaty did not permit him to recall this and the prevailing high spirits left no room for bad temper. Tryphaena however was settled on Giton's lap, covering his chest with kisses and occasionally titivating his depilated appearance. Being depressed and annoyed with the recent treaty, I took nothing to eat or drink, but looked at both of them with oblique and hostile glances. All the kisses and all the endearments that the lecherous woman thought up wounded me deeply. Yet I still wasn't sure whether I was more angry with the boy for stealing my mistress or with my mistress for seducing the boy. Both acts were offensive to my eyes and more saddening than my past captivity. Added to this was the fact that Tryphaena would not talk to me like an old friend and once pleasing lover, and Giton did not regard me as worth even the usual toasts – at least he didn't address me in the general conversation, which was the least he could do. He was nervous, I imagine, of opening some fresh scar in the initial stages of the reconciliation. Tears of vexation choked me, and my groans, which I smothered into sighs, almost made me faint.

*

[*Lichas*] tried to get invited to the party, putting on no lordly airs but acting like a friend asking a favour.

*

[*Tryphaena's maid to Encolpius*] 'If you had any decent blood in your veins, you wouldn't regard him as anything more than a whore. If you were a man, you wouldn't go to such a perverted creature.'[29]

*

Nothing embarrassed me more than the possibility of Eumolpus' realizing what had gone on, and, with his usual fluency, taking revenge in verse.

*

Eumolpus swore in the most solemn terms

*

114. While we were talking about this and similar things, the sea grew rough; clouds gathered from all directions and turned the day into darkness. The sailors scampered nervously to their duties and took down the sails before the storm. But there was no consistent wind driving the waves and the helmsmen did not know which way to head the ship. Sometimes the south-east wind blew towards Sicily, then time and again the north-east wind, dominating the Italian shoreline, would take over and turn the helpless ship this way and that.[30] And what was far more dangerous than all the gales, the sudden pitch-black darkness had quenched the light so completely that the navigator could not even see the length of the prow. When the strength of the storm was at its height, Lichas, trembling, stretched out his hands to me pleadingly and said:

'You're the one, Encolpius. Save us from this danger. Just restore to the ship that sacred robe and the goddess's rattle.[31] In heaven's name, have some pity for us, as surely you used to.'

And then in mid-shout the wind flung him into the sea. He was caught up in a raging whirlpool and the blast whirled him round and sucked him under. Loyal servants however caught hold of Tryphaena, who was almost lifeless, put her in a boat with most of the luggage and snatched her from certain death ... Clasping Giton to me with a cry, I wept and said:

'We deserved this of heaven – death alone would unite us. But our cruel luck does not allow it. Look, the waves are already overturning the ship. Look, the angry sea is trying to break our affectionate embraces. If you ever really loved Encolpius, kiss him while you can and snatch this last pleasure from the jaws of death.'

As I said this, Giton took off his clothes and, covered in my tunic, brought up his head for a kiss. And in case the envious waves should drag us apart even when clinging together like this, he tied his belt round both of us and said:

'If nothing else, we will float longer if we are tied together in death, or if out of pity the sea is likely to throw us up on the same shore, either some passing stranger will throw stones over us out of common humanity or, as a last favour that even the angry waves cannot refuse, the heedless sand will cover us.'

For the last time I felt bonds about me and as though laid out on a bier I waited for death – no longer an enemy. Meanwhile the storm executed the commands of fate and carried away all that was left of the ship. No mast, no helm, no rope or oar was left, but like a rough and shapeless log it went with the waves.

*

Fishermen came hurrying out in little boats to do some looting. When they saw there were people to defend their property, their greed was replaced by the wish to help.

*

115. We heard a strange murmur and moaning from the captain's cabin, as though an animal were trying to escape. We followed the sound and found Eumolpus sitting there and turning out verses on a great sheet. Surprised that he had leisure in the face of death to write poems, we dragged him out protesting and told him not to worry. But he was blazing with anger for being interrupted, and said:

'Allow me to get this line right. The poem is almost finished.'

I grabbed the lunatic and told Giton to come and drag the bellowing poet to land.

*

Finally the job was done and we sorrowfully entered the fisherman's cottage. Satisfying ourselves somehow with spoilt food from the wreck we passed a very miserable night. Next day, when we were discussing where in the world we could safely go, I suddenly saw a body turning in a gentle eddy and drifting to the shore.

I stopped sadly and began gazing at this example of the sea's treachery with moist eyes.

'Perhaps somewhere,' I said aloud, 'a carefree wife waits for him, perhaps a son, not knowing about the storm. Or perhaps it was his father he left, at least someone he kissed when he set out. So much for mortal schemes and mortal desires. Look at him – how the man floats!'

I was still mourning for what I supposed was a stranger, when the tide turned his undamaged face to the shore and I recognized almost underneath my feet what had been a little while ago the terrible and implacable Lichas. I could hold back my tears no longer. In fact, I beat my breast again and again and said: 'Where are your bad tempers and your ungovernable rages now? You have been at the mercy of fishes and other horrible creatures. A little while ago you boasted of your power and your position, but you haven't even a plank left from the wreck of your great ship. Go now, mortals, and fill your hearts with great schemes. Go and carefully invest your ill-gotten gains for a thousand years. Yesterday he must have looked at the accounts of his investments, he must have fixed the day he would reach his home town. O heavens, how far away he lies from his destination! Yet it is not only the seas that serve mortals like this. Weapons play a man false in wartime; the collapse of his family shrine buries a man giving thanks to heaven; a man falls from his carriage and hastily gasps his last. Food chokes the glutton, abstinence the abstemious. If you think it over properly, there is shipwreck everywhere. Mind you, a man drowned at sea does not get buried – as though it matters what destroys a perishable corpse – fire, water, or time! Whatever you do, all these things come to the same thing. But of course, wild beasts will mangle the carcass. As though it were better that fire should have it – and yet we consider this the severest possible punishment when we are angry with our servants. So what is the point of this craze to make sure that no part of us is left behind after burial?'

*

And the pyre, built by his enemies' hands, reduced Lichas to ashes.

While Eumolpus was composing an epigram on the dead man, he gazed into the distance in search of inspiration.

*

116. We gladly performed this duty and then we took the road we had decided on and in a short time we were sweating our way up a mountain, from which we saw in the near distance a town situated on a lofty height. Being lost, we did not know what town it was until we learnt from some farm overseer that it was Croton, a very ancient city, once the foremost in Italy.[1] We then inquired most carefully what sort of people lived in this noble area and what type of business they particularly favoured, since their wealth had been diminished by a long series of wars.

'My dear sirs,' he said, 'if you are businessmen, change your plans and look for some other source of livelihood. If, however, you are a more sophisticated type and you can take incessant lying, you are following the right road to riches. You see, in this city no literary pretensions are honoured, eloquence has no standing, sobriety and decent behaviour are not praised and rewarded – no, whatever people you see, you must consider as divided into two classes. Either they have fortunes worth hunting or they are fortune-hunters. In this city no one raises children because anyone who has heirs of his own is not invited out to dinner or allowed into the games; he is deprived of all amenities and lives in ignominious obscurity. But those who have never married and have no close ties attain the highest honours – only these have real courage, or even blameless characters. You are on your way to a town that is like a plague–ridden countryside, where there is nothing but corpses being pecked and crows pecking them.'

117. Eumolpus, the wiser head, turned his thoughts to this novel situation and confessed that this method of enrichment appealed to him. I imagined that the old man was joking, just like a poet, until he said:

'I wish we had more elaborate stage-properties, more civilized costumes, and a more splendid set-up to give plausibility to the imposture. I wouldn't postpone grabbing it, by god! I'd lead you straight to a fortune. Even so, I promise ...'

*

... whatever he should ask for, provided that our old companion in crime, the robe I'd stolen, would do and also whatever Lycurgus' burgled villa had yielded.[2] The mother of the gods with her usual good faith would send us money for immediate use.

*

'Why delay the start of the show then?' said Eumolpus. 'Make me your master, if you like the business.'

No one dared condemn a scheme that would cost nothing. And so, to safeguard the imposture in which we were all involved, we swore an oath dictated by Eumolpus, that we would be burned, flogged, beaten, killed with cold steel or whatever else Eumolpus ordered. Like real gladiators we very solemnly handed ourselves over, body and soul, to our master. After swearing the oath we saluted our master in our role as slaves, and we were all instructed that Eumolpus had buried his son, a young man of great oratorical abilities and high promise, and the unhappy old man had therefore left his native city so that he should not have daily cause for tears at the sight of his son's followers and friends or his tomb. Shipwreck was next added to this grief, in which he had lost more than twenty million sesterces. But he was not worried by the loss, except that being deprived of his servants he did not see about him what was proper to his rank. Besides, he had thirty million invested in Africa in farms and loans; in fact, he had such a large number of slaves spread among his estates in Numidia that they could even capture Carthage.

Following this pattern, we told Eumolpus to cough a lot, get first constipation, then diarrhoea, and curse all his food openly. He was to talk about gold and silver, unreliable farms and his invariably unproductive lands. Moreover he was to sit down every day at his accounts and renew the terms of his will every month. And, to complete the farce, whenever he tried to call one of us he was to call out the wrong name, to make it clear that their master remembered even the ones who were no longer with him.

After making these arrangements, we prayed to heaven that it would all turn out well and happily, and set off down the road. Giton however, could not manage the unaccustomed pack and Corax the hired man, a constant grumbler in his job, kept putting his bag down, hurling insults at us for hurrying, and vowing that he'd throw away the bags and run off with his load.

'What *is* this, you people?' he said. 'Do you think I'm a beast of burden or a ship for carrying stones? I contracted for a man's job, not a dray-horse's. I'm a free man as much as you are, even if my father did leave me poor.'

Not content with cursing, every so often he lifted his leg right up and filled the road with obscene sounds and smells. Giton laughed at his bad behaviour and followed each of his farts with an equally loud imitation.

*

118. 'Poetry,[3] my young friends,' said Eumolpus, 'has cheated many people. As soon as each of them has made his lines scan and woven some idea into a delicate web of words, he thinks he's gone straight up Helicon. Tired by their legal practice they often fly to the calm waters of poetry, as though it were a lucky port in a storm, believing it must be easier to construct an epic poem than a speech that glows with scintillating epigrams. But noble inspiration hates empty verbiage and a mind cannot conceive or bear fruit unless it is soaked in a mighty flood of great works. One must avoid all vulgarity of language and one must select expressions not in common use; the effect should be "I hate the vulgar crowd and fend them off". Besides this, one must be careful that witty lines are not made to stand out from the body of the narrative, but add their colour and brilliance to the texture of the poem. Witness Homer and the lyric poets, Roman Virgil, and Horace's careful felicity. Other poets either have not seen the way to approach poetry, or if they have seen it have been frightened to take it. Above all, whoever attempts the great theme of the Civil War without being full of the great writers will fail under the task. For it is not historical fact that has to be handled in the poem – historians do this far better. No, the unfettered inspiration must be sent soaring from the catapult of wit through dark messages and divine interventions and stories, so that it gives the impression of prophetic ravings rather than the accuracy of a solemn speech before witnesses.

'As an example, if you like, here's this bold attempt, even though it has not yet received the final touches:[4]

I

119.   'All-conquering Rome was mistress of the globe,
     By land and sea an empire to the poles,
         but still unsatisfied.
     Sea-lanes battered by heavy hulks;
     A hidden bay, a gold-producing region –   5
         this was the ENEMY.
     The Fates are bent on war,
     The search for wealth continues.
     Ordinary pleasures,
         plebeian enjoyments   10
            are tedious,
     Soldiers connoisseurs of Corinthian bronze.
     Gems from deep mines
         flash challenges to purple.
     From Numidia marble –   15
         From China new silks –
     The Arabian countryside
         stripped bare for profits.
     Further disasters, more stabs at a stricken Peace (hear ye!):
     Wild beasts are stalked in the woods of Taurus,   20
     Ammon in darkest Africa
         flushed for the monster
     "which is slain
         because his tooth sells dear".
     Starvation in strange forms   25
         weighs down the ships;
     The prowling tiger hauled in a bronze cage
     To gorge on human blood for the cheering PLEBS.
     Shame chokes my spleen and voice.
     How to reveal those doomed lives?   30
     The genitals removed,
     Organs mutilated under the knife
     And broken into the services of lust.
       The solemn march of time is checked,
       The speeding years retarded,   35
       Nature seeking herself finds nothing.
       Each man has his catamite
       (The soft enervated gait,
       The floating hair,
       The fashions in clothes,   40
       Tokens of absent virility.)

Eye-catching tables of citron-wood from Africa (look ye!)
Mirror the splash of purple and lackeys;
Imitate in mottled surfaces disvalued gold.
About the useless wood, the pride of fools,   45
The mob moves tipsily.

Footloose, the soldier hefts his tackle,
      an esurient mercenary.

The Belly, miracle of ingenuity,
Brings the parrot-wrasse,   50
Submerged in Sicilian water,
Alive to the table;
Pulls oysters from the Lucrine Lake,
To make a sale to the palate,
The high price most of the flavour.   55

The Phasian Lake emptied of birds,
Along that silent shore
Only the wind breathes upon the deserted leaves.
The same madness in politics:
A bribed electorate changing sides for silver.   60
On sale: one people and one senate

CHEAP!

Votes are for selling.
Even old men forget
      the strenuous requirements of freedom.   65
A change of government for small change,
Auctoritas corrupt and humiliated.
   Cato is defeated,
      rejected by the electorate;
The victorious candidate is embarrassed,   70
Ashamed to snatch
      the *fasces* from Cato.
Not the defeat of a candidate,
The death-blow of a great people –
Rome a lost city,   75
      merchant and merchandise,
      plunderer and plundered.
A vile vortex, a gaping whirlpool,
The people drowning.

With *Usura* comes there greed,   80
With usura hath no man a house,
With usura hath no man a hand free,
A canker born in the hidden marrow,
A madness raging in the limbs of the body politic
And wandering with its sorrows   85
Like a pack of hounds.
And out of this Revolution,
Revolution from poverty.

War tempts the poor.
Dissipated fortunes are recouped by murder,   90
Boldness with nothing has nothing to lose.
Drowned in this filth, sodden with this sleep,
What practitioner's skill can rouse Rome surely?
Furor militaris
None but the soldier's, *furor militaris*,   95
          desire pricked by the sword.

II

120.   'Fortune produced three captains.
Enyo, murderous goddess of War,
Crushed each on different battlefields.
Parthia kept Crassus,   100
In the Libyan Sea lay Pompey (surnamed Magnus)
And Julius –
          his blood incarnadined ungrateful Rome.
The earth,
Intolerant of so many tombs together   105
Divided their ashes.
Such are fame's privileges.
   The scene:
   Deep in a hollow cleft
   Between Neapolis and Puteoli,   110
   A cleft awash with water from Cocytus,
   Hot with eternal exhalations,
   Damp with a deadly dew.
   No autumn green here,
   No green fields of pleasant turf,   115

No echoing thickets
    Or sweet discords of spring song.
But CHAOS,
    foul black pumice rock,
In triumphant isolation,   120
And a ring of depressed cypresses above.
Father Dis, appearing from below,
Head powdered with white ash
And flames from funeral pyres,
Sardonically to Fortune, winged goddess: 125
    "O mistress of all divine and human things,
    Hater of all security of power,
    Lover of the new, forsaker of triumphs,
    Art thou not crushed
    By the weight of Rome?   130
    Canst thou raise higher that doomed mass?
    The new generation frets at its strength,
    Burdened by accumulated wealth.
    See, everywhere rich pickings of victory,
    Prosperity raging to its ruin.   135
    They build in gold and raise their mansions to the stars.
    The seas are dammed by dykes of stone
    And other seas spring up within their fields –
    A rebellion against the order of all things.
    The tunnelled earth yawns under insane buildings;   140
    Caverns groan in hollowed mountains;
    As long as frivolous employments are found for stone,
    My ghosts confess their hopes of heaven.
    On then, Fortune –
    Change thy looks of peace for the face of war.   145
    Rouse Rome and give my kingdom its dead.
    I have felt no blood on my face,
    My Tisiphone has not bathed her parched limbs,
    Since Sulla's sword drank deep
    And the bristling earth produced its bloody crops."   150

121.   'He tries to take her right hand,
    But the ground breaks into a yawning chasm.

Fickle-hearted Fortune so replies:
    "Father, lord of inmost Cocytus,
    If I may with impunity reveal   155
        what must come to pass,

Thy wishes are granted.
The mad rage inside me no less than thine,
A more wayward fire eats my heart.
All I have heaped upon the Roman citadels   160
I now detest,
    resenting my generosity.
The same power that built
    will destroy their mighty works.
I have in mind   165
    to immolate their warriors,
Choke their decadence with blood.
Now rings through timorous ears the clash of arms:
I see Philippi strewn with double slaughter,
Thessalian pyres, Spanish and Libyan dead;   170
I see Nile's barriers groaning,
The bays of Actium,
    warriors terrified of Apollo's
      martial port.
Go then, open the thirsty territories of thy kingdom   175
To beckon in new ghosts.
The ferryman Charon will be too weak
To ferry the shades in his boat –
    there will be need of a fleet.
Glut thyself on the great disaster, pale Tisiphone,   180
Bite into the open wounds.
The torn world is led to the Stygian shades."

122.   'As she finished a cloud shook
And with abrupt flashes of fire
Broke apart for a gleaming thunderbolt,   185
Closing behind the jetting flame.
The father of the shades retreated,
Pater umbrarum
Closed the gaping breast of the earth
in panic,   190
Paling before fraternal bolts.

III

'At once mankind's disaster, the dooms to come,
Are revealed by heavenly omens.

Hyperion, ugly with bloody face,
            hid his orb in darkness,   195
As though he saw civil war already.
Elsewhere Cynthia dimmed her full face,
Withdrew her light from the scene of the crime.
Mountain ridges thundered into fragments,
   As peaks collapsed,   200
And rivers wandered no longer free,
     dying slowly between familiar banks.
Heaven a pandemonium of military excursions;
A tremulous trumpet from the stars
     took Mars by the ears.   205
Etna, eaten by strange fires,
    flung its eruptions into the skies.
Amid the tombs and unburned bones
    the faces of the dead appear
With terrible menacing shrieks.   210
A comet trailing new stars, bearing fire;
A new Jove,
A new sky descending in bloody rain.
Portents soon clarified by God.

Caesar brooks no delay,   215
Pricked by lust for revenge
He abandons the Gallic,
       begins the Civil
       War.

IV

'In airy Alps   220
Where the rocks once pounded by a Greek divinity
Slope softly to let men enter,
Est locus,
   a holy place with altars there to Hercules.
Winter blocks it with tight-packed snow   225
And lifts it to the stars with a blanching peak.
The heavens might have fallen from its top.
It does not melt in midsummer rays, spring breezes,
Its packed surface stays stiff with ice and winter frost,
It could carry the globe on its threatening shoulders.   230

When Caesar tramped these ridges with his exulting
        soldiers and chose his site,
He looked out
  over the wide Italian plains from the summit,
Pointed both hands to the stars: 235
  "Jupiter Omnipotent,
  Saturnian land once glad of my armies,
  And loaded down with my triumphs,
  I call you to witness:
  Mars summons me to war,   240
        an unwilling warrior.
I bring unwilling hands to the execution,
Forced by my grievances,
Driven from my city
  while I reddened the Rhine with blood   245
And blocked the Gauls from the Alps
(Their second attempt on the Capitol).
Exile the surer for my victory!
In German blood my guilt is rooted,
        in a hundred triumphs.   250
Yet who are they my glory terrifies?
Who are they who would end my wars?
Cheap operators bought and sold,
        hirelings,
My Rome their step-mother.   255
But not with impunity, nor without revenge, I think,
Shall a coward tie my hands.

Run mad, my victorious ones!
Go, comrades, plead my case with a sword!
The same charge laid at our doors,   260
The same disaster over us all.
I owe you thanks –
        I did not win alone.
So, since there are penalties
  for the acquisition of trophies,   265
And victory celebrations see us in convicts' dress,
        Fortune be the judge –
Let the die be cast.
Begin the war and try your mettle.
Yet my case is already won –   270
With so many brave around me

            I do not know the meaning of defeat."
      'At the trumpet of his voice
      A raven, *Delphicus ales*,
      Was a glad omen in the sky,   275
      Cleaving the air.
      From the left of the dread grove
      Strange voices sounded
                  and flames rose.
      The brightness of the Sun grew brighter than its wont   280
      And set a burning halo of gold about its face.

123. 'Caesar deployed his standards of war,
      Heartened by omens,
      First to attempt these new audacities.
      The icy surface and frost-hard ground   285
      Made no resistance,
                  lay quiet, crunching gently.
      But the squadrons shattered the bound clouds,
      The horses panicking unfettered the ice,
                  the snow melted.   290
      Rivers of sudden origin ran from the mountain heights,
      Yet these too (as at a command)
      Halted and the flow was still,
                  (chained downpour).
      One moment a mire, then a hardened floor.   295
      Treacherous before, it now mocked at their steps,
                  deceived each foot.
      Men, horses equally, arms and armour
      Lay piled in sorry confusion.
      Now the clouds, hit by the cutting wind,   300
      Let fall their loads,
      Winds torn by whirlwinds,
      Skies rent by swollen hailstones.
      The very clouds were tatters
                  and fell about their armour.   305
      The frozen ice heaved like ocean waves.
      The earth was covered by the storm of snow,
      The stars were covered
      And the rivers stuck to their banks
                  covered too.   310
      Only Caesar above it –
      Leaning on his great spear,

With sure strides breaking across the cracking fields,
Like Hercules, Amphitryonides, striding, head-high,
From the Caucasian peak,   315
Or like a frowning Jupiter,
Rushing from the towering tops of Olympus,
Hurling his bolts at the doomed race of Giants.

V

While Caesar angrily trod underfoot
                    the haughty pinnacles,   320
Winged Rumour, wings fluttering in terror,
Took flight to the high ridges of the Palatine,
And with this thunder of rumours smote
Every statue in the city:
    "The fleets are on the sea,   325
     The whole Alps a blaze of squadrons
     Spattered with German blood."
Armies, blood, slaughter, fire, whole wars
Flit before their eyes.
Their hearts battered by this din   330
Were torn in two and much afraid.
Flight by land, said one –
The sea is better, said another:
The sea is now safer than our country.
Not wanting were those who favoured fight,   335
Accepting the command of Fate.
The people trailed from the desolate city,
To wherever their stunned minds moved,
                    saddest of scenes.
Rome's heart is in the rout,   340
Beaten already the Quirites
Leave their sad homes when they hear the rumour.
One clutches his children in trembling hands,
One hides his family gods beneath his coat,
Leaving the sad hallway   345
                    cursing to death the distant enemy.
Some clasp wives to their sad breasts
And young men who never felt a load
Clasp aged fathers,
Carrying only what they fear for most.   350
Others unwarily take all they have,

Carrying booty to battle.
In a storm at sea,
When great Auster starts to roughen the deep
And sends the driven waves toppling,   355
When rigging and rudder fail,
One man battens down,
Another looks for safe harbour, tranquil shore,
And another hoists sail to fly the storm,
Trusting his all to Fortune.   360

An end to these minor catastrophes:
Pompeius Magnus with both consuls,
Pompey, terror of the Pontus,
Explorer of savage Hydaspes,
The rock that wrecked the pirates,   365
For all his three triumphs that made Jupiter tremble,
For all the veneration of Pontus
After he sheered through its maelstrom,
And the submission of the waves of the Bosphorus,
Took to flight,   370
            Shame on 't!
His title to power forgotten,
So fickle Fortuna might see the back
            Of even Pompeius Magnus.

VI

124.   'Such a great infection spread even to the skies,   375
        The timorousness of heaven set the seal on flight.
        And through the world a gentle host of gods,
        Abominating earth's madness, abandoned earth,
        Avoiding the armies of the doomed.
        First Pax, first of them all,   380
        Bruising her white arms, hid her defeated head
        In a helmet, left earth in haste
        For the implacable kingdom of Dis.
        Submissive Honour her companion,
        And Justitia, hair ragged,   385
        Concordia sobbing in her torn dress.
        The flight not all in one direction:
        Where the realm of Erebus yawned,
        Emerged in broad array the troop of Dis:

Bristling Erinys, Bellona, menacing,   390
Megaera with her armoury of torches,
Doom, Treachery and the pale image of Death.

In their midst went Furor, Madness,
Like a horse trailing broken reins,
Her bloody head held up to the world   395
Her face, pitted with a thousand wounds,
Hid in a bloodstained helmet:
The battered shield of Mars,
                 heavy with innumerable arrows,
Gripped in her left hand,   400
In her right the threat of a burning torch
Carrying fires to earth.

VII

The earth feels the weight of the gods,
Stars shifted, losing equilibrium,
The whole kingdom of heaven divided.   405
Dione first heads the armies of her Caesar,
Pallas moving to her side and Romulus (Mavortius)
                 beating his great spear.
Phoebus and Phoebus' sister,
And Mercury, on Cyllene born, took Pompey away,   410
And Hercules Tirynthius like him in all his deeds.
          The trumpets sounded.
Discordia with her torn hair
Raised to the gods above her Stygian head.
Clotted blood in her mouth,   415
Tears in her battered eyes,
Her teeth mailed with a scurf of rust,
Her tongue dripping with foulness,
Her face in a ring of snakes;
With bosom convulsed beneath her tattered dress,   420
She waved in a shaking hand a bloody torch.
Left Tartarus, the darknesses of Cocytus,
Striding up to the high ridges
Of the lordly Appennines,
Vantage-point for all lands, all seas,   425
And the forces flooding the world.
From her mad breast these cries erupted:

"To arms, ye nations – now your hearts are on fire.
To arms and throw your torches
           into the hearts of cities.   430
Whoever hides will be defeated.
Let no woman lag behind, or child,
           Or age-torn man.
Earth trembles, the ripped houses revolt.
Cling to your Law, Marcellus.   435
Shake up the masses, Curio.
Lentulus, quench not that brave and martial ardour.
And you, son of heaven,
Why do you delay with your armies?
Why are you not battering at gates,   440
Tearing away town walls, hauling off treasure?
Can you not guard the Roman fortress, Pompey?
Look then to the walls of Epidamnus,
And dye Thessalian bays with human blood."
And all Discordia commanded   445
           so came to pass on earth.'

CROTON

When Eumolpus had poured all this out in a great flow of words, we finally entered Croton. Here we recuperated at a little inn and next day, looking for a house on a larger scale, we fell in with a crowd of legacy-hunters, who asked us what sort of people we were and where we came from. Following our concerted plan we told the gullible inquirers where we were from and who we were.

Immediately they did their best to outdo each other in putting their financial resources at Eumolpus' service ... All of the legacy-hunters vied with each other to get into Eumolpus' good graces with presents.[1]

*

125. While all this was taking place in Croton over a considerable period of time ... Eumolpus, full of happiness, was so forgetful of his previous fortune, that he often boasted that no one in the place could stand up against his influence, and his own people, through the good offices of his friends, would get off scot-free for any crime they committed.

Personally, although I fattened myself up every day with more and more of these over-abundant luxuries and thought Fortune had taken her eyes off me, yet quite often I was worried not from any real cause, but from thinking of my usual luck: 'What if some shrewd legacy-hunter sends a spy to Africa and exposes our whole deception? What if the hired man gets tired of our present happy position, turns over evidence to our friends, and uncovers the whole scheme by his spiteful treachery? We'll obviously have to run away once more and just when we were rid of it, we'll be reduced to poverty again for a fresh period of beggary. Heavens above, how terrible it is to live outside the law – one is always expecting what one rightly deserves.'[2]

*

126. [*Circe's maid, Chrysis, is talking to Polyaenus, i.e. Encolpius*] 'Because you're aware of your sexual charms, you put on an arrogant air and sell your favours instead of giving them free. Otherwise, what's

the point of your combed wavy hair, the heavy make-up, the soft sulkiness in your eyes, the self-conscious walk, the carefully measured steps? What's the object unless you're prostituting your good looks for money? You look at me – I'm no fortune-teller, and I don't go in for astrology, but I tell people's characters from their faces, and when I've seen how someone walks, I know what he's thinking. If you're selling what I've come for, there's a customer waiting. Or if you're giving it free – which is nicer – put me under an obligation for your kindness. You say you're just a poor slave, but you're only exciting her desire to boiling point. Some women get heated up over the absolute dregs and can't feel any passion unless they see slaves or bare-legged messengers. The arena sets some of them on heat, or a mule-driver covered with dust, or actors displayed on the stage. My mistress is one of this type. She jumps across the first fourteen seats from the orchestra and looks for something to love among the lowest of the low.'[3]

I said in a voice full of sweetness: 'Tell me, are you the one who is in love with me?'

The maid laughed heartily at such an unlikely notion.

'I wouldn't make you so pleased with yourself. I have never yet gone to bed with a slave, and heaven forbid I should ever see a lover of mine crucified. That's for ladies who kiss the whip-marks. Even though I'm a servant, I've never sat anywhere except in the lap of knights.'

I couldn't help some surprise at such contrasting sexual desires. I thought it very strange that the maid should cultivate the superior outlook of a lady and the lady the low taste of a maid.

Then as the joking continued, I asked her to bring her mistress to the copse of plane trees. The girl agreed to the suggestion. She tucked up her tunic and turned into the laurel grove bordering the walk. Without any long delay she brought out of the shadows a woman who was lovelier than any work of art, and led her to my side.

No words could do justice to her charms – whatever I said would not be enough. Her curls flowed naturally over the whole breadth of her shoulders and waved back at the hairline from her exquisitely narrow brow. Her eyebrows ran down to the contour of her cheeks and almost met over the bridge of her nose. Her eyes were brighter than stars shining outside the glow of the moon. Her nostrils curved in a little, and her little mouth was as Praxiteles[4] imagined Diana's.[5] Now her chin, now her neck, now her hands, now the pearly lustre of her feet clasped by a thin gold chain – each in turn would have put Parian marble[6] to shame. Then for the first time I despised my old passion for Doris.[7]

*

> What has happened, Jove, what has happened
> To make you throw down your arms,
> To become an old story in heaven,
> To disdain these terrestrial charms?

> Now here was a worthy occasion
> To beetle your brows and put on
> Two horns or cover your white hair
> With the feathers and form of a swan.[8]

> Here, here is a real Danaë –
> She would kindle your lust even higher.
> One touch, one mere touch of her body
> And your limbs would be melting in fire.

*

127. She was delighted and smiled so sweetly I thought the full moon had shown her face out of a cloud. Then modulating her voice to her gestures, she said:

'If you don't find a smart lady distasteful, one who had a man for the first time only this year, let me introduce to you a new girl-friend, young man. Of course, you have a boy-friend too – I wasn't ashamed of making inquiries, you see – but what's to stop you adopting a girl-friend as well? I shall come on the same footing. You have only to agree to put up with my kisses as well, whenever you like.'

'On the contrary,' I replied, 'I must beg you, you beautiful creature, not to disdain to number a poor stranger among your adorers. You will find him religiously devoted if you permit him to worship you. And don't imagine I am entering this temple without an offering. I give up my boy-friend for you.'

'What?' she said. 'Are you giving up for me the boy you cannot live without, the lips you cling to, the one you love the way I want to love you?'

As she said this, there was such charm in her voice, such a sweet sound caressed the enraptured air that it was as though the song of the Sirens sang through the breezes. And then in my amazement – the whole sky seemed somehow brighter – it occurred to me to ask the goddess her name.

'So my maid hasn't told you,' she said, 'that I'm called Circe?' Not
that I am the child of the Sun – my mother never stopped at will the
course of the revolving heavens. Yet if the fates unite us, I shall have
something to thank heaven for. A god, in fact, is already working his
mysterious purposes to some end. It is not by chance that Circe is in
love with Polyaenus – a great flame is always kindled between these
names. Take me in your arms, if you wish: there is no reason to fear
any prying eyes. Your beloved boy is a long way from here.'

Saying this, Circe drew me, entwined in arms softer than swansdown,
on to the grassy ground.

> Flowers such as the Earth Mother spread on Ida's top
> When Jove and his wifely love united[10]
> (His breast one raging fire).
> Roses, violets, soft rushes glinting there
> And the white lilies smiling
>   from the green meadows.
> Such a place cried for love on its soft grass
> The day brightened like a blessing
> On our secret amours.

Side by side there in the grass we kissed a thousand times in our love-
play, groping towards more strenuous pleasures.

*

128. [*Circe to Polyaenus*] 'What is it?' she said. 'Does my mouth offend
you in some way? Does my breath smell through not eating? Is it the
unwashed sweat from my armpits? If it's not any of these, am I to
suppose you're somehow frightened of Giton?'

Flushed with obvious embarrassment, I even lost whatever virility I
had. My whole body was limp, and I said:

'Please, my queen, don't add insults to my misery. I've been
bewitched.'

*

[*Circe*] 'Tell me, Chrysis – but the truth, mind! Am I somehow
unpleasant? Am I untidy? Am I somehow obscuring my beauty because
of some natural defect? Don't deceive your mistress. I've done something wrong.'

Then as Chrysis remained silent, she snatched a mirror from her and
after trying every expression that lovers usually put on to amuse each
other, she shook out her dress, rumpled from contact with the ground,
and rushed into the shrine of Venus. On my part, like a guilty thing,

trembling as though I'd seen a horrible vision, I began asking myself mentally whether I had been robbed of the chance of true pleasure.

> Any soporific midnight an instance,
> When the unfocused eyes are dream-deluded:
> The spaded earth exposing gold,
> Guilty hands fingering criminal gains,
> Snatching at jewels,
> Sweat too bathing the face,
> And a deep fear in the mind
> That mere awareness of gold on the person
> May dislodge it
> > even from the breast pocket.
> The images of joy recede from the mocked brain;
> Reality returns
> To a heart longing for lost pleasures
> Lingering in vanished illusions.

*

[*Giton to Encolpius*] 'So thank you for loving me in such an honourable Platonic way.[11] Alcibades himself couldn't have been safer when he slept in his teacher's bed.'

*

129. [*Encolpius to Giton*] 'Honestly, dear lad, I can't realize I'm a man, I don't feel it. The part of my body that once made me an Achilles is dead and buried.'[12]

*

The boy was frightened of being discovered alone with me and giving rise to gossip, so he rushed off and took refuge in the inner part of the house.

*

Chrysis however entered my room and delivered to me a letter from her mistress, which read as follows:

Dear Polyaenus,

If I were a sensual woman, I would complain I had been tricked. As it is, I am positively grateful for your weakness. I've played too long in the mere shadows of pleasure. However I'm writing to ask how you are and whether you got home on your own feet. Doctors say a man can't walk if he has no strength. I'll tell you something, my young friend – beware of paralysis. I have never seen a sick man in such great danger – you are as good as dead, for heaven's sake. If that same chill got into your knees and hands, you could send for the undertaker. To come to the point: although I was deeply offended, still I don't begrudge a sick man his prescription. If you wish to get better, send Giton away. You will get your strength back, I can tell you, if you sleep without your darling boy for three days. As far as I am concerned, I'm not afraid of meeting someone who will like me less. The mirror doesn't lie, nor does my reputation.

Get well soon – if you can.

Circe

When Chrysis saw I had read the whole insulting screed, she said:

'These things tend to happen, particularly in this part of the country, where women even drag down the moon . . . This problem will be taken care of too. Just write a soothing reply to my mistress and restore her good spirits with a frank and natural answer. If the truth must be told, from the moment she was so insulted, she has not been her usual self.'

130. I gladly took the maid's advice and wrote some such letter as this:

Dear Circe,

I admit I have done many bad things. After all, I am a man and still young. But I have never till today committed a really deadly sin. You have the culprit's confession. Whatever you order, I deserve it. I have been guilty of treachery, I've killed a man, and I've robbed a temple – find a punishment for these crimes. If you wish to kill me, I'll come and bring my sword. If you are content with just whipping, I'll run naked to my beloved. Remember this one thing, not I but my instruments were at fault. The soldier was ready, but had no weapons. Who caused this trouble I don't know. Perhaps my thoughts ran ahead of my lagging body; perhaps in my keen desire to enjoy every last thing, I used up the pleasure in dallying. I have not discovered what I did. Still, you tell me to beware of paralysis – as though it could become any worse, now it has deprived me of the ability to possess you of all women. However this is what my excuses come to: I will give you satisfaction, if you allow me to atone for my fault.

Your slave,
Polyaenus

*

I sent Chrysis off with this sort of promise and carefully attended to my treacherous body. Omitting a bath, I used a very moderate amount of oil to rub myself down, then dining on more solid dishes than usual, onions and the heads of snails without seasoning, I drank a sparing quantity of wine. After this, setting myself up with a very gentle stroll before bed, I went to my room without Giton. So great was my anxiety to placate her that I was afraid my boy-friend might impair my virility.

131. Getting up next day without any mental or physical strain, I

went down to the same grove of plane-trees, although I was nervous of such an inauspicious place, and began waiting among the trees for my guide, Chrysis. I walked round for a short while and I had only just sat down where I had been the day before when she turned up, bringing a little old woman with her. When she greeted me, she said:

'How are you, my fine friend? Have you begun to feel in better spirits?' . . .

The old woman brought out of her dress a string of variously coloured threads twisted together and bound it round my neck. Then mixing some dust with spittle, she took it on her middle finger and ignoring my repugnance, marked my forehead with it.

*

After completing this spell, she instructed me to spit three times and drop down my chest, again three times, some pebbles which she had charmed and wrapped in purple. Then she began to test my virility with her hands. Faster than you could speak, the nerves obeyed the command, and the little old woman's hands were filled with a mighty throbbing. Leaping with joy, she said: 'Do you see, my dear Chrysis, do you see how I've started a hare for others to hunt?'

*

> The lofty plane-tree spreads its summer shade,
> Metamorphosed Daphne near by,[13] crowned with berries.
> Cypresses tremulous, clipped pines around
> Shuddering at their tops.
>> Playing among them
> A stream with wandering waters,
> Spume-flecked, worrying the stones
>> with a querulous spray.
>> A place right for love.
> Witness the woodland nightingale,
>> and Procne[14] turned urban swallow –
> Everywhere amid the grass and soft violets,
> Their woodland homes a temple of song.

*

She lay relaxed, her marble neck resting on a golden couch, and she beat the tranquil air with a branch of flowering myrtle. When she saw me, she blushed a little, obviously remembering yesterday's affront. Then when everyone had gone, and I had sat down beside her at her invitation, she placed the branch over my eyes, and with this wall between us she became bolder.

'How are you, you paralytic?' she said. 'Have you come intact today?'

'Why ask me?' said I. 'Try me!' and I threw myself bodily into her arms and kissed her till I could kiss no more – no magic spells there.

*

132. Her sheer physical beauty cried out to me and she pulled me down to make love to her. Our lips ground noisily together in kiss after kiss. Our locked hands found every possible way of making love. Our bodies wrapped in a mutual embrace united even our very souls.[15]

*

Smarting from these open insults, the lady finally rushes to have her revenge. She calls her attendants and has them hoist me up and whip me. And not content with such a drastic punishment she calls round all her wool workers and the lowest types of servant and has them spit at me. I put my hands over my eyes, and without any begging for mercy because I knew what I deserved, whipped and spat on, I was flung through the door. Proselenus is thrown out too, Chrysis is beaten, and the whole household gloomily muttered to each other and wondered who had dashed their mistress's high spirits . . .

*

And so, after weighing things up, I became more cheerful. I concealed the marks of the whips with some doctoring so that my ill-treatment would neither amuse Eumolpus nor sadden Giton. Then I did the only thing I could do to save my face, I feigned weariness; and wrapped up in bed, I directed the whole blaze of my anger on what had been the cause of all my troubles.

> Three times I took the murd'rous axe in hand,
> Three times I wavered like a wilting stalk
> And curtsied from the blade, poor instrument
> In trembling hands – I could not what I would.
> From terror colder than the wintry frost,
> It took asylum far within my crotch,
> A thousand wrinkles deep.
> How could I lift its head to punishment?
> Cozened by its whoreson mortal fright
> I fled for aid to words that deeper bite.

And so leaning on my elbow I made quite a speech, abusing it for its disobedience. 'What have you got to say?' I said. 'You insult to mankind, you blot on the face of heaven – it's improper to give you your real name when talking seriously. Did I deserve this from you – that you should drag me down to hell when I was in heaven? That you should betray me in the prime of life and reduce me to the impotence of the last stages of senility? Go on, give me a serious argument.' As I poured this out angrily:

> Turning away, she kept her eyes down-cast,
> Her visage no more moved by this address
> Than supple willow or drooping poppyhead.[16]

Once this vile abuse was finished, I too began to feel regret – for talking like this – and I blushed inwardly at forgetting my sense of shame and bandying words with a part of the body that more dignified people do not even think about. Then after rubbing my brow for some time, I said to myself: 'Still, where's the harm in relieving my feelings by some natural abuse? Anyway, how is it we curse such parts of the body as the stomach or the throat and even the head, when we have the occasional headache? In fact, didn't Ulysses argue with his heart, and don't some tragic heroes abuse their eyes as though they could hear them? People with gout curse their feet, people with arthritis their hands, people with ophthalmia their eyes, and when people stub their toes, they often blame the pain on their feet.

> Cato[17] frowns and knits his brows,
> The Censor wants to stop us,
> The Censor hates my guileless prose,
> My simple modern opus.
> My cheerful unaffected style
> Is Everyman when in his humour,
> My candid pen narrates his joys,
> Refusing to philosophize.

> Find me any man who knows
> Nothing of love and naked pleasure.
> What stern moralist would oppose
> Two bodies warming a bed together?
> Father of Truth, old Epicurus[18]
> Spoke of bodies, not of soul,
> And taught, philosophers assure us,
> Love is Life's sovereign goal.

*

There is nothing on earth more misleading than silly prejudice and nothing sillier than hypocritical moralizing.

*

133. After finishing this speech, I called Giton and said:

'Tell me, my dear, but on your honour. That night Ascyltus stole you away from me, did he stay awake and assault you or was he content with a lonely and honourable night?'

The lad touched his eyes and solemnly swore that Ascyltus had offered him no violence.

*

Kneeling on the threshold, I offered up a prayer to the hostile deity:[19]

> 'Comrade of Nymphs, comrade of Bacchus,
> Deity of the rich forests
>   whom fair Dione appointed,
> Famed Lesbos, green Thasos obey your wishes
> And the Lydians spread over the seven rivers
> Bow before you –
> They built you a temple in your own Hypaepa –
> Come to me, guardian of Bacchus, darling of Dryads,
> Hear my timid orisons.
> I come before you –
>   unstained by guiltless blood.
> I was no enemy of religion
>   when I robbed the temples.[20]
> Need and the attrition of poverty,
>   these were the agents –
> Not my true self.
> The man who sins through poverty
>   is a venial offender.
> My prayer is:
>   Relieve my mind,
>   Forgive the venial sin,
> And whenever fortune smiles on me,
> I shall not let your glory go unhonoured –
> A horned goat, O holy one, sire of his herd,
> Will come to your altars,
> The farrow of a grunting sow, a milky victim,
> Will come to your altars.
> Wine of the newest vintage will foam in the chalices
> And inebriated young men
> Will march in triumph
> Three times around your shrine.'

*

While I was doing this and keeping a close eye on the dear departed, the old woman entered the temple. She looked a sight with her torn hair and black clothes. She put a hand on me and led me outside the vestibule.

*

134. [*The old woman, Proselenus, to Encolpius*] 'Were they witches who enervated you? Did you tread on some shit in the dark at a crossroad? Or a corpse? You haven't even rescued yourself from the boy. Instead, you're soft, weak, and tired, like a cart-horse on a slope; you just wasted all this effort and sweat. And not content to be a sinner on your own, you've set heaven against me too.'

*

And without any protest from me, she led me through into the priestess's room where she threw me on a bed, and snatching a rod from behind the door, still without a murmur from me, gave me a thrashing. If the rod had not shattered at the first stroke and lessened the force of the blows, she might perhaps have broken my arms and head as well. I howled particularly at the cuts aimed at my groin. With my tears flowing freely I leaned my head on the mattress and covered it with my right hand. She was equally upset and tearful. She sat on the other side of the bed and complained in tremulous tones of living too long, until the priestess came in and found us . . .

'Why have you come to my room like mourners to a funeral?' she said. 'Especially on a holiday, when even miserable people show a smile . . .'

*

[*Proselenus to Oenothea,*[21] *priestess of Priapus, talking of Encolpius*] 'Oh, Oenothea,' she said, 'it's this young man you see here. He was born under an evil star. He can't make a sale to boy or girl. You've never seen a man so unlucky – he's got a piece of wet leather, not a prick. In fact, what do you think of someone who could get out of Circe's bed without having had any pleasure?'

Hearing this, Oenothea sat down between us and shook her head for quite a time.

'I'm the only one who can cure that trouble,' she said. 'And don't think I'm doing anything puzzling – I want the young man to sleep the night with me. May I drop dead if I don't make it as stiff as a horn:

'All things on earth obey me. At my wish
The flowering earth grows arid, the sap dry.
At my wish its benisons spill forth.
Rocks and jagged cliffs gush out Nile waters;
For me the ocean flattens its white tops;
The zephyrs lay their blasts hushed before my feet.
The rivers obey me,
Hyrcanian tigers,[22] and dragon sentinels.
Small things to boast of! –
The orbed image of the moon descends
At the pull of my spells.
                    The Sun-god
Turns round his foaming horses
And fear-driven retraces his orbit.
Such power have words.
The hot breath of bulls is quenched
By the rites of virgins;
Sun-child Circe transformed Ulysses' crew
With magic spells.[23]
Proteus[24] turns into whatever shape he likes.
Expert in magical experience,
I will root Idaean trees in the sea.
Plant rivers on the topmost height.'

135. I shuddered: I was terrified by such a fabulous promise and I began scrutinizing the old woman very warily ...

'Well,' cried Oenothea, 'now do what I tell you.' ... And carefully washing her hands she lay on the bed and kissed me a couple of times ...

Oenothea placed an old table in the middle of the altar and heaped red-hot coals on it. She took down a broken old cup and repaired it with some warmed pitch, then she replaced in the smoky wall a wooden nail which had come out with the cup as she pulled it down. Wearing a square cloak, she placed a great kettle on the hearth and drew out from her larder with a fork a cloth bag containing beans and an ancient piece of pig's cheek, very knocked about and with a thousand bruises on it. When she unfastened the string of the bag, she poured part of the beans on the table and ordered me to shell them carefully. I obeyed her instructions and with meticulous fingers separated the beans from their filthy pods. But with some caustic comments on my slowness, she took them herself, stripped the pods off with her teeth and spat them to the ground like dead flies.

*

I was amazed at the ingenious shifts of poverty and the sort of artistry individual objects displayed:

> No gleam of Indian ivory inlaid in gold,
> No radiance of marble underfoot,
> The earth not mocked by the earth's profusion;
> Just a thicket of husked straw on a willow frame,
> New ... clay pots,
>   the hasty products of cheap wheels.
> Here a tank of soft limewood,
> Tough platters of wicker work,
> A wine-stained cup.
> The walls around were a stiffness
> Of dry straw and random mud –
> Held by a scattering of rustic nails,
> And hanging there a slim broom of green rushes.
> The provisions of the humble place
> Hung from its smoky beam:
> Bland sorb-apple,
> Dried savory and raisins in bunches,
> Twined in sweet-smelling wreaths ...
> In such a hut on Attic ground
> Lived Hecale,[25] hostess worthy of worship,
> Whom in the years of eloquence
> The Muse of inspired Callimachus described
> With wond'rous art.

*

136. While she cut off a small piece of the meat too, ... and as she put back the cheek, which was as old as she was, into the cupboard with the fork, the rotten stool, which had given her short body the necessary height, broke and, because of her weight, sent the old woman sprawling into the hearth. The neck of the kettle was broken and put out the fire, just as it was beginning to blaze up. She burnt her elbow on a glowing piece of wood and blackened the whole of her face with ashes she stirred up. I got to my feet in alarm and set the old woman on her feet, not without some amusement ... To prevent anything delaying the sacrifice, she immediately rushed off to some place in the neighbourhood to relight the fire ...

I went to the door of the cottage . . . when all of a sudden three geese –
I suppose they generally got their daily rations from the old woman at
midday – made a rush at me and to my dismay surrounded me with an
obscene and infuriated hissing. One tore my tunic, another undid my
shoe-laces and tugged at them, and the ring-leader in this savage assault
went so far as to peck at my leg with its serrated beak. Without any
messing about, I tore a leg off the tiny table and with this weapon began
hammering at the most ferocious of the birds. And not content with a
half-hearted stroke, I avenged myself by killing the goose:

> They fled like the heavenward flight
> Of Stymphalian birds[26]
> From Hercules' powerful arts;
> Like the Harpies, dripping with filth,
> When Phineus' deceptive feasts dribbled poison;
> The aether tremulous and afraid,
> The heavenly kingdoms confused
> At the strange wailing . . .

*

The rest had already snapped up the beans, which had rolled away and
spread out over the whole floor; and now, deprived, I suppose, of their
leader, they had returned to the temple.

Pleased with both my bag and my revenge, I throw the dead goose
behind the bed and bathe the wound in my leg, which was not deep,
with vinegar. Then, fearing a row, I made up my mind to leave.
Collecting my clothes I began to make my way out of the cottage, but
I had not crossed the threshold when I noticed Oenothea on her way
with a potful of fire. I naturally retreated, threw off my clothes and
stood in the doorway as though waiting for her impatiently.

She placed the fire in the hearth   it was in some dry reeds   and
after putting a lot of sticks on top, she started to explain her delay. Her
friend had not let her go without her getting through the ritual three
drinks.

'Here,' she said, 'what have you done while I was away? Well, where
are the beans?'

I thought I'd done something to be proud of, so I gave her the whole
battle in detail, and to cheer her up I offered her the goose as
compensation for the loss. When the crone saw it she raised such a loud
shriek that you'd have thought the geese were back in the place again.
Naturally confused, in fact thunderstruck, as though my action was

some strange crime, I asked her why she had flared up and why she was more sorry for the goose than for me.

137. She beat her hands together:

'You criminal,' she said, 'why go on talking? You've no idea of the great offence you've committed. You've killed Priapus' darling, the pet goose of all the ladies. Don't think it's a mere nothing you've done. If the authorities knew of this, you'd be crucified. You've polluted my house with bloodshed – the first time it's ever happened, and you've given any enemy who likes an opportunity to expel me from my post as priestess.'

*

'Please don't shout,' said I, 'I'll give you an ostrich in place of the goose.'

*

While I stood stupefied at all this, and she sat on the bed and wailed over the fate of the goose, Proselenus arrived with the provisions for the sacrifice. Seeing the dead goose, she asked how it happened and then began to cry copiously herself, and said she was deeply sorry for me – as though I'd killed my father, not a communal goose.

So, bored and tired of it all, I said:

'Tell me, can one pay compensation for sacrilege? ... even if I insulted you, even if I'd committed a murder. Look, I'm putting down two gold pieces – you can buy gods and geese with this.'

When Oenothea saw them, she said:

'I apologize, young man. I'm worried for your sake. It's a sign of affection, not ill-will. We'll do our best to prevent anyone knowing about it. You just pray heaven forgives you for what you've done.'

> With money you've a yacht with a following breeze;
> With money you've got Lady Luck on her knees;
> You could marry Danaë[27] with cash on the nail
> And make her and her father believe the same tale.
> If you're a poet or speaker, the crowd thinks you're great,
> If you plead at the bar, Cato[28] sounds second-rate.
> You can prove and disprove, be a lawyer of note,
> Whose cases are vital for textbooks to quote.
> Whatever you wish for, if you can disburse,
> Will be there – you've a Jupiter locked in your purse.

*

She put a cup of wine under my hands and after rubbing my outstretched fingers clean with leeks and garlic, she threw some filberts into the wine, murmuring a prayer. She made various deductions from whether they came to the top or settled, but I didn't fail to notice that the empty nuts filled with air naturally stayed on the surface of the liquid, while the heavy, full nuts were carried to the bottom.

*

Cutting open the goose's breast, she extracted a very fat liver and foretold my future from it. And more, to get rid of every trace of the crime, she cut up the whole goose, spitted the pieces and prepared an elegant feast for a man who a little while ago, by her own account, was doomed . . .

Cups of strong wine passed quickly round as this went on.

*

138. Oenothea brought out a leather dildo: this she rubbed with oil and ground pepper and crushed nettle seed, and began inserting it gradually up my anus . . .

The vicious old woman then sprinkled my thighs with this liquid.

*

She mixed the juice of cress with some southern-wood, and after soaking my genitals in it, she took a green nettle-stalk and began whipping me steadily everywhere below the navel.

*

Although staggering with drink and desire, the old crones took the same route and followed in my tracks for several streets, shouting 'Stop thief!' But I got away, every one of my toes bleeding through my headlong rush.

*

'Chrysis, who detested your earlier position, intends to follow you in your present situation even at the risk of her life.'[29]

*

'What did Ariadne or Leda[30] have to compare with her loveliness? What could Helen or Venus do against her? Paris himself, judge in the contest of goddesses, if he'd seen her with his roving eyes when making his comparison, he would have given up Helen *and* the goddesses for her. If I were allowed just to take a kiss, or embrace that divine and heavenly breast, perhaps my body would recover its strength and the parts that I'm positive are drugged by some witches' brew would revive. It's not her insults that make me reluctant. I overlook the whipping. I was thrown out, but I regard that as a joke. Only let me back into her good graces ...'

*

139. I tossed and turned in bed, groping continually, after some image of my beloved ...

*

> Others have been hounded by gods
> And implacable fate, not I alone.[31]
> Hercules hounded from Argos,
> And propping heaven on his shoulders.
> Impious Laomedon
> And those two angry immortals:
> He paid the price of his offences.
> Pelias felt the weight of Juno.
> Then there was Telephus –
> He took up arms in his ignorance.
> Even Ulysses went in fear of Neptune's power.
> Now I too take my stand among these –
> Over land and white Nereus' sea, I am hounded
> By the mighty rage of Priapus of Hellespont.

*

I started by asking my dear Giton whether anyone had been asking for me.

'No one today,' he said, 'but yesterday quite an elegant lady came to the door and after a long conversation, when she wore me out with irrelevant chatter, she finally said you ought to be punished and you would suffer as a slave should if you took offence and persisted in your ill-feelings.'

*

I had not yet finished when Chrysis arrived and clasped me in a most unrestrained embrace, saying:

'I've got you in my arms just as I'd hoped. You are my only desire, my only pleasure in life. You will never put out the fire I feel unless you quench it in my blood.'

*

One of the new servants hurried up and swore that our master was furious with me because I'd been absent from my duties for over two days. I'd be well advised to prepare some suitable excuse, as it was highly unlikely his rage would calm down without someone getting the whip.

*

140. There was one highly respectable matron, Philomela by name, who had extorted a great many legacies while she had the advantages of her youth. By now she was an old woman and her bloom had gone, so she forced her son and daughter on childless old men and by means of these deputies managed to continue her profession. Naturally she came to Eumolpus and started by handing over her children to his wisdom and upright nature; to him alone could she entrust herself and her prayers. He was the only one on earth who could manage every day to instil sound principles into young people. In fact, she was leaving her children in Eumolpus' house so that they could listen to his talk ... which was the only legacy that could be given to young people.

She was as good as her word. She left the very pretty daughter with her youthful brother in his room and pretended she was going off to the temple to say the appropriate prayers.

Eumolpus, who was such a sexual miser that he even regarded me as a boy, did not hesitate a moment to invite the girl to the rituals of the buttocks. But he had told everyone that he had gout and a weakness in the loins, and if he did not keep this pretence intact, he would be in danger of ruining the whole show. So to ensure that his deception was not discredited, he begged the girl to sit on top of the upright nature to which she had been entrusted, and ordered Corax to get under the bed he was lying in and, with his hands placed on the floor, to move his master with his own thighs. He carried out the order phlegmatically and the expertise of the girl responded with similar movements. When things were looking forward to the climax, Eumolpus called loudly to Corax to press on with the job. Placed in this way between his servant and his lady friend the old man looked as though he was playing on a swing. Eumolpus repeated this performance a few times amid howls of laughter, including his own.

And so I for my part, not to get out of the habit through lack of practice, approached the brother, as he admired his sister's tricks through the key-hole, and tried to see if he would accept my advances. The well-trained little fellow did not withdraw from my caresses, but divine hostility dogged me there too.

*

'There are mightier gods who have restored me to full health. Mercury, who leads souls away and leads them back,[32] by his kindnesses has returned me what was cut off by the hand of vengeance. So you may

take it that I am more favoured than Protesilaus[33] or anyone like him
in history.'

With this I lifted my tunic and showed all I had to Eumolpus. At
first he was horrified, then to convince himself fully, he held in both
hands the gifts of the gods.

*

'Socrates, the wisest of all in the opinion of the gods and men, used to
boast that he had never looked inside a tavern and never trusted his
eyesight at any assembly with a large crowd. There is nothing more
profitable than a continuous dialogue with wisdom' ...

'All of that is true,' I said, 'and no one should come to grief quicker
than those who are after what belongs to others. How would a confidence
man or a pickpocket survive, if he didn't drop little boxes or chinking
purses into the crowd to hook his victims? Just as dumb animals are
snared with food, so men can't be caught unless they are nibbling
hopefully at something.'

*

141. 'The ship with your money and servants has not arrived from
Africa as you promised. The legacy-hunters are already drained dry
and are cutting down on their generosity. So if I'm not mistaken,
fortune is beginning to have her regrets again.'

*

'All those who have legacies in my will, except for my freedmen, will
receive what I have left them only on this condition – that they cut up
my corpse and eat it in front of the people.'

*

'We know that among certain races the custom of the dead being eaten
by their relations is still observed. So much so that sick people are often
reproached for causing their flesh to deteriorate. I therefore call on my
friends not to shrink from my demands, but eat my body in the same
spirit as they damned my soul ...'

The enormous reputation of his money blinded the eyes and hearts
of the poor fools.

Gorgias was ready to carry out the terms ...

*

'I have no worries about your stomach's balking. It will obey your
command if you promise it a lot of luxuries as compensation for one
hour's disgust. Just close your eyes and pretend you are eating a million
sesterces, not human offal. Then for another thing, we'll find some

seasonings to change the taste. After all, no meat is pleasant by itself; it's artfully adulterated in some way and made acceptable to the reluctant stomach. And if you want the idea to be justified by examples too, there are the Saguntines,[34] who ate human flesh when they were besieged by Hannibal – and they weren't expecting a legacy. The Petelians did the same in the last stages of a famine and all they were after with this feast was to avoid dying of starvation. When Numantia was captured by Scipio, there were some mothers found carrying around at their breasts the half-eaten bodies of their own children.'

THE FRAGMENTS
AND
THE POEMS

I

Servius (late 4th c. A.D.) on Virgil, *Aeneid* 3.57: *auri sacra fames*] *sacra*
means accursed. The expression derives from a custom of the Gauls.
Whenever the inhabitants of Massilia suffer from a plague, one of their
poor people offers himself to be fed at the public expense for a whole
year on special religious foods. Afterwards he is dressed in sprigs of
sacred foliage and certain ritually prescribed clothing and led round the
whole city with curses, so that the ills of the whole city will fall upon
him. He is then cast out. This is in Petronius.

II

Servius on Virgil, *Aeneid* 12.159 (on the feminine gender of nouns
ending in *-tor*): If, however, the nouns are not derived from a verb, they
are of common gender. Both the masculine and feminine end similarly
in *-tor*, e.g. a male and a female *senator*, a male and female *balneator*
(bath attendant), although Petronius employs a form *balneatrix* in his
writings.

III

Pseudacro (*c.* A.D. 400) on Horace, *Epodes* 5.48: *Canidia rodens pollicem*]
he has described the bearing and movements of Canidia in a fury.
Petronius, to describe someone in a rage, says 'with her thumb bitten
to danger point'.

IV

Sidonius Apollinaris (*c.* A.D. 450), *Carmen* 23:

145. What shall I say to you, glories of Latin eloquence,
   Cicero of Arpinum, Livy of Padua, and Mantuan Virgil . . .
155. And you, Arbiter, worshipper of the sacred stump
   Amid the gardens of Massilia,
   A match for Priapus of the Hellespont.

V

Priscian (early 6th c. A.D.), *Principles of Grammar* 8.16 (GL 2.381) and
11.29 (*ibid.* 567) (among examples of past participles of deponent verbs

with passive meaning): Petronius 'soul embraced (*amplexam*) to our breast'.

Vb

Boethius (A.D. 480–524) in his comments on Porphyry's *Introduction to Aristotle's Categories* (translated by Victorinus), *Dialogue* 2.32: 'I will do that very willingly,' I said, 'but since the morning sun, as Petronius has it, has smiled upon the roofs, let us get up and if there is anything in that matter, it will be discussed later with more careful consideration.'

VI

Fulgentius (A.D. 532–567) *Mythologies* 1 p. 12 ff. (*Helm*): You do not know ... how much ladies shrink from satire. Although even lawyers give way under a woman's flood of words and schoolteachers do not even mumble, although rhetoricians are silent and public announcers hush their noise, there is one thing alone that imposes some moderation on their madness, though it be Petronius' character Albucia who is in heat.

VII

Fulgentius *ibid.* 3.8 p. 73 (on the extreme heat of myrrh extract): So Petronius Arbiter too tells us he drank a draught of myrrh to arouse his sexual desires.[1] [This is in Book XIV, where Quartilla is in the company of Ascyltus and Encolpius and, to allow the latter to drink a second toast, gave him Ascyltus' portion to drink. Then Quartilla says 'Has Encolpius drunk all the satyrion there was?']

VIII

Fulgentius in his *Treatise on the Contents of Virgil's Works* p. 98 ff.: Now we earlier explained the fable of the three-headed Cerberus by way of a quarrel and litigation in court; compare Petronius' hostile description of Euscios – 'he was a Cerberus in court'.

IX

Fulgentius in his *Explanation of Archaic Words* 42 p. 122: A mess of various meats is called a course or dish (*ferculum*), compare Petronius – 'after the course was brought to the table'.

X

Fulgentius *ibid*. 46 p. 123: *valgia* (wry twists) are contortions of the lips due to vomiting; compare Petronius 'with his lips wryly twisted'.

XI

Fulgentius *ibid*. 52 p. 124: *alucinare* (to have hallucinations) is the term for dreaming nonsensical dreams. It derives from *alucitae*, which we call mosquitoes. So Petronius says, 'for the mosquitoes (*alucitae*) were bothering my companion'.

XII

Fulgentius *ibid*. 60 p. 126: *manubies* (booty) means the ornaments that kings wear; compare Petronius, 'the *manubies* of so many kings found in the possession of a runaway slave'.

XIII

Fulgentius *ibid*. 60 p. 126: *Aumatium* (little eye) is the term for a public privy of the sort found in theatres or in the circus; compare Petronius, 'I flung myself into a privy'.

XIV

Isidorus Hispalensis (A.D. 602–36) in the *Origines* v. 26.7: *dolus* (guile) is mental cunning, so termed because it beguiles (*deludat*): it does one thing and feigns another. Petronius thinks otherwise for he says: 'What is guile, gentlemen of the jury? Surely when something has been done which guys the law. You have your guile, now let me tell you about an evil (*malum*).'

XV

From the *Glossary of St Dionysius* (*Petrus Daniel*): *petaurus* (= *petaurum*, a spring-board or see-saw) is a kind of game; compare Petronius, 'and at the demand of the spring-board now higher (now lower)'.

XVI

Ibid.: Petronius, 'there was general agreement that they did not usually go through the Neapolitan tunnel without bending'.[2]

[XVII *Bücheler*][3]

[Another Glossary (used by Pierre Pithou): *suppes suppumpis*, that is 'with feet bent backwards.' *Tullia, media vel regia* (Tullia, middle or royal).]

[XVIII *Bücheler*]

[Nicoló Perotti, *Cornucopiae* p. 200, 26 (Aldine edition, 1513) Cosmus was an excellent manufacturer of perfumes and Cosmian perfumes are named after him.[4] The same author has 'and though he be smothered in a whole jugful from Cosmus (Juvenal 8.86). Petronius, 'bring us, he said, an alabaster box of Cosmian'.]

XIX

Terentianus Maurus (late 2nd c. A.D.), *On the Metres of Horace* (*G L* 6.399):

> We see the poet Horace
> Nowhere used such verses[5]
> In regular succession,
> But the Arbiter so eloquent
> Packs them in his writings.
> You can recognize them
> In lines we like to chant, as:
> 'Girls of Memphis origin,
> Trained for godly services'

> 'Tinged with darkness' colouring,
> Boy with hands loquacious'.

Marius Victorinus (d. *c*. A.D. 360) 3.17 (*GL* 6.138): We know that certain lyrical poets inserted some verses of this metre and form in their poems, as we find also in the Arbiter. An example of his is:

> 'Girls of Memphis origin,
> Trained for godly services'

and again,

> 'Tinged with darkness' colouring,
> Choruses Egyptian.'

XX

Terentianus Maurus *op. cit.* (*GL* 6.409, 2849–2858, 2861 2865):

> The division which we speak of
> Gives the metre old Anacreon
> Used in his sweet singing.
> We find Petronius used it,[6]
> When he says that lyric poet
> Sang songs befitting Muses
> (And many others used it).
> But that verse of our Petronius –
> *iuverunt segetes meum laborem*:
> (The harvest helped my labour)
> I'll show you its caesura –
> *iuverunt* starts as hexameter:
> What's left, *segetes meum laborem*
> Is like *triplici vides ut ortu*
> 'Seest thou with triple rising
> The Moon her fire revolving,
> And Phoebus with swift axle
> Traverse the rapid globe.'

Marius Victorínus 4.1 (*GL* 6.153): ... The metre will be Anacreontic, inasmuch as Anacreon used it most frequently, but many poets used it in our literature, among them the Arbiter has this in his writings:

> 'Seest thou with triple rising
> The Moon her fire revolving,

And Phoebus with swift axle
Traverse the rapid globe.'

XXI

Diomedes Thrax (late 4th c. A.D.) in his *Grammar* (*GL* 1.518): From this comes also that caesura, an example of which Petronius offers in:

'An old woman stewed in wine,
With trembling lips.'

XXII

Servius (late 4th c. A.D.) in his *Exposition of the Grammar of Donatus* (*GL* 4.432, 22): Again, he uses '*Quirites*' (citizens) only in the plural. But we read in Horace '*hunc Quiritem*' (this citizen) as though the nominative were 'this *Quiris*'. Again Horace also writes '*quis te Quiritem?*' ('Who – you a citizen?') where the nominative would be *hic Quirites*, a form used by Petronius.

Pompeius (5th c. A.D.) in his *Commentary on the Grammar of Donatus* (*GL* 5.167, 9): No one says '*hic* (this) *Quirites*' (citizen) but '*hi* (these) *Quirites*' (citizens), although we will find the former. Read in Petronius and you will find this done with the nominative singular, and so Petronius says '*hic Quirites*'.

XXIII

Anonymous, *On Nouns of Uncertain Gender* (*GL* 5.578, 23): *Fretum* (sea-strait) is neuter and its plural is *freta*, cf. Petronius '*freta Nereidum*' (straits of the sea-nymphs).

XXIV

St Jerome (*c*. A.D. 348–420) in his *Letter to Demetriades* 130.19: curled and waved boys, their skins smelling like foreign mice, the virgin should avoid like some plague and poison of chastity. The Arbiter's line refers to them:

['he who always smells nice has not a nice smell']⁷

XXV

Fulgentius, *Mythologies* 2.6 p. 45 f. (*Helm*): although Nicagorus[8] tells us that (*Prometheus*) first gave rise to the image and describes the exposure of his liver to the vulture as an allegory of spite. Hence too Petronius' lines:

> The vulture that picks through the torn liver,
> Tears out the breast, each inmost part,
> Is not the creature witty poets aver,
> But Lust and Spite, the cankers of the heart.

XXVI

A L 690:

> So the crow flies against Nature's way
> By laying eggs when the corn is high;
>
> So the bear gives birth, then licks its cub
> Into shape; fish spawn, uncoupled in love;
>
> So Apollo's tortoise, free of parental chains,
> Cares for its eggs with warm nostrils in the sand;
>
> So the sexless bee, roused from its web of wax,
> Swarms and refills its empty ranks.
>
> Nature's not happy with a limited range,
> But delights in all variety and change.

XXVII

A L 466:

> Fear invented the gods.
> Lightning flashing from a high heaven,
> Walls riven by the flame,
> Athos kindled beneath the blow,[9]
> Phoebus descending beneath the traversed earth
> For his new risings,
> The decay of the moon and its glory recovered,

Stars scattered over all the world,
And the year divided into changing months.
The vice took hold – vain superstition
Bade farmers offer first fruits to Ceres,
Bind Bacchus with full palms,
Let Pales rejoice at the shepherds' hands.
A hazard to every sailor,
Neptune from the depths claims the waters,
Pallas the streets and inns.
Every guilty wish, every venial instinct
Invents its own gods in greedy competition.

XXVIII

A L 476:

People would rather swallow a lighted candle
Than keep a secret that smacks in the least of scandal.
The quietest whisper in the royal hall
Is out in a flash buttonholing passers-by against a wall;
And it's not enough that it's broadcast to the nation –
Everyone gets it with improvement and elaboration.
So the servant, not being sufficiently stealthy
To play the gossip and stay alive and healthy,
Dug a hole and spilt the news into that
About the ears His Majesty was hiding under the royal hat.[10]
The hole took the story to its bosom and in less time than
    it takes to utter,
The reeds started to mutter
And begin
To let out the whole story that Midas was trying to keep in.

XXIX

A L 650:

Our eyes deceive, the vagrant senses lie,[11]
When reason's overborne. Yon tower hard by
Rises four-square, but from the distant ground
Looks circular, its angles worn and round.
Full stomach shrinks from honey, often the nose
From cinnamon. Conflicts in taste arose,

Because the senses in predestined suit
Wrangle in their continual dispute.

XXX

AL 651:

Dreams,[12]
The fleeting shadow-play that mocks the mind,
Issue from no temples,
No heavenly power sends them –
Each man creates his own.
When prostrate limbs grow heavy
And the play of the mind is unchecked,
The mind enacts in darkness
The dramas of daylight.
   The shatterer of cities in war,
   Who fires unlucky towns,
   Sees flying spears, broken ranks, the death of kings,
   Plains awash with spilt blood.
   The barrister pleads again in nightmare,
   Sees the twelve tables, the court, the guarded bench.
   The miser salts away his money
   To find his gold dug up.
   The hunter flushes the woodland with his hounds.
   The sailor dreams he is doomed,
   Drags out of the sea the upturned poop,
   Or clings to it.
   The mistress scribbles a note to her lover;
   The guilty lover sends a gift . . .
   And the hound in his slumbers bays at the hare's tracks.
   [The pangs of unhappiness last
   Into the watches of the night.]

XXXI[13]

AL 464:

Each to his taste: what this one scorns
Another likes; roses one plucks, another thorns.

XXXII

AL 465:

> Autumn had shattered the shadows' glowing line,
> The cool-reined sun looked down on colder skies,
> The plane-tree's leaves were falling and the vine
> Had stripped to count its grapes: before our eyes
> The old year's promises were now redeemed.

XXXIII

AL 467:

> I would not steep my hair in the same old oil,
> Nor woo my stomach with too familiar wine.
> Bulls love to change the valley where they graze;
> And wild beasts fill their maw with changing prey

XXXIV

AL 468

> I should love my wife like my income:
> But I must confess to my shame
> That I wouldn't love my income
> If I thought it would stay the same.

XXXV

AL 469:

> Youth, leave your home for alien shores.
> For you now dawns a mightier day;
> Be strong, and the Danube, that last boundary,
> The icy North and the safe Egyptian realms,
> The nations of the morn and setting sun,
> Will learn of you: he who descends
> On distant sands becomes a greater man.

XXXVI

AL 470:

> There's some use in everything, sometime, somehow –
> In trouble, what you've thrown away seems so useful now;
> When the boat goes down and the strongroom bullion too,
> It's the floating oars that save the drowning crew;
> When the trumpet sounds, the sword's at the rich man's throat,
> And the poor man stands there safe, in his ragged coat.

XXXVII

AL 471:

> My little house has its safe roof above;
> Wine-laden grapes hang from the fruitful elm.
> The boughs are hung with cherries; my orchards grow
> Their reddening apples and the olive grove
> Is cracking with its lavish freight. And where
> The airy garden drinks its channelled streams,
> The saffron plant, the creeping mallows thrive,
> And poppies promising their carefree sleep.
> Then, should I wish to weave my snares for birds,
> Or set my traps to catch the quivering deer,
> Or pull up timid fish on slender lines,
> . These are the only tricks my fields have known.
> So go and sell the hours of life that flies
> For rich men's feasts. The same death waits for me:
> May it find me here to judge the time I've spent.

XXXVIII

AL 472:

> Is it not enough, engulfed by maddened youths,
> With damned and blackened name, we're swept off course?
> Look, slaves and home-born rabble run amok
> And wanton through our hard-won hoard of wealth.
> Cheap slaves have kings' estates, and prison cells
> Scorn Vesta and the hut of Romulus.
> So virtue lies abject in deepest mud:
> The fleet of the unjust flaunts whiter sails.

XXXIX

AL 473:

> So the body will immure the belly's wind,
> Which, labouring to emerge from those deep depths again,
> Searches with blows for a way; and the cold shiver
> That masters the constricted bones will never cease
> Till the warm sweat bedews the loosened frame.

XL

AL 474:

> O shore and sea more sweet to me than life!
> What luck to come so soon to lands I love!
> O lovely day! In these fields long ago
> I used to rouse the Naiads as I swam.
> The pool of the spring is here; yonder the kelp
> In the bay. A haven safe for secret loves.
> I have lived. And Fortune's bite can never wrench
> From me those joys time past once gave.

XLI

AL 475:

> This said, he tore white hair from 's trembling head,
> And rent his cheeks; from 's eyes a rain of tears,
> But as the evil flood sweeps through the dales,
> When melts the frigid snow, and soft south wind
> Brooks not the ice to press the prison'd earth,
> So in full spate his face ran tears; his heart
> In deepest grief resounds with troubled moans.

XLII

AL 477:

> There sea and sky in battle win by turns;
> Here smiles the sward, pierced through with dainty streams.
> There sailors mourn their sunken barque;
> Here shepherds water sheep from gentle banks.

There death confronts and stops the gape of greed;
Here Harvest gladly bows to sickle blades.
There thirst, dry-jawed, burns up amid the foam;
Here lavish kisses shower on faithless men.
Let Ulysses in tatters tire the tide;
The fair Penelope will live on land.

XLIII

AL 478:

If there's no haste to die, to force the fates
To break the tender threads with eager hands,
Then test thus far the anger of the deep.
Look where the ebbing tide flows back and bathes
One's feet, still safe, with gentle waves.
Look where the mussel rolls in seaweed green
And the slipp'ry shell with raucous whorl is trapped.
Look where the tides toss back the rolling sands,
And coloured pebbles end on rippled flats.
Whoever can tread here, here let him play,
Safe on the shore, and think just this is sea.

XLIV

AL 479:

Beauty is not enough; who wishes to be fair
Must not content herself with average care.
Talk, be witty and smile to show your wit –
If Nature's unaided, nothing comes of it.
Art is Beauty's aid, her finest dress:
Beauty, if scornful, dies of nakedness.

XLV

AL 691:

India bore me on shores purple as Tyre,
Where the white dawn rises in an orb of fire;
A creature born here, divine honours among,
I changed a barbaric noise for the Latin tongue;

Delphic Apollo, dismiss your every swan –
My parrot voice a worthier myrmidon.

XLVI .

A L 692:

Shipwrecked, a sailor finds another
    stunned by the same blow
And tells his story.
Crops ruined by hail,
    a whole year's labour with them,
The farmer weeps out his troubles
On a breast similarly afflicted.
At funerals the bereaved weep in concert –
Death the leveller.
We too will hammer at the stars
    with antiphonal complaints.
I have heard that prayers
Fly more bravely linked.

XLVII

A L 218:

You send me golden apples, Marcia dear,
You send me gifts of shaggy chestnut too;
For those I'm grateful, but if you came here,
You'd bring your choicest gift, my love, just you.
And if you wish, crab-apples you may bring,
Your honeyed lips would make them sweet to taste.
Yet if you must deny my welcoming,
Just kiss the fruit; I'll eat it up in haste.

XLVIII

A L 693:

If you are Phoebus' sister, I entrust my cause
To you to plead it in your brother's ears,
Delia.[14] Address him so: O Delphic one,
I built for you a temple of Sicilian stone,

And sang you honest songs on slender reed.
O God Apollo, show me the coins I need.

XLIX

A L 694:

All that might hush our piteous earthly cries
An honest god has set before our eyes.
These common herbs, the berries in the rough
Brambles are for our belly pangs enough.
With rivers near, who but the fool feels drought,
Or leaves his hearth to face East winds without?
The sword of law blocks in the ravening bride;
No girl in lawful sheets needs ever hide.
Rich Nature gives enough to satisfy:
Endless the claims of unchecked vanity.

L

A L 695:

In a soldier's bonnet there nested a dove
To prove the alliance of Mars and of Love.

LI

A L 696:

A Jew may adore his god in the sty
And pour out his woes in the ears of the sky,
But unless he will shorten his scabbard to see
That the tip of his penis will always hang free,
He'll be driven from home to a city in Greece
And spend all his Sabbaths – eating in peace.

LII

A L 697:

Brave hands are the one nobility,
Sole sign of a heart that is free.

LIII

AL 698:

My bed was soft, the early night was bliss.
My drowsy eyes surrender – Love broke my rest
And shook me by the hair in wild protest.
Nails ripped my flesh. 'To waste a night like this!
You're mine,' he said. 'You broke a thousand hearts,
Can you, hard-hearted, lie alone and rest?'
I leap from bed, barefoot and barely dressed;
I try each road, but all roads are false starts.
I run, but hate to go or to retreat,
Then stand ashamed to halt, so late abroad.
No song of birds, no watchdog even roared,
No human voice, no bustle in the streets.
Alone of all, I fear my bed and sleep:
At your command, great Love, your watch I keep.

LIV

AL 699:

Long may our hearts, Nealce, guard that night,
When first you came to me as I lay still;
The bed, its guardian spirit, the silent light[15] –
They saw your soft submission to my will.
So come, let us endure, though youth has passed,
And use those years that have so short a stay.
Justice and Law allow old loves to last:
Make our quick love go not so quick away.

LV[16]

AL 700:

Its joys are short and nasty,
And end in quick disgust
So let us not be hasty:
In blind and beastly lust
Love wanes, its glow departing –
So let's be slow in starting;
Let's lie here sharing kisses

On an endless holiday.
There's no sweeter rest than this is
(Without a blush to pay),
An endless new beginning
That never dies away.

LVI

AL 701.

Reproach and Love, all in one moment,
For Hercules himself would be a torment.

LVII[17]

AL 786:

Before my birth the gods, they say,
Discussed what sex I'd be.
'Boy!' said Phoebus; 'Girl!' said Mars;
Said Juno, 'I disagree.'
So I was born hermaphrodite,
But how was I to die?
The goddess was first with the answer:
'The sword!' Said Mars, 'The cross!'
But Phoebus decided on drowning.
So I had to die of them all.
A tree hung over a stream,
Wearing my sword, I climbed –
A slip, we were driven together:
My feet caught in a branch,
My head dipped into the stream –
Not woman, not man, yet both:
River and Sword and Cross.

LIST OF CHARACTERS*

AGAMEMNON: Teacher of rhetoric at Puteoli, with whom Encolpius is arguing at the opening of the work. He takes the three heroes to dinner with Trimalchio. He is named after Agamemnon, leader of the Greek expedition to Troy, and his assistant is appropriately named Menelaus after Agamemnon's brother, the husband of Helen.

AGATHO: A cosmetician (74.15). Literally, 'Goodman'.

ALBUCIA: An unknown woman (Fgt. VI). Literally, 'Littlewhite'.

ASCYLTUS: Encolpius' companion and later enemy. In Greek his name means 'untroubled' or 'unmolested' or perhaps 'indefatigable'.

BARGATES: A landlord and friend of Eumolpus. The name is Semitic.

CARIO: A slave of Trimalchio. The name signifies a Carian and was a common slave name.

CARPUS: Another common slave name. Here it is the name of Trimalchio's carver (36 ff.). It means 'harvest' in Greek.

CERBERUS: The three-headed watchdog of Hades. Used metaphorically in Fgt. VIII.

CHRYSANTHUS: A lately dead friend of Seleucus and others in Trimalchio's circle (42.3). Literally 'Goldflower'.

CHRYSIS: Circe's supercilious maid (128 ff.). Literally, 'Golden Girl'.

CINNAMUS: Trimalchio's steward. Literally, 'Cinnamon'.

CIRCE: The would-be mistress of Encolpius, named after the witch who captivates Odysseus in Homer's *Odyssey*.

CORAX: Eumolpus' hired servant. The name, often given to slaves, means literally 'raven'.

CORINTH: Trimalchio's manufacturer of Corinthian ware (50.4).

CROESUS: Trimalchio's little favourite (64.5). The name of a wealthy king of Lydia.

DAEDALUS: Trimalchio's ingenious cook. In mythology Daedalus was the prototype of the great inventor.

---

* I have listed the main characters in the *Satyricon* and the accepted Fragments, giving where requisite the literal meaning of the names which, no doubt, Petronius chose deliberately.

DAMA: A friend of Trimalchio's (41.10). The name is Greek for 'tamer'.

DIOGENES: C. Pompeius, a friend of Trimalchio's (38.10). Literally, 'Heaven-born'. The reader might think of Diogenes the Cynic.

DIONYSUS: A young slave of Trimalchio's. In mythology, the great god of wine and ecstasy.

DORIS: Apparently a former mistress of Encolpius. Literally, 'a Dorian woman'.

ECHION: A friend of Trimalchio's, a rag-collector. Literally, a sort of plant.

ENCOLPIUS: The hero (or anti-hero) of the work. In other authors, such as Martial, his name is given to homosexual favourites. Literally, the name means 'embraced'.

ENDYMION: A mysterious boy who appears in the novel, probably due to an interpolator. In mythology, he is a beautiful and eternally sleeping youth, beloved by the moon-goddess, Selene.

EUMOLPUS: A pederastic poet, critic, and fraud, who befriends Encolpius and masterminds the affair at Croton. In Greek the name means 'sweet singer'.

EUSCIOS: A vague character mentioned in Fgt. IX. Literally in Greek, 'Pleasantly Shadowy'.

FORTUNATA: Trimalchio's wife. Literally in Latin, 'Blessed by Fortune'.

GAIUS: See TRIMALCHIO.

GANYMEDES: A guest of Trimalchio's. In mythology Ganymede, a Trojan prince, became cup-bearer and lover of Zeus. The English noun 'catamite' is derived from the name.

GITON: Encolpius' beloved. His name is Greek for 'neighbour'.

GORGIAS: A Crotonian legacy-hunter, who seems to stop at nothing. His famous namesake was a great orator and Sophist.

HABINNAS: Close friend of Trimalchio's, a monumental mason and one of the more important men at Puteoli. The name is Semitic.

HEDYLE: Apparently the wife of Lichas, whom Encolpius seems to have seduced (113.3). Literally, 'Little Sweety'.

HERMEROS: A guest of Trimalchio's. He seems to be sitting next to Encolpius and takes exception to Ascyltus' sneers. Literally, 'Love of Hermes'. A gladiator of the period with the same name is mentioned in c. 52.

HESUS: A superstitious passenger on board Lichas' ship. The name has connotations of 'clinging'.

JULIUS PROCULUS: A guest of Trimalchio (38.16).

LICHAS: A ship captain from Tarentum and an old enemy of Encolpius. The name would be connected with 'licking'.

LYCURGUS: A mysterious figure from some missing portion of the work; he had been a cruel host to Encolpius, who has apparently murdered him. His villa may have been the source of the trio's gold. The wolfish name also belonged to a cruel mythical King of Thrace.

M. MANNICIUS: Owner of the block of flats in which Encolpius and Eumolpus are staying.

MASSA: A favourite young slave of Habinnas. Literally, 'Lump'.

MENELAUS: Agamemnon's second in command at his school.

MENOPHILA: The mate of Philargyrus, one of Trimalchio's slaves. Literally, 'Lover of Strength'.

NICEROS: One of the most interesting guests of Trimalchio. The name connotes both victory and passion.

OENOTHEA: A dissolute priestess of Priapus at Croton. Her name means literally 'wine-goddess'.

PANNYCHIS: An immature slave-girl, belonging to Quartilla. Literally, 'the All-night Girl'.

PETRAITES: 'Rocky' was a gladiator of the period.

PHILARGYRUS: A slave belonging to Trimalchio. Literally, 'Lover of Silver'.

PHILEROS: A guest of Trimalchio. Literally, 'Fond of Love'.

PHILOMELA: A corrupt matron at Croton, who sells her children for legacies. The name also of the song-loving nightingale.

PLOCAMUS: A guest of Trimalchio. Literally, 'Lock of Hair'.

POLYAENUS: Encolpius' pseudonym at Croton. An Homeric epithet of Ulysses, meaning 'much-praised'.

C. POMPEIUS: See DIOGENES.

PRIAPUS: The god of fertility who hounds Encolpius through the book and whom he constantly and inadvertently offends.

PROCULUS: See JULIUS PROCULUS.

PROSELENUS: An old bawd adept at magic. Literally, 'Older than the Moon'.

PSYCHE: The maid of Quartilla. Literally, 'Soul'.

QUARTILLA: Priestess of Priapus. The name is a diminutive of the Roman first name for 'fourth in sequence'.

SCINTILLA: The wife of Habinnas. Literally, 'Spark'.

SCISSA: Literally, 'Cut Up'; a sentimental friend of Habinnas.

SCYLAX: Trimalchio's dog. The name is Greek for 'puppy'.

SELEUCUS: A guest of Trimalchio. The name belonged to various powerful Eastern rulers in the fourth and third centuries B.C.

SERAPA: Trimalchio's astrologer. The name belonged to an Egyptian deity.

STICHUS: A slave of Trimalchio, who is in charge of Trimalchio's funeral arrangements. Literally, 'Line', a common slave name.

TRIMALCHIO (the name means literally 'thrice-blessed' and is basically Semitic): the great vulgarian ex-slave, whose dinner occupies most of the extant fragments of the work.

TRYPHAENA (the Greek meaning of the name is 'luxury'): a prostitute from South Italy with whom Encolpius and Giton had dealings in some lost part of the work and who figures in c. 100.7 ff.

NOTES ON THE *SATYRICON*

Puteoli

1. Petronius' complaints in these chapters are echoed by the elder Seneca, Quintilian and Tacitus among others. The prestige of oratory under the Republic made higher Roman education primarily a training in rhetoric. Under the Empire political conditions reduced the importance of oratory enormously, but education continued in the same set mould, becoming progressively more remote from everyday life. The unreal topics of the school, briefly enumerated here by Petronius, left room only for ingenious argumentation and epigram and attention to sound and cadence. The lack of subject matter is paralleled by the attention paid to formulae and arrangement. It should be remembered, however, that Encolpius is putting forward these criticisms for his own selfish purposes and the discussion between him and Agamemnon should not be taken as proposals for serious educational reform. Indeed, some of the analysis is reminiscent of textbook histories of oratory.

2. Petronius seems here to be referring to the linguistic and thematic realism of Sophocles and Euripides, which he attributes to fifth-century Greek education. This was certainly more literary than rhetorical (the art of rhetoric was just coming in with the Sophists and was intensely studied only at a much later stage). In fact Euripides does show many signs of Sophistic rhetoric, but Petronius is right in making the point that the language is at the service of real problems and not artificial set themes.

3. The nine lyric poets normally include Pindar. The others are Bacchylides, Sappho, Anacreon, Stesichorus, Simonides, Ibycus, Alcaeus and Alcman. Corinna is sometimes added to the list and would give us the required total here. Although these lyric poets often drew extensively on the Homeric *Iliad* and *Odyssey* for both subject matter and language, yet Petronius is here probably referring to their great contributions in style and form to the development of Greek poetry. The lyric age of Greece was in its way as impressive and inventive as the age of the Homeric epics.

4. This sort of training: i.e. training in declamation on sterile themes, either in the form of *controversiae*, the ingenious discussion of complicated or unreal legal or moral problems (e.g. should sons provide for their parents, no matter

what the parents have done?) or *suasoriae*, speeches recommending some course of action to an historical or fictitious character (e.g. advice to a dictator to retire into private life). Plato's philosophical style and Demosthenes' oratorical style are in their different ways the greatest of Greek prose styles. Both belong to fourth-century Greece and of course would have had the traditional Greek literary training.

5. Petronius is here making the traditional distinction between the Attic and the Asianic styles. The first was simple and natural; the second was flowery and appealing to the emotions. Asianism proper began in the middle of the third century B.C., and thereafter the debate between the rival protagonists of the two main styles continued. There was a strong Atticist movement about the middle of the first century B.C. which looked back to the great period of Attic oratory for its models, and there was a revival of Asianism at the beginning of the second century A.D. But the struggle was perennial and sometimes resolved by compromise, as with Cicero. The debate extended to more than oratory proper. Petronius' own style is clearly intended as Attic by contrast, for example, with Seneca's (cf. c. 132). In view of the recurring nature of the controversy there is no need to decide which particular period Petronius had in mind for the coming of Asianism to Athens.

6. Thucydides was the great fifth-century historian of the Peloponnesian War; Hyperides, a fourth-century Greek orator, was regarded as second only to Demosthenes. Although their styles are radically different, the one being tortuous and highly individual in style, the other being much more in touch with ordinary speech, Petronius obviously has in mind their grasp on real life and their imperviousness to sterile and academic formulae.

7. The exact technique involved here is still mysterious despite certain puzzling references in Pliny the Elder. As far as we can see, it seems to be a method of rapid sketching which allowed of easy reproductions.

8. Cicero, *Pro Caelio*, 17.41.

9. Spongers in drama: i.e. parasites who live off rich men. They are familiar characters in comedy and are credited with great shrewdness as flatterers.

10. C. Lucilius (*c*. 180–102 B.C.) was the earliest and most fearless Roman satirist. He boasted that he could improvise 200 verses an hour standing on one foot, a feat for which the more painstaking Horace reproaches him and his admirers.

11. The scheme of education Agamemnon offers in this poem begins with moralizing and then moves on to a more or less standard classical education in literature, and one which from all the evidence fits in with Petronius' own fairly conventional views on the right authors and the right approach to literature. There is a certain incongruity in putting it in the mouth of Agamemnon, who seems from his behaviour at Trimalchio's house to be a fairly worthless sort of teacher, but then as Petronius has chosen his characters almost entirely from

the lower and less reputable classes, he has no other mouthpiece available even for his own sincere views, and it seems part of his ironic intention that this should be so. The 'home of the Sirens' is roughly the Naples area, where Agamemnon now is, and the 'Lacedaemonian colony' may be Tarentum. The purport of these lines is simply 'be you born in Greece or S. Italy'. Homer is to be the first author in accordance with Greek custom, then the various writers of Socratic dialogues (including Plato). Demosthenes is then followed by a course in Roman writers, probably the Roman orators, which will profit from the sound preliminary training in Greek literature. After this oratory should be left for a while in order that history may be studied, including military history and such events as Cicero's fight for the freedom of the Republic. With this training, the student may then begin writing himself.

12. It is clear that Encolpius and his companions have but recently arrived in the town. Elsewhere in the work we discover certain facts about it, notably that it is on the sea and an important mercantile port. It was almost certainly Puteoli, the modern Pozzuoli.

13. This was *satyrion*, one of the best known of ancient aphrodisiacs. Pliny (*NH* 26.10) describes its strange shapes and properties and distinguishes three kinds. It was supposed to be stimulating even if held in the hand – otherwise, as here, it was drunk in dry wine.

14. Lucretia was raped by Tarquin, son of the last Etruscan king of Rome. She was a model of wifely virtue. The story was the basis of Shakespeare's *Rape of Lucrece*. The relationship between Encolpius and Giton is of course clear. It is difficult to reproduce in translation the flavour of the words used by Encolpius, e.g. *frater*, which means literally 'brother' but signifies a very different relationship.

15. This and the next episode with Quartilla occur after a lacuna. It is not unlikely that both of these episodes are misplaced in the text as we have it and perhaps came from a slightly earlier section of the work, perhaps their first arrival in Puteoli before they meet Agamemnon. In any case the present episode presupposes an adventure in the country where they steal the cloak, but through Encolpius' fault they also lose the gold which they have stolen (perhaps from the mysterious Lycurgus whom Encolpius murdered).

16. Cynics: followers of the Cynic philosopher Diogenes. The word *Cynic* literally means 'dog-like': they professed to bark at all normal human values, including money, which they regarded as useless for happiness.

17. Priapus: this is one of the many incidents involving Priapus in the extant fragments and the lost parts of the work. It is fairly clear that the general framework of the *Satyricon* is a sort of comic parody of the wrath of Poseidon against Odysseus, but with Priapus, the ancient god of sexuality and fertility, hounding Encolpius (cf. cc. 133, 139, and Fragment IV). In his more domesticated aspects in Rome he was a garden god, represented with a huge red

phallus, who acted as scarecrow against birds and thieves as well as promoting vegetable fertility; in the novel, however, he is a slightly comic lord of sexuality and potency. He was originally worshipped in and around Lampsacus on the Hellespont (his sacrifice was an ass, the ancient symbol of lust), and he was a considerably more important deity than the tame Roman Priapus. Indeed some legends made him the son of Dionysus and Aphrodite. His cult spread to Greece, Alexandria, and finally Rome in the period after the conquests of Alexander the Great, but he never matched his original local significance.

18. The text at this point becomes extremely fragmentary. It is quite likely that we have two collections of fragments or two recensions to deal with. The sequence of events is very confused and it is, for instance, unlikely that two *cinaedi* ('pansies', as I have translated) enter to harass Encolpius, particularly as they behave in much the same way and between each incident the atmosphere is one of jovial friendliness. It would be difficult and confusing in a translation such as this to reallocate the fragments, so I have translated them in the received order. The plot, such as it is, although jerky and repetitious, is fairly clear.

19. The Latin pun cannot be properly translated. In the original, *embasicoetas* (which I have translated as 'night-cap') means both an obscene drinking-vessel and also an obscene bed-partner.

20. What follows is a sketchy parody of a Roman marriage, with veil, marriage torches, decorated marriage chamber, and even a matron of honour in the person of Quartilla.

21. This is the first obvious example of the scopophilic element that runs through the work.

Dinner with Trimalchio

1. In Roman toasts a little wine was poured in the group as a libation to the gods. Trimalchio's pretensions to popularity with his household become even more absurd later. The masseurs, of course, are not drinking his health at all.

2. Such representations seem to have been common – mosaic examples may be seen in Pompeii and the Naples Museum. Lifelike representation of the *trompe l'oeil* sort was a main object of ancient art.

3. The allegory of the mural is fairly simple. Mercury as the god of trade (and thieves) is an appropriate patron for Trimalchio. Minerva as the goddess of general and technical wisdom is there to reflect Trimalchio's own high estimation of his education and capabilities. The platform or *tribunal* to which Mercury rushes him by the chin (the special bodily seat of power) is where the seats of magistrates are placed. In this case it would represent the position of *sevir*, one of the municipal officials, often freedmen, who were in charge of the Imperial cult in the towns outside Rome. The rest of the symbolism is obvious and conventional.

4. The first shave was symbolic of a boy's reaching man's estate and donning the *toga virilis*. The event was celebrated, and the trimmings might be put in a box and dedicated to a god at some temple. It was obviously an upper-class custom – Nero dedicated his beard clippings to Capitoline Jupiter – and Trimalchio's observance of it is part and parcel of his self-importance.

5. The rods and axes were the Roman symbols of magisterial authority. Trimalchio has them as a *sevir Augustalis*, a fact of which we are constantly reminded.

6. i.e. a *sevir*.

7. The date of the action in Puteoli is some time in the summer. Trimalchio's lavish hospitality is such that he is boasting of being out to dinner only twice a year, which, therefore, has to be carefully noted as a reminder.

8. The first reference to Trimalchio's superstitious nature. The slave we find later warning guests not to step over the threshold on the wrong foot is another. The left was regarded by the Romans (and still is by moderns) as unlucky. Superstitions about thresholds and boundaries are legion. Later we find that Trimalchio's guests may not enter and leave by the same threshold.

9. At a Roman dinner normally three large couches were placed around a large central solid table, the diners reclining diagonally on their left sides and eating with their right hands. The fourth side was open to allow the slaves to serve the food. More than three could take their places on these couches, and it is clear from the number of guests that Trimalchio had far more than the usual nine, the number of the Muses, even if we exclude *umbrae* (uninvited guests who would come with an invited friend), wives (e.g. Fortunata), who would just sit on the edge of a couch, and attendants such as Giton who would be at the feet of their masters. Trimalchio has also set out small tables to allow more room, and the traditional seating has been changed, Trimalchio reclining in the top place on the highest couch (no doubt in order to be nearer the bathroom). Encolpius is probably reclining below Hermeros and Habinnas will later take the honoured praetor's place on the middle couch.

U P P E R	Trimalchio			Diogenes	L O W E S T
	Agamemnon			Proculus (freedman's place)	
	Hermeros			Scintilla & Fortunata	
		Encolpius	Ascyltus	Habinnas (place of honour	

MIDDLE

10. This first course is typical of the rest of the dinner: elaborate servers of

various precious metals; expensive delicacies such as dormice (European field-mice); and above all the attempt on the part of the cuisine to represent natural foods as something that they are not – here damsons and pomegranate seeds look like a fire beneath the griddle. Later pork will be presented as fowl, and so on.

11. Trimalchio's appearance is rightly laughed at by the guests. The close crop is a sign of the slave or ex-slave; the napkin ostentatiously displays the broad purple stripe which was worn by the senatorial order on their togas; gold rings are the specific privilege of Roman knights, so Trimalchio wears a gilt ring and a gold ring studded with iron – thus sailing as close to the wind as he dares.

12. Probably the game called *latrunculi* – a game something between draughts and chess, although sometimes dice played a part in it. The object was to put an opponent's piece between two of one's own and so capture him. There is at least one Egyptian picture of a solo game, although normally it was played between two people.

13. This label has given commentators a lot of trouble. Opimius was consul in 121 B.C., but although this vintage produced long-lived wines (some bottles, almost undrinkable, surviving to the middle of the first century A.D., according to the elder Pliny), we cannot, therefore, date the time of this episode to 21 B.C. The point is that Trimalchio is trying to impress his guests with the age and quality of his wine, but no vintner puts a label like this on a bottle unless he is trying to cheat a customer. Trimalchio does not know his dates – all he knows is that Opimian was the best (like Napoleon brandy). He is either lying or he has been cheated.

14. The skeleton is a frequent motif in fresco or mosaic on dining-room walls or house floors. Its purpose is to admonish the diners to eat, drink, and be merry, for tomorrow we die.

15. Each of the foods placed over the signs of the Zodiac is either a sort of rebus, e.g. over Aries, *cicer arietinum* (chickpeas), or has some appropriate connection with the sign in question, e.g. the goose is connected with rain and is placed over the rainy constellation of the Water-carrier. The rebuses will not always come through in translation, so I have substituted where necessary a reasonable English equivalent.

16. Pegasus was the winged horse of Bellerophon, on which he killed the Chimera.

17. The satyr Marsyas lost a musical contest with Apollo; for daring to challenge the god he was flayed alive.

18. Millions of millions: the sums are generally given in sesterces, which are now calculated as worth about a pound or a dollar (1985). One sesterce would buy two good loaves of bread. Even so the total sums, even Trimalchio's thirty million (approx. £30,000,000), will not seem impressive to us with our

knowledge of modern millionaires. But we are dealing with a non-industrial, non-technological society and, given this, Trimalchio is quite rich, although we know of some much richer freedmen of the Emperor Claudius, such as Pallas and Narcissus; the latter was allegedly worth 400 million sesterces.

19. A quotation from Virgil (*Aeneid* 2.44). The original context was pejorative.

20. Trimalchio's explanation of the various types born under the different signs of the Zodiac is an amalgam of popular superstition and fairly obvious astrological symbolism. I have tried to make the connections alleged by Trimalchio self-evident in the translation. The only ones which might cause difficulty are the following: 'those who find their own feed', i.e. independent people, who are generally associated with the Bull in other astrological authors; 'runaways' are born under the Virgin, because she is Astraea, who 'fled' the earth after the Golden Age and became the constellation; she is also associated with a certain astrological *nodus* or knot, hence the chain-gang association. A complete discussion may be found in J. G. W. M. de Vreese, *Petron 39 u. die Astrologie* (Amsterdam, 1927).

21. Hipparchus and Aratus: Aratus (*c.* 270 B.C.) was the author of two astronomical poems which survive; Hipparchus (*c.* 190–125 B.C.) was the greatest of Greek astronomers.

22. The set of puns on which this little farce depends is untranslatable. Dionysus or Bacchus, the Greek god of the vine and ecstasy, was identified by the Romans with their own god of the vine and agricultural fertility, Liber or Liber pater. The slave boy Dionysus, after imitating the various cult-aspects of Dionysus, is asked by Trimalchio to be *Liber*, a request he takes as meaning that he is liberated (*liber* meaning 'free'). Trimalchio goes along with this no doubt pre-arranged joke and so makes the unlikely claim that he has a *liber pater*, i.e. a 'free father', punning on the Italian god's name.

23. *Morra* is the modern Italian equivalent of the Roman game whereby two players put up a number of fingers and each tries to guess the total. 'Up-Jenkins' is the English equivalent.

24. *Bestiarii*, the animal fighters, were generally put on in the morning shows and were of decidedly inferior status to the real gladiators.

25. This was one of the various types of gladiators. A 'Thracian' was comparatively lightly armed and was often matched against a 'Samnite', who was more heavily armed.

26. Tarracina, a town of Latium, is midway between Rome and Naples; Tarentum is at the top of the heel of Italy. The distance between them would be a little over 200 miles.

27. Trimalchio's learning, like that of the Calvisius Sabinus described by Seneca (*Letters from a Stoic* XXVII), is defective and pretentious. Homer does

not narrate the twelve labours of Hercules and the Cyclops did no physical damage to Ulysses, but had his own eye put out by that hero.

28. This is one of the famous Sybils of antiquity: she was Aeneas' guide to the underworld. Sybils were regarded as immortal but, unfortunately, grew old and withered like Tithonus, hence this reply, used by T. S. Eliot as the epigraph of *The Waste Land*. Cumae is just up the coast from Puteoli and, like Puteoli, it was a town colonized by Greeks. The ancient and impressive Cave of the Sybil and Virgil's entrance to the underworld via Lake Avernus are a few kilometres up the road from the modern Cuma.

29. Corinthian bronze was a special amalgam of copper, gold and silver in varying proportions; it was highly prized, by the Emperor Augustus among others. Trimalchio's history is as defective as his mythology. He is probably thinking of the false story that Corinthian bronze was discovered by accident when Corinth was set on fire in 146 B.C. by Mummius, but he confuses this sack with the sack of Troy (*c.* 1184 B.C.) and replaces Mummius by the great Carthaginian general Hannibal who died *c.* 183 B.C.

30. The Caesar referred to here is the Emperor Tiberius, according to a similar story in Pliny.

31. Cassandra, of course, had no children; she was the Trojan priestess who became the concubine of Agamemnon and was killed by his wife Clytemnestra. Daedalus was responsible for many things, including flying, but he did not build the Trojan horse. Niobe had twelve children, but they were killed by Apollo and Artemis because she insulted their mother Latona when boasting of her own fecundity. Hermeros and Petraites were contemporary gladiators, and cups like those described here have been found by archaeologists.

32. The *Cordax* was originally a coarse choral dance from Old Greek comedy. It would correspond to our cancan or the bump-and-grind.

33. Crucifixion was the punishment of criminals and slaves.

34. Atellan farces were at first improvised Italian character sketches in Oscan dialect; they revolved round certain low-life stereotypes – Maccus, the clown, Bucco, the babbler, Pappus, the old man, etc. They had developed a certain parodic and satirical humour, in fact certain Romans even wrote them, although they eventually degenerated and became more like mimes.

35. Mopsus is otherwise unknown except as a mythological figure connected with Apollo and is perhaps an invention of Trimalchio's. He might have been some very minor writer of the period whom it is absurd to rate so highly. There is a similar absurdity in comparing Cicero, the great orator, to Publilius Syrus, his contemporary, who was only a writer of mimes. The fragment that follows is probably an imitation by Petronius.

36. The game was a great favourite with Augustus, according to Suetonius. It is impossible to translate the passage with absolute literalness, but I have

kept as close to the Latin as possible. The poverty of the puns and the rebuses is equally apparent in the Latin as in the English.

37. Roman citizens did not pay tribute, and manumission, which could be purchased, was a fairly common privilege for a hard-working slave.

38. December was the month of the Saturnalia when a great deal of licence was allowed to slaves. At this period the festivities proper lasted five days, beginning 17 December. It was very like our Christmas.

39. The liberation tax was five per cent of the slave's value, payable on manumission either by the master or the slave.

40. The riddle has generated various solutions. The most plausible answers are the shadow or the penis.

41. Another mishmash of mythology. Diomede was a Greek hero at Troy, quite unrelated to the Trojan Ganymede, who became Jove's cup-bearer. Helen was the sister of Castor and Pollux. Helen was stolen by Paris, and Agamemnon, her brother-in-law, was trying to recover her. Trimalchio introduces also a half-memory of the story of the hind being substituted by Diana for Iphigenia, daughter of Agamemnon, who was to be sacrificed at Aulis to allow the Greek fleet to sail. The Trojans, of course, were fighting against the Greeks, not the inhabitants of the Italian town of Tarentum. Iphigenia was only promised to Achilles, who died unmarried, and Ajax went mad over the award of the armour of Achilles to Ulysses.

42. The Lares were the household gods responsible for the prosperity of the house. They were generally depicted as young men in tunics and it was frequent practice to show with them a picture of the genius of the house, which was usually modelled from the master's face. Trimalchio has given appropriately commercial names to his Lares. It was customary to sacrifice to the Lares during the evening meal, generally just before dessert. Kissing the image of Trimalchio is, however, a little extreme.

43. Encolpius seems to be getting drunk.

44. Apelles was a famous tragic actor of the time of Caligula (assassinated in A.D. 41), so Plocamus is referring to a period approximately twenty-five years before the date of the action.

45. The place of honour meant here is the praetor's seat at the lower end of the middle couch and usually next to the host's seat, which however in this case is occupied by Fortunata and Scintilla.

46. The ninth-day dinner was a regular feature of Roman funeral arrangements; it followed the ninth-day sacrifice to the dead to which Habinnas refers when deploring pouring half his wine over the wretched slave's bones. Such elaborate treatment for a dead slave was extremely uncommon and hints at a very special relationship between him and Scissa.

47. One tenth of one per cent to Mercury: paid by the month by the grateful

merchant to the patron god of traders. The size of the bracelet indicates a high revenue.

48. The horse-play here depends on the fact that Roman women usually sat rather than reclined at table.

49. The joke here depends on the slaves taking Trimalchio's order for dessert (*secundae mensae*) literally and bringing in a second set of tables (*secundae mensae*).

50. The opening line of *Aeneid* 5.

51. On Atellan verses see n. 34 above.

52. Cappadocians were regarded as the slyest and most difficult slaves.

53. Daedalus was the legendary craftsman who built the Cretan labyrinth etc., and invented wings to escape from that island; he was the standard prototype of inventiveness.

54. A practice introduced to Nero's court by the later Emperor Otho: its presence at Trimalchio's dinner might indicate that Petronius thought it vulgar.

55. It was bad manners to dance in public; the incident might indicate that the women are drunk.

56. The Greens were one of the chariot teams who raced in the Circus, the others being Red, White and Blue, although other colours were added later. Partisanship ran high and bets such as that described below were a great feature of the sport.

57. Ephesus is otherwise unknown.

58. As a *sevir* Trimalchio would be entitled to such official dress; he would not, however, be entitled to the gold rings which were the privilege of the knights.

59. Slaves generally adopted their master's family names. 'Pompeius' would suggest that Trimalchio once belonged to the family of the Pompeii; 'Maecenatianus' may have been ostentatiously adopted to suggest a connection with the great Maecenas, Augustus' Minister of State; it is unlikely that he ever was a slave of Maecenas.

60. Presumably the Neronian harp-player mentioned in Suetonius and Dio. If so, it would be further evidence for the Neronian date of the work.

61. Cock-crowing is a well-known omen and the transference of the ring from one hand to the other is akin to the superstition of changing money from one pocket to another for luck.

62. Cassandra mournfully prophesied the fall of Troy and Agamemnon's death; here she stands for a crude spoil-sport, a prophet of gloom and doom.

63. It was a common practice to list the Emperor as an heir, both as a compliment to him and as a precaution against his setting aside the provisions of the will and confiscating the estate.

64. The evidence of Dio and Suetonius is conflicting, but the most reasonable theory is that Augustus fixed the senatorial property qualification at 1,000,000

sesterces, at which it presumably stayed for the next few reigns. So, like many modern senates in practice, it was an assembly of millionaires.

65. Apulia is part of lower Southern Italy.

66. One for each season of the year.

67. Scaurus is perhaps the famous Pompeian manufacturer of fish sauce, rather than a member of the noble family of the Scauri.

Eumolpus

1. The Theban brothers were Eteocles and Polyneices, the sons of Oedipus. Polyneices led an army against Thebes and the two brothers killed each other in single combat.

2. These lines seem to have been introduced from elsewhere in the work. They are singularly inappropriate here.

3. Tantalus, one of the great sinners in Hades. He was punished by being stood in a river whose water ran from his lips; while overhead branches with fruit on them always eluded his grasp.

4. Zeuxis (*fl.* 424 B.C.), a famous Greek painter renowned for the realism of his still lifes. His figure painting seems to have been rather idealized.

5. Protogenes (*fl.* 332 B.C.), a diligent and self-taught artist of Rhodes; his works were rare because of the time he took over them. Like most great Greek artists he was renowned for his accurate draughtsmanship.

6. Apelles was a contemporary of Protogenes and regarded as one of the greatest of all Greek artists. One of his best works was Aphrodite rising from the sea (the *Anadyomene*). He prided himself particularly upon the *grace* of his paintings.

7. This was Ganymede, who became Zeus's cupbearer. Hylas was the beloved companion of Heracles; during the voyage of the Argo, while getting water, he was pulled in by an amorous Naiad. The boy accidentally killed by Apollo with a discus was a Spartan prince called Hyacinth: the flower of that name was supposed to have sprung from his blood.

8. Lycurgus is a mysterious character in the novel whom Encolpius seems to have killed after being entertained by him and, apparently, ill-treated. His villa may have been the source of the trio's mysterious gold.

9. Pergamum was the capital of the Roman province of Asia. A quaestor was in charge of the financial side of Roman provincial administration.

10. Democritus of Abdera (*c.* 460–370 B.C.), a voluminous writer on natural science and ethics, who elaborated the atomic theory and is important for his contribution to Epicureanism. He wrote a book on the powers of seeds, plants and fruits, which Eumolpus may have in mind here.

11. Eudoxus of Cnidos (*c.* 408–355 B.C.) was a famous Greek mathematician and astronomer; far from growing old on a mountain, he engaged in politics in

later life. Chrysippus (*c*. 280–207 B.C.) was the great systematizer of Stoicism and the author of innumerable works. Hellebore was a well-known purgative, supposedly effective against mental illness.

12. Lysippus of Sicyon (*fl*. 328 B.C.), the most famous sculptor of the time of Alexander, produced about 1,500 works according to one authority; he was noted for his fidelity to detail and for introducing new and more slender proportions to his figures. Myron of Eleutherae (*fl. c.* 480–455 B.C.) was a revolutionary Greek sculptor, especially known for the radically novel postures of his works, which were made possible by the relatively new technique of bronze-casting. A copy of his *Discobolus* survives and well illustrates this tendency.

13. Dialectic by this time was probably very like our logic; in effect, the study of the laws of thought and argument.

14. Apelles (see n. 6 above); Phidias of Athens (*c*. 490–417 B.C.) is the great sculptor of the Elgin marbles, brought to England from the Parthenon. Two other great works of his were the chryselephantine statue of Athene Parthenos and the statue of Zeus at Olympia.

15. The Capture of Troy was a common subject of poetry; Nero wrote on the subject. Eumolpus' narrative is a pastiche in different metre of Virgil's account in the first half of *Aeneid* 2, and there are constant Virgilian echoes. The following notes on the classical allusions are keyed to the line numbers of the translation: l.3 – Calchas was the priest of Apollo who predicted the war would last ten years. l.5 – the Delian is Apollo; one of his cult-sanctuaries was the island of Delos where he was born; through Calchas he urges the building of the Trojan horse out of hatred for Troy. l.6 – Ida is a mountain in the Troad. l.12 – gods' vail: the Horse was supposed to be a Greek offering to the gods. l.17 – Sinon pretended to be a deserter and told the Trojans that the Horse, if taken into Troy, would keep the city from capture. l.24 – Laocoön's death with his two sons is the subject of the famous statuary group in the Vatican; it is a late first century B.C. work of three Rhodian sculptors of the Pergamene school, and was regarded by the elder Pliny as the finest work of plastic art ever produced. l.35 – Tenedos is a small island off the coast of the Troad. l.48 – sacred ribbons: the boys are dressed as acolytes for a sacrifice.

16. Giton is carrying out his usual function of attending his lover. He is guarding Ascyltus' clothes in the public baths, holding the towels and scrapers for the oil.

17. Eumolpus is clearly the speaker and is presumably responding to some moralizing from Encolpius.

18. Another example of the constant persecution of Encolpius by Priapus.

19. Epicurus of Athens (342–270 B.C.), the great founder of Epicureanism. He proposed moderate pleasure as the sole good for man and tried to eliminate all religious fear of the gods, of death, of omens, etc. Naturally he would

discount oneiromancy as superstitious; in his system the gods lived in carefree happiness and did not interfere at all in the affairs of men.

20. It has been plausibly suggested that Fragment XXX was originally located here.

21. Consequently to do this when there was no storm was regarded as inviting disaster.

22. See Homer, *Odyssey* 19.473 ff., where the nurse Eurycleia recognizes Odysseus' hunting scar while bathing him.

23. Hercules: a reference to a missing part of the work. This episode probably took place in Baiae. Lichas' wife was named Hedyle. The public humiliation of Tryphaena referred to next may have been a public trial for some alleged sexual offence resulting in a sentence of exile.

24. Eumolpus offers here a parody of forensic oratory, just as later he will parody the language of treaty-makers.

25. Medea cut her brother Absyrtus in pieces and scattered them in the sea to delay her father's pursuit of Jason and herself.

26. Ephesus was a large Ionian city on the coast of Asia Minor. The story of the Widow of Ephesus has its parallels in many literatures including Chinese; its classic statement here has been the basis of many other versions, such as Christopher Fry's play *A Phoenix Too Frequent*.

27. Virgil, *Aeneid* 4.34.

28. Virgil, *Aeneid* 4.38.

29. Although the MSS attribute this fragment to Tryphaena's maid who is talking to Encolpius, it is more likely that it belongs to Encolpius, who is jealously protesting over Giton's behaviour with Tryphaena, who as a prostitute is more likely to be described by him as a *spintria* (an adept in innovative sexual practices such as the 'daisy-chain'). Tryphaena's maid in any case likes Giton, saved him from punishment and improved his appearance.

30. The description of the winds and the storm makes it difficult to put the shipwreck in the Straits of Messina, as is generally done; more likely, it took place in the Gulf of Squillace or off Cape Rizzuto, which makes their landing near Croton more easily explicable.

31. The robe and rattle to which Lichas refers would belong to the tutelary goddess of the ship, the Egyptian deity Isis. Encolpius has apparently stolen them in the lost episode which deals with Lichas.

The Road to Croton

1. Croton, the modern Crotone, on the coast of the toe of Italy, was colonized by Greeks about 710 B.C.. The height of its power was marked by the defeat of Sybaris in 510 B.C., but thereafter its defeat by Locri and Rhegium in the fourth century, its capture by Dionysius of Syracuse, and a series of internal

and external wars (the Lucanian, the Bruttian, the Pyrrhic, and the Hannibalic) ruined it. A Roman colony sent there in 194 B.C. failed to revive the town. This part of the work, whose theme is the common satirical topic of legacy-hunting, is placed in a less realistic setting than the events centring on Puteoli, presumably because Petronius was less familiar with the area and because his satire here is of a more literary and far-fetched nature than heretofore.

2. Further references to certain lost episodes. The robe is probably the robe of Isis which Encolpius had stolen from Lichas' ship and about which Lichas was so concerned during the storm. Lycurgus, who has been alluded to earlier, seems to have been a host of Encolpius, whose ill-treatment had driven Encolpius to kill him and then, with Ascyltus and Giton, plunder his villa.

3. This piece of literary criticism, with its famous epigrammatic description of Horace, gives us a very good idea of Petronius' views on literature. He is a traditionalist, an admirer of the standard classics such as Homer, the Greek lyric poets, Virgil, and Horace (whom he quotes below (*Odes* 3.1)), and is opposed to the glittering epigrammatic style of such contemporary authors as Seneca and Lucan. His ideal is a smooth, sober Atticism. In particular, his criticism of the innovations in the epic made by Lucan in his *Pharsalia* is clear from his insistence on wide reading in traditional authors and a retention of the divine machinery of Homer and Virgil which Lucan had dropped. Although Lucan is not mentioned by name, it is obvious that he is referred to because the criticisms are appropriate only to the *Pharsalia*. No doubt Lucan was by now out of Nero's favour on account of the latter's jealousy, but the mention of Lucan would be inappropriate in the fictional situation, even if the purport of the criticism is plain. The poem that follows is full of reminiscences of Lucan Books I–III (which had probably been published by this time) and, to a lesser extent, of certain later books of Lucan (cf. the end of the *Pharsalia*). The purpose of the poem which follows has been long disputed. It has been regarded as a parody (but then why are there not hits at Lucan's Stoicism, the excessive use of portents, etc.?); or an attempt, particularly appropriate in Eumolpus' mouth, to show how easily it can be done; or a model for the proper handling of such an epic theme (but in this case, by making it a very unfinished effort of Eumolpus', Petronius is certainly disclaiming much poetic responsibility for it); and other suggestions have been made. My own rather hesitant opinion is that Petronius has taken the subject matter of Lucan Book I and rewritten it in the light of his own (and Eumolpus') strictures. He has expanded, combined, and changed some of the material – by substituting the crossing of the Alps for the crossing of the Rubicon, for example, and by introducing more deities in place of Lucan's portents – but he has kept Lucan before the reader's mind by the use of direct references and allusions and imitations of Lucan's frigid conceits (e.g., the statement that Charon's boat will be insufficient to carry over the ghosts of the dead, a fleet will be needed). Nevertheless, by giving the

whole criticism and rehandling to the poetaster Eumolpus (who says the work is still unrevised) he disclaims any great responsibility for its merits, although no doubt he thought it as good as Lucan's work. For the style of the translation, see the Introduction.

4. I have divided the poem into sections as a convenient way of clarifying its structure. The notes on the poem are given by the line numbers of the translation: l. 21 – Ammon was the name of Jupiter, worshipped as a ram in Africa. The temple stood on the present oasis of Siwah. Here the name means little more than Libya. l. 24 – Wild beasts for use in the amphitheatre commanded heavy prices. l. 53 – Oysters from the Lucrine Lake were particularly valued. l. 56 – These were pheasants. l. 72 – Cato (the Younger) was the very type of stern unbending Roman virtue. He was one of Caesar's most vehement opponents and finally committed suicide when defeated by the Caesarian party in Africa. He was defeated by Vatinius for the praetorship. l. 97 – The three captains were Julius Caesar, Pompey and Crassus, who formed the first triumvirate until Crassus' death while fighting the Parthians allowed the jealousy of Pompey to turn him against Caesar. Pompey was assassinated on the shore of Egypt, and Caesar, of course, was killed in Rome by the conspirators. l. 108 – The scene takes place in the Phlegrean Fields, the modern Solfatara, a heavily volcanic region of mud-pits and hot sulphur holes and caves. Cocytus is one of the rivers of the underworld. l. 122 – Dis is the lord of the underworld. l. 148 – Tisiphone is one of the Furies, the avenger of murder. l. 149 – Sulla's was the last instance of civil war, when he proscribed and murdered hundreds of followers of Marius in order to become dictator in Rome. This was over thirty years before the civil war between Caesar and the senate began. l. 169 – The battle of Philippi (42 B.C.) saw the defeat of Brutus and Cassius by Octavian and Antony. Although the battlefield is in Macedonia on the borders of Thrace, Roman poets sometimes wrongly locate it at Pharsalus, in Thessaly, where Caesar routed Pompey in 48 B.C. Hence the double slaughter. There is a reference here also to the battles that took place in Spain and in Africa. l. 171 – Nile's barriers: a reference to Caesar's Egyptian campaign. l. 172 – Antony and Cleopatra were decisively defeated by the forces of Octavian at the Battle of Actium in 31 B.C. Apollo was on Octavian's side: Propertius has a laudatory poem describing the god's intervention. l. 177 – Charon took souls across the River Styx in an old leaky boat. l. 191 – The lightning bolts came from Jove, the brother of Dis. l. 194 – Hyperion is the sun. l. 197 – Cynthia is the moon. l. 215 – Caesar has just pacified Gaul in a long and bloody series of battles. The civil war ostensibly began over the senate's refusal to prolong his command of an army. l. 237 – Saturnus was an ancient Italian deity, honoured as the god of agriculture: his land is therefore Italy. l. 246 – The Gauls were a constant fear to Romans; they had already sacked the Capitol in 390 B.C. l. 249 – Caesar had also conquered a number of

German tribes. l. 274 – The raven was the bird of Apollo, who had a shrine at Delphi, and it was therefore considered prophetic. l. 314 – Hercules, formally son of Amphitryon, had gone to the Caucasus to release Prometheus from his chains and shoot the vulture that perpetually devoured his liver. l. 318 – This is a reference to the war between the Gods and Giants. l. 322 – The Palatine Hill was one of the oldest and most important areas in Rome. l. 341 – Quirites was the formal name for Roman citizens. l. 354 – Auster is the South Wind. l. 362 – The two consuls of the year 49 B.C. were C. Claudius Marcellus and L. Cornelius Lentulus Crus, both Pompeian supporters. l. 363 – Pontus: Pompey had conquered Mithridates of Pontus in 63 B.C. l. 364 – Hydaspes is a river in India, the scene of a victory won by Alexander the Great. Pompey had never in fact gone so far. l. 365 – Pompey had been charged with clearing the Mediterranean of pirates in 67 B.C. He effected this great task in three months. l. 388 – Erebus, the god of Darkness. l. 390 – Erinys, a Fury; Bellona, the goddess of War. l. 391 – Megaera, another Fury. l. 406 – Dione, a poetical allusion to Venus, as this was her mother's name. She was the mythical ancestor of the Julian line. l. 407 – Pallas Athene (the Roman Minerva) was, of course, notable for her martial abilities; Romulus, the mythical founder of Rome, was a son of Mars, hence his epithet Mavortius. l. 409 – Apollo and Diana. l. 410 – Mercury was born on Mount Cyllene in Arcadia. l. 411 – Pompey is like Hercules both because of his extensive travels and because he freed Rome from so many perils, as Hercules freed Greece. Hercules was born in Tiryns. l. 435 – Marcellus: the most appropriate person for this reference would be M. Claudius Marcellus, consul 51 B.C., who proposed to recall Caesar on 1 March 50 and certainly ensured that the question would be discussed on 1 March 49. Petronius may have confused him with his brother, C. Claudius Marcellus, consul in the fateful year of 49. l. 436 – C. Scribonius Curio was tribune of the people in 50 B.C. and a staunch supporter of Caesar. Here he is called on to agitate the mob to ensure the advent of war. l. 437 – Lentulus was a consul of 49 B.C. (cf. l. 362 above). Lentulus was, in fact, a determined advocate of civil war, despite all the pleas of his friend Balbus, one of Caesar's lieutenants. l. 438 – Son of heaven: Julius Caesar, later the divine (*divus*) Julius. l. 443 – Epidamnus (or Dyrrachium) in Epirus was Pompey's main base on the Adriatic after he left Rome, and he managed to ward off Caesar's first attack there. Later he moved into Thessaly for the disastrous battle of Pharsalus, where he was defeated.

Croton

1. This reduplication is probably due to an abbreviated text, which was then incorporated into the main text.

2. Possibly this fragment is out of place in its present position and should occur later in the Crotonian adventure.

3. This type of female character occurs fairly frequently in ancient and modern literature: in Greek and Latin authors such as Herondas, Martial and Juvenal, she appears as an object of fear and contempt. The modern paradigm of the temperament is provided by D. H. Lawrence's *Lady Chatterley's Lover*, but similar portraits may be found in Thomas Mann's *Felix Krull* (Madame Philibert) and L. P. Hartley's *The Go-Between*. The fourteen rows referred to are those reserved in the theatre for the knights by the *Lex Roscia* of 67 B.C., frequently reaffirmed in the imperial period.

4. Praxiteles, an Athenian sculptor (*fl.* perhaps 364 B.C.) was famed for his statues of Aphrodite. Unlike the earlier Athenian school, he produced statues which were full of emotion and sensuality.

5. Reading *Dianam* despite the difficulties. Diana, the puritanical goddess of the hunt, is hardly appropriate in an erotic context such as this. Possibly an allusion to Venus was originally intended, e.g. *Cnidiam* or *Dionen*, as Jahn suggested.

6. Parian marble from the island of Paros was renowned for its pure whiteness.

7. A reference to some lost episode in the work.

8. References to the rape of Europa by Jupiter in the form of a bull, Leda in the shape of a swan, and Danaë as a shower of gold.

9. Circe, the daughter of the Sun, was the name of the enchantress who turned the companions of Ulysses into swine, but fell in love with the hero (cf. *Odyssey* 10). *Polyaenus* is one of the epithets used by Homer to describe Ulysses (*Odyssey* 12. 184); it means 'much-praised' or, alternatively, 'with many a tale', a meaning which is more appropriate for Encolpius' assumption of it as a pseudonym.

10. A reference to Juno's distraction of Jupiter from the Trojan War, when they went to bed together on Mount Ida: the description roughly follows Homer's (cf. *Iliad* 14.347 ff.).

11. Platonic way: *Socratica fide* in the original. A reference to Alcibiades' description in Plato's *Symposium* (217 ff.) of the chaste and honourable way Socrates treated him, even when he spent the night with him. It is almost certainly this passage which is the origin of our concept of Platonic love.

12. Achilles is the natural prototype of prowess. Encolpius, however, seems to have found his own Achilles' heel.

13. Daphne, in the myth, was turned into a laurel to escape from Apollo's amorous pursuit.

14. Procne, the wife of Tereus, was turned into a swallow. Her sister Philomela was changed into a nightingale.

15. In the MSS this paragraph is prefaced by the words '*Encolpius de Endymione puero*', which are clearly an intrusion. The paragraph itself is not necessarily out of place. A close reading reveals that, however active their hands

are clasping each other and however close their embraces and kisses, 'the right true end of love' is not to be inferred and the next paragraph comes as no surprise.

16. A pastiche of Virgil: *Aeneid* 6.469–70 (a description of Dido on meeting Aeneas); the last line is half a line from *Eclogue* 5.16, and half a line from *Aeneid* 9.436.

17. Cato – in the original *Catones*, those who were stern and censorious puritans like the elder Cato, Censor in 184 B.C. The poem seems a key to the whole work. It pleads for naturalism of attitude, language and subject-matter.

18. Epicurus (341–270 B.C.) admittedly held that pleasure was the only good, and this included corporeal enjoyments. But he advocated moderate, non-violent pleasures, not such pleasures as involved as much pain as delight. Roman Epicureans, however, tended to interpret his doctrines more crudely.

19. Priapus, the divine antagonist of the novel, is being addressed. Bacchus was Priapus' father; Dione is poetic for Aphrodite, his mother. As a country god, he would be a natural companion of nymphs. The islands of Lesbos and Thasos would be cult-centres. Hypaepa (-orum) is a small town in Lydia, now Bereki.

20. Encolpius' confessions refer to parts of the work now lost. He may refer to the slaying of his host Lycurgus, but the incident involving temples (of Priapus or Isis?) is more obscure.

21. Both of these old crones are skilled in the magical arts; their names are appropriately chosen, cf. the comments in the List of Characters.

22. Hyrcania was on the Caspian Sea. Hyrcanian tigers were no doubt familiar to Roman writers; there is a line of Virgil that mentions them (*Aeneid* 4.367).

23. Cf. n. 9 above.

24. Proteus was the old man of the sea and had the power to assume any shape he liked to elude those who wished to take advantage of his prophetic powers.

25. Hecale was a poor old woman who gave hospitality to Theseus when he was on his way to kill the Bull of Marathon. She was the subject of an *epyllion* or epic vignette by Callimachus, the great Alexandrian poet and scholar (*c.* 305–240 B.C.); he is referred to a line or so later in the Latin text as Battiades because he was a native of Cyrene and Battus was the mythical founder of that city. His poem would be congenial to the Alexandrian literary tastes of the Neronian period.

26. Stymphalian birds: rapacious birds who were driven by Hercules from their original haunt near the Stymphalian lake in Arcadia to the island of Aretias in the Euxine. Harpies were winged creatures sent to punish Phineus for the ill-treatment of his sons by his first marriage; they swooped down and

removed part of any food served to him and soiled the rest. According to some stories, he was rescued from them by the Argonauts.

27. Acrisius, king of Argos, shut up his daughter Danaë in a bronze tower because of a prophecy that a son of hers would kill his grandfather. Zeus nevertheless got to her in the form of a shower of gold and she gave birth to Perseus.

28. Marcus Porcius Cato Licinianus, son of Cato the Censor, was the most celebrated jurist of his time. The other 'lawyers of note' specified in the original are Servius Sulpicius Lemonia Rufus, contemporary and friend of Cicero, who was a famous orator and jurisconsult, and M. Antistius Labeo, a learned and revolutionary jurist in the reign of Augustus.

29. The order of the fragments in this section (138–9) seems seriously dislocated. I have decided however to keep the order as found in the manuscript tradition, leaving it to the reader to work out a more satisfactory order of events.

30. Famous mythical beauties. Ariadne was a Cretan princess, first the mistress of Theseus, who abandoned her, and then wife of Dionysus. Leda was seduced by Zeus in the shape of a swan and became the mother of Helen, who ran off with the Trojan Paris, providing the cause of the Trojan War. Paris was granted her as a reward for giving the prize of beauty to Venus in the contest of the three goddesses on Mount Ida.

31. This poem is the clue to one of the main motifs of the work – the wrath of Priapus. The mythical comparisons Encolpius adduces are all cases of divine hostility against some mortal. Hercules was hated by Juno and had the twelve labours imposed upon him, one of which entailed his taking the sky off the shoulders of Atlas for a time. Laomedon was king of Troy and took Apollo and Neptune into his service, but he cheated them of their pay and for that Neptune sent a sea-monster to ravage Troy. He is called impious because he broke his contract with the two gods. Pelias killed Sidero, his mother's cruel stepmother, before the altar of Juno. It may have been this piece of impiety which led eventually to his dismemberment by his daughters on the advice of Medea who had promised a method of rejuvenating him. Telephus was king of Mysia at the time of the Trojan War; while repelling the Greek invasion of his land he encountered Bacchus who was helping the Greeks. The god caused him to stumble over a vine root and he was then wounded by Achilles. The wrath of Neptune against Ulysses is of course a major theme in the *Odyssey*; Ulysses incurred this enmity for his blinding of the Cyclops Polyphemus, who was one of Neptune's sons. Nereus was the old man of the sea, father of the Nereids, and his domain was the Mediterranean, in particular the Aegean.

32. The Roman Mercury was identified with the Greek god Hermes; the latter did have a fertility aspect as well as being the god of sudden and unexpected gains. Here, however, Encolpius seems to be attributing his

restoration to the god's power as the guide of the dead. Encolpius, after all, is dead in that part where he was once an Achilles.

33. Protesilaus was the first Greek killed at Troy. He was granted a few hours of return from the underworld to visit his dearly beloved wife, Laodameia. Encolpius, too, has come back from the dead.

34. Saguntum, a city in Spain, was captured by Hannibal in 219 B.C. after an eight-month siege. Petelia, a town in Southern Italy, was captured by Himilco, a lieutenant of Hannibal, after a siege of several months. Livy described the extremities to which the inhabitants were reduced from lack of food, but makes no mention of cannibalism. Numantia, a Spanish town, was captured in 133 B.C. after an eight-month blockade by Scipio Aemilianus. Tales of cannibalism in times of siege are common in ancient literature and should be taken with a pinch of salt. Josephus' description of the siege of Jerusalem is equally sensational.

Notes on the Fragments and Poems

1. Fgt. VII – Fulgentius may be confusing the real Petronius' myrrhine drinking vessel, which gave wine a delicate aromatic flavour, with the aphrodisiac potions mentioned in the *Satyricon*.

2. Fgt. XVI – The *crypta Neapolitana*, still surviving, goes through under the rocky ridge of Cape Posilippo and provides a shorter route to Puteoli and Baiae from Naples. Seneca has a vivid description of its discomforts, dust and noise (*Epistle* 57).

3. Fragments XVII and XVIII were with good reason excluded from Müller's editions. XVII makes very little sense and was wrongly attributed to Petronius through a misreading of a marginal note by Scaliger.

4. Fgt. XVIII – Cosmus was a real first-century manufacturer of perfumes and cosmetics, mentioned by Martial and Juvenal, but the name may have been handed down or assumed as a trade name.

5. Fgt. XIX – no verses of the type referred to (catalectic iambic dimeter in the Latin text) are extant in the Petronian corpus as we have it.

6. That is, the Anacreontic metre.

7. Fgt. XXIV – the line is found in Martial (2.12.4). It may have been mistakenly attributed to Petronius, or possibly he and Martial were both quoting a common dictum.

8. Fgt. XXV - Nicagorus was an Athenian sophist who lived during the reign of the Emperor Philippus (A.D. 244–249) and wrote a series of biographies of famous men.

9. Fgt. XXVII – Mount Athos is a mountain in Macedonia, now famous for its monastery. Phoebus is the sun. Pales was a Roman divinity of flocks and shepherds and was worshipped during the Palilia (21 April). Pallas claims the

streets and inns perhaps because she was the goddess of all useful and domestic arts. The whole poem is based on the Epicurean explanation of religion and would fit Eumolpus' philosophy.

10. The story of King Midas, who was afflicted with ass's ears for a wrong decision as judge in the musical contest between Apollo on the lyre and Marsyas the satyr on the flute, was popular in the Neronian period, being used in Persius' first satire. His 'golden touch' is a separate legend.

11. This is an exposition of Epicurus' doctrines on the senses. Perception is conveyed by thin films of atoms shed by physical objects; these are eroded the further they have to travel through space. Taste and smell are dependent on the interaction of differently shaped atoms in the sensory source and the human receiver.

12. This poem, which is also based on Epicurean doctrines, would fit appropriately into c. 104 as another poetic effusion by Eumolpus.

13. The Fragments or Poems that follow are not printed in Müller's 1983 edition. Texts may be found in the editions of Bücheler and the Loeb Library.

14. Delia: i.e. of Delos, the island on which Diana, addressed here, was born along with her brother Apollo.

15. Reading *lampas* (Bücheler) for *longa*.

16. A number of versions of this famous poem, including that by Ben Jonson, may be found in *Arion* 2 (1963), pp. 83–4.

17. This poem is clearly not by Petronius. I include it here as a typical example of what has been sometimes attributed to him, in this case by Maurice Rat, editor and translator of Petronius, in the *Classiques Garnier*.

SENECA

INTRODUCTION

The Authorship and Date of the *Apocolocyntosis*

The following work, variously entitled in the MSS as *Divi Claudii Apotheosis per saturam*, *Ludus de morte Claudii*, or *Satira de Claudio Caesare*, or *Apotheosis Annaei Senecae per Saturam* and attributed to Seneca, was early identified with the *Apocolocyntosis* mentioned in the well-known passage of Dio Cassius (60.35):

> [Claudius] received the state funeral and all the other honours accorded to Augustus. Agrippina and Nero made a show of mourning for their victim and they elevated to heaven the man they'd carried out from the banquet in a litter. This prompted Lucius Junius Gallio, Seneca's brother, to a very pungent witticism. Seneca himself had written a piece he called the *Apocolocyntosis*, playing on the word *Apotheosis*, and Gallio is credited with the following pithy remark. As the public executioners used to drag the bodies of those executed in prison to the Forum with large hooks and hauled them from there to the river, he commented that Claudius had been hauled into heaven on a hook.

There is little reason to doubt the identification of the Senecan authorship. The main objections are that the work is not given the title *Apocolocyntosis* in the MS tradition and that there is no mention in the text of Claudius' metamorphosis into a gourd or colocynth (or pumpkin, as modern translators have preferred), although there should be on the strict analogy of the word *apotheosis* (deification). It has therefore been suggested that the last part of the work, where this might take place, is lost; that the gourd really refers to the broken dice box that Claudius is given or to a bizarre and humiliating punishment; that Seneca wrote two works about Claudius' death or even that the work before us is by Petronius, the author of the *Satyricon*. None of these suggestions carry conviction. The traditions of contemporary Menippean satire and current colloquialisms may account for the resemblance between the language of the *Satyricon* and that of the *Apocolocyntosis*; again, Seneca would hardly write two similar pamphlets when the job would be effectively done by one; the dice box explanation is far-fetched even for a first-century joke, and it does not meet the point about the 'gourdification'; and although the work ends fairly hastily and abruptly, the ending is satisfactory and final in terms of probability and plot. The best solution so far offered to the problem of the meaning of the title is that the pun, like many puns, is not an exact linguistic parallel to the host word, since verbal jokes frequently break philological rules.[1] (Martial provides numerous examples of this.) On this theory *Apocolocyntosis* is not *Transfiguration into a Pumpkin*, but *Transfiguration of a Pumpkin-head*. The association of *gourd* (in Latin *cucurbita*) with folly and empty-headedness is analogous to the nineteenth-century association in England and the United States of the pumpkin (*Cucurbita Pepo*) with stupidity and self-importance.[2]

Whatever the joke was, if it was represented in the title the preservers of the MS tradition did not understand it. And they might easily have changed the unique coinage *Apocolocyntosis* to the more understandable *Apotheosis*. It would be equally literal-minded to protest that the whole point of the satire is that Claudius' claim to be made a god is rejected.

As if the dispute about the title was not enough, the piece itself excited a certain amount of scepticism and distaste among scholars. Could this pamphlet be the work of the same author as the *Consolatio ad Polybium* with all its flatteries of Claudius and his powerful freedman, or, for that matter, the work of the author of Nero's funeral speech over his predecessor? Could this humour spring from the same pen that wrote the humourless exhortations that fill the *Letters to Lucilius*? Seneca's defenders argue unconvincingly that the praise of Claudius in the *Consolatio* is insincere and satirical; his critics, when they do not deny the Senecan authorship of the *Apocolocyntosis*, find it a cruel and disgusting piece of work.

---

1 There are also a few Greek words similarly compounded from a noun which do not follow the pattern of *apotheosis* in forming their meaning (e.g. *apodontosis, aposomatosis, aporaphanidosis,* and some technical terms in medicine), but this would be irrelevant if one were making a joke. One might rather rely on the listener's familiarity with compounds from verbs such as *apobiosis* (Plutarch), which means 'the leaving of life'

2 The association in Latin is to be found in Petronius, *Satyricon* 39.12 and Apuleius, *Metamorphoses* 1.15, both colloquial contexts. For the connotations in English, see the *OED s.vv.* 'pumpkin' and 'pumpkin-headed' Similar connotations attach to the Italian *zucca* and the Spanish *calabasa*. US colloquial speech provides analogous examples: 'off one's gourd' for 'mad'; and 'squash-rot' for 'senility'

It may help to look first at the time and circumstances of its composition, whoever wrote it, and then see whether it will fit our picture of Seneca the philosopher and statesman and his Neronian ambience. The Emperor Claudius died, perhaps from a poisoned preparation of mushrooms served him by his wife Agrippina, on 13 October A.D. 54. His influential freedman Narcissus, who is described as though recently dead in the *Apocolocyntosis* (13.2), committed suicide very shortly thereafter. The satire was written within the year after Claudius' death, according to the author (*Apocolocyntosis* 1.1), but satire against those long-dead, *pace* Juvenal, tends to fall flat. Moreover, the obtrusive flattery of Nero as the young emperor inaugurating a new Golden Age, a constant theme in Neronian propaganda,[1] seems more appropriate to a coronation than to an established scheme of things. The obloquy and the eulogy both point to a courtier who had much to resent from Claudius and much to expect from Nero. The author had also an intimate acquaintance with the imperial household[2] and a high degree of literary skill in both prose and verse. There is no better candidate, then, for the authorship of the work than the younger Seneca who may have thought its composition and informal, perhaps anonymous, publication a humorous way of compensating for, if not actually disowning, the politic but fulsome speech he had written for Nero to deliver at Claudius' funeral.

The sooner this was done the better, even if it meant that the writing might display some signs of haste. And Furneaux's suggestion, in his edition of Tacitus' *Annals*, that the *Apocolocyntosis* was written for the celebrations of the Saturnalia in mid-December, is highly plausible. But we need not attribute to the author any one single motive in writing the piece.

There is no internal evidence against Senecan authorship; indeed, linguistic resemblances between the *Apocolocyntosis* and the *Satyricon* anchor it in the Neronian era, and some of the verse passages are

---

1. Particularly prominent in the first and fourth Eclogues of Calpurnius Siculus.

2. Would some tactless remarks about incest, which is treated really in a humorous way on the whole, have offended Agrippina, who after all wrote a highly indiscreet set of *Memoirs*? It is noticeable that the pivotal part she played in stage-managing, if not actually procuring, Claudius' death and in arranging the accession of Nero over Claudius' own son, Britannicus, is firmly suppressed in the work. There are no jokes about mushrooms or any indication at all that Claudius may have been poisoned.

reminiscent of Seneca's style in his tragedies, particularly and significantly in the *Hercules Furens*.[1]

The Place of the Work in Seneca's Writings

The main objections then to attributing the *Apocolocyntosis* to Seneca seem largely subjective. How could a stoic philosopher, regarded by some as a proto-Christian, write such stuff? A glance at Seneca's career as a writer may illuminate the question.

Lucius Annaeus Seneca (*c.* 2 B.C.–A.D. 65) was born at Cordoba in Southern Spain into a wealthy equestrian family with strong political interests and connections.[2] No one would doubt his early and continued interest in philosophy, but he was also an eminent orator and a barrister, and his keen involvement in public and court politics is reflected in his chequered career. He was elected quaestor about A.D. 33 and his reputation as an orator did not endear him to Caligula. In 41 he was accused of adultery with Julia Livilla, Caligula's sister, and was banished by Claudius to Corsica, where he remained until his recall in 49, at the urgings of Agrippina, to become tutor to her son, the future Emperor Nero. He then re-entered politics with a praetorship.

Seneca's earlier works are lost, but it is clear from his writings in exile that his philosophical pen was scarcely ever unguided by practical or political motives.

During his eight years of exile on Corsica he wrote poetry complaining of his misery on the barren island, and philosophical tracts in which he actively campaigned for a remission of his sentence. His attitude to exile then does not correspond to his views on it in his *Epistles* (cf. e.g. 24.17). In the consoling philosophical essays on bereavement, addressed first to his mother Helvia and then to the respected Roman lady Marcia, he tries to clear his reputation of the sexual charges, and also disavow some dangerous political connections with the party of Sejanus. In the *Consolatio ad Polybium* the flattery of Claudius' powerful freedman and his imperial master is so arrant that Seneca later tried to suppress the piece. In the last part of his treatise *On Anger*, however, which was written after his return to Rome and under the protection of Agrippina,

---

1. For a sampling of Seneca's dramatic work, see *Seneca: Four Tragedies and Octavia*, translated and introduced by E. F. Watling (Harmondsworth, 1966).

2. For fuller information on his life and works, see M. T. Griffin, *Seneca, A Philosopher in Politics* (Oxford, 1976).

there is covert criticism of Claudius' capricious and tyrannical behaviour. In yet another dissertation, this time *On the Shortness of Human Life*, he ridicules Claudius' pedantry. Both provide satirical themes for the *Apocolocyntosis*. Similarly, the high hopes expressed for the Golden Age of Nero in the slighter work are reflected and articulated in the hortatory tracts directed at the young emperor later. In his tracts *On Mercy* and *On Benefits*, Seneca mixes flattery into his practical advice on the proper treatment of the Senate and of Nero's subjects in general. As in the *Apocolocyntosis*, the Emperor Augustus and all that he supposedly stood for figure prominently.

The scurrility of the *Apocolocyntosis* is often thought to militate against Seneca's authorship, but that argument may be disposed of by a glance at the savage concluding ripostes in *On the Happy Life*, written about 58. This highly personal treatise overlays the high-minded philosophy with a mixture of abuse and threats against opponents, very like P. Suillius, who had openly accused Seneca of hypocrisy in wallowing in the wealth and luxury which, as a Stoic, he professedly despised. There are similar shrill attacks on thinly disguised enemies at court in his *Epistles*.[1] Even in the *Natural Questions*, written in retirement after A.D. 62, he manages to insert a passage of praise for Nero's poetry.

The objection that the *Apocolocyntosis* is too light and humorous for a serious writer such as Seneca may be quickly disposed of. First of all, beneath the banter, there are some serious aims, not least the discrediting of Claudius and the fulsome defence of the youthful Nero, in the eyes of some a usurper of the throne. Secondly, the genre of Menippean satire, as practised by Varro, let alone his Greek precursors, furnished adequate guidelines for the composition of an amusing work in prose and verse, two skills in which Seneca was equally adept. Is one surprised that the Attic tragedians produced satyr plays as well as tragedies? Or that respected Roman worthies such as the younger Pliny wrote erotic epigrams as well as serious prose? Moreover, much of the humour is essentially wit, often plays on words, of which most Romans were inordinately fond, and Seneca is no exception here.

---

1. See Seneca, *Letters from a Stoic*, translated by Robin Campbell (Harmondsworth, 1969), pp. 220 ff. The last tirade is probably a veiled attack on Petronius and others like him, who by their congenial tastes and unorthodox style of life had usurped Seneca's place in Nero's grace at court. Compare with Seneca's description of this coterie the description of Petronius given by Tacitus, cited on pp. 11–12 of this volume.

In short, the surprising thing is that doubt about Senecan authorship of the *Apocolocyntosis* should have persisted for so long and, as is not unusual in such disputes, without any plausible alternative candidate or any explanation of what could motivate some highly talented but otherwise unknown writer to produce such a politically indiscreet and personally biased lampoon.

The Literary Qualities of the *Apocolocyntosis*

The piece then is a somewhat hastily written squib. It was perhaps primarily prompted by some personal and not entirely unjustified malice against Claudius – eight years on Corsica is a long time – and the necessity of flattering that emperor, whether for selfish reasons as an exile or for political purposes as a statesman, must have left a sour taste. With his death the covert criticism of the *De Brevitate Vitae* (*On the Shortness of Human Life*) could become overt. Some broader considerations of state were then involved. The circumstances called for white-washing Agrippina, positively gilding Nero, and painting Augustus in colours that might have surprised some of his contemporaries. Nor was Seneca one to pass up an opportunity for displaying his considerable literary expertise for the court circle and a ruler whose preoccupation with art was to become later an obsession.

Speed of composition does not entail faulty construction or lack of artifice. The narrator adopts and then parodies the pose of the historian, solemnly laying out his credentials and authorities. The exigencies of the Menippean genre[1] then lead him into a parody of the periphrases that bad poets use to express time in their verses, a pet topic with Seneca to which he will revert again in the criticism of Julius Montanus in the *Epistles* (122.11 ff.). This in turn paves the way for the lengthy verse digression on the promises of a new Golden Age under Nero. This is the literary structure imposed on the events of the narrative, which are simply that Claudius is finding it hard to die; Mercury takes pity on him and invokes one of the Fates to help him on his way. She cuts his life-line and spins a more propitious thread for his successor with the help and encouragement of Nero's tutelary deity, Apollo.

Once released, with a suitable set of last words on his deathbed,

---

1. For the characteristics of Menippean satire, see the Introduction to the *Satyricon* above, pp. 20 ff.

Claudius is taken up to heaven, where he is gingerly treated as a monster. Jupiter sends Hercules to cross-examine him, a suitable choice because of his past experience with monsters and because he too was a mortal who has been recently granted Olympian status.

The character of Hercules in his well-established comic role as buffoon and braggart is well realized. The humorous use of Homeric quotations in his interchange with the dead emperor keeps the conformity of the piece with Menippean rules, just as later in the narrative the verse tags and proverbs remind us intermittently of the origins of the genre. Claudius' evasive Homeric answers are intended to imply that he is the ruler of Rome, but his companion in death as in life, the goddess Fever, will have none of this and maliciously exposes him as a Gaul by reason of his place of birth and so belonging to a race unpopular with Romans as well as Spaniards. This prompts the insertion of a bravura piece of mock-tragic verse by Hercules, boasting of his heroic exploits involving that area. Claudius then appeals to the god for help with a mixture of flattery and self-pity.

How Claudius succeeds in winning Hercules over to his cause we do not know, since the text fails us at this point. Given the leisurely pace of the narrative so far, with as much attention given over to literary parody as to plot proper, we may surmise that we have lost more than one double page of text.[1] The least we have lost is not inconsiderable. Gone is the conclusion of Claudius' speech winning over Hercules to support of his claim to be a god with full divine privileges. Doubtless some inducements were offered to justify Hercules' later enthusiasm. Hercules must have forced his way into the senate-house of the gods along with Claudius and introduced his proposal to elect the dead emperor as a god to the divine ranks. General disorder must have ensued despite Jupiter's attempt to allow for only orderly procedures in questioning him (witness his critical remarks in c. 9). The work reopens with the concluding part of a speech by a god who is hostile to Hercules' proposal.

What more may be missing? Weinreich suggests a caricature of Claudius' own speeches, which were discursive and often laced with Homeric quotations (Suetonius, *Claudius* 42). This would have followed Hercules' presentation of Claudius' claim to deification and Jupiter's

---

1. A reconstruction of the missing parts is offered by O. Weinreich, *Seneca Apocolocyntosis. Die Satire Auf Tod/Himmel – und Höllenfahrt des Kaisers Claudius* (Berlin, 1923).

granting the candidate the right to speak. The speech presumably would stress his qualifications, perhaps as a judge or reformer, the sort of claim challenged by the first speaker we encounter when our text resumes. (He may not have been the only one, of course.)

The most intriguing question is then: Who is the god who speaks out of order in his indignant rejection of the case put by Hercules and Claudius? One may assume that it was a minor deity, like Janus and Diespiter, who might also afford occasion for some descriptive humour at his expense. His somewhat learned approach to the matter, with philosophical and physiological references, would point to a minor Greek deity such as Aesculapius, but that has certain problems.[1]

It is clear, however, that the centre, indeed the heart, of the *Apocolo-cyntosis* is the Council of the Gods, an epic theme borrowed for satiric uses by Menippus, and later used by the Roman satirist Lucilius for his specific purposes. Seneca's deployment of the theme, like Petronius' parallel use of the Symposium or *Cena* motif, naturalized by Horace in *Satire* 2.8, is a brilliant adaptation to Roman circumstances and to the author's own aims.

The speech by Janus, who is against the proposal on general grounds, might hint at Seneca's own disquiet, doubtless shared by many conservative Romans, at the frequent deifications not only of emperors, but also of members of the imperial household, but the point is made with tact and not belaboured.

Diespiter, after a personal appeal by Hercules, offers somewhat flimsy arguments for his yea-vote. Claudius is related to Augustus and Livia, his aunt and Augustus' wife, whom Claudius had deified personally, so he deserves the honour. His dubious claim that Claudius is also the wisest of men must be understood against Diespiter's own background. Claudius' antiquarianism had given him a new lease on life; Diespiter was included in the old religious formula to ratify a treaty with foreign rulers. In his old-fashioned views Claudius would be ideal company for Romulus. His extension of the citizenship presumably counted in his favour also.

This, of course, is preliminary banter to introduce the set speech by

---

1. Weinreich's suggestion (*op. cit.* p. 93) that the speakers missing from the text as we have it, if more than one, would be gods of Greek origin who were comparative newcomers to the Roman pantheon runs up against the objection that the last speaker quotes Varro. Romans and Romanized deities might be expected to know Greek, but Greeks were notoriously ignorant of Latin and Roman literature.

Augustus which is obviously the political core of the piece. The gravamen of Augustus' charges in opposing Claudius' admission to heaven is that Claudius capriciously murdered various relatives and sundry members of the Roman aristocracy. Augustus' indignation, given his own record as a cold and calculating terrorist and an unsympathetic *paterfamilias* towards his own daughter Julia, not to mention her friends, is somewhat surprising, unless we remember that Seneca has found it politic to have Nero declare that he would govern in accordance with the rules laid down by Augustus, and he would use Augustus constantly as an example for Nero to follow in his various political writings directed at Nero. Unfortunately Claudius had made the same political declaration at the opening of his reign. Augustus' rejection of him has therefore political significance.

After this, any further debate in heaven would be anti-climactic and the action therefore speeds up. Without delay Mercury hauls him off. Only as they pass through the Sacred Way does the action slow down for a dirge to be heard for Claudius at a handsome funeral, fit for a divinity. This di ~e, which structurally parallels the praises of Nero at the opening of the work, and which employs one of Seneca's favourite choral metres, is shot through with irony, extolling his empty or vicariously earned triumphs and his arbitrary legal judgements, and enumerating the classes of disreputable mourners who have a real cause for grief at his passing: lawyers because of the extra business lost; new poets because of Claudius' general sympathy for literary pursuits and his willingness to attend recitations; and, finally, gamblers, whose addiction Claudius himself shared.

The last section allows Seneca to remind his audience of the casualties inflicted by Claudius on his own family circle and entourage and the upper classes in general. Claudius is then faced with the summary justice he himself was alleged to deal in. Aeacus grants no delay in the trial and listens to no defence, even though his counsel is a respectable nobody. (Whatever political considerations Seneca had in mind in this choice of Publius Petronius for this task are lost on us.) After considering various alternatives the prosecution decides on an appropriate eternal penalty – throwing dice from a dice box with a hole in it. The ending is abrupt, as though inspiration or enthusiasm were flagging on the author. Claudius is claimed as his slave by his *bête noire* Caligula and appropriately given the task of handling the former emperor's legal business under proper supervision. The two punishments are again related to several of Claudius' weaknesses; his dependence on freedmen; his supineness under harsh treatment; and his obsession with the law and with gambling.

On the Text and Translation

Unlike the *Satyricon*, the *Apocolocyntosis* was fairly fortunate in its textual transmission. A couple of pages or perhaps more are missing after c.7, but there are no real grounds for believing that the apparently hurried conclusion to the piece is due to damage to the text rather than the author's own inclinations. There are nearly fifty MSS of it extant, and they divide into three families: the Sangallensis, the Valentianensis and the Londinensis.[1] I have sometimes preferred the MS readings to the emendations of later editors.

In the original version of this translation I had followed for the most part the text of C. F. Russo (Florence 1948), but in the revision, for the reader's convenience, I have brought the translation into conformity with the latest text which is that of P. T. Eden, *Seneca Apocolocyntosis* (Cambridge 1984). This supplies also an excellent introduction, bibliography, apparatus and notes, to which I am much indebted. I have adopted different readings from this text in the following places: 5.1, *impresserit* (Bücheler) for *impresserunt*; 7.5, *tulerim* (Haase) for *contulerim*; 8.2, *illud nedum ab Iove* (Gronovius) for *illum deum [induci] ab Iove*; 8.3, *inquit* (Lipsius) for *inquis*; [*ut deum*] (Mariotti); 9.1, *existimabit* (Sangallensis) for *existimavit*; 9.3, *lanistis* (Maehly) for *larvis*; *Canis excidit* (Valentianensis) for *canis adsidit*; 10.4, *sed* (Sangallensis) for *et*; 11.2, *tres homines assarios* (Bücheler) for [*tristionias*], [*non*] *Assar[aci nat]ionem* from *tristionias assarionem* (MSS); 11.6, *a caelo ad inferos unde* (Birt) for *ad inferos a caelo unde*; 12.1, *concentus* (Lipsius) for *conventus*; 14.1–2, *XXX* and *CCXXI* (MSS) for *XXX[V]* and *CC[X]XXI*.

As is customary, I have tried to give the translation a modern ring without doing too much injustice to the original. I have used equivalencies where necessary for the legal and political terminology. Not all of the Latin puns survived their transition in their pristine form, but at least the reader is made aware of them.

---

1 For a succinct summary of the transmission, see L. D. Reynolds, '*Apocolocyntosis*', in *Texts and Transmission: A Survey of the Latin Classics* (Oxford, 1983), pp. 361 ff

THE APOCOLOCYNTOSIS
OF THE
DIVINE CLAUDIUS

1. I wish to give future generations an account of the events in heaven on the thirteenth of October of this new year of grace that inaugurated our present period of prosperity. No offence and no flattery have any part in it. What follows is the honest truth. If the reader asks for my sources, in the first place I will refuse to answer if I am not so inclined. Who is going to make me? I know that I'm a free agent ever since the death of the fellow who proved the old saying – *be born a king or a fool*! Should I wish to answer, I'll say the first thing that comes to my lips. Whoever demanded sworn certification from an historian? But if it is necessary to reveal my source, you should ask the man who saw Drusilla's ascent into heaven.[1] This person will claim he saw Claudius making the same journey, though 'with unequal steps'.[2] Willy-nilly, he has to watch everything that goes on in heaven – he's in charge of the Appian Way,[3] the way by which, as you know, both the Divine Augustus and Tiberius Caesar joined the company of the gods. If you ask him, he'll tell you in private. He'll never say a word to more than one. Ever since he swore in the senate that he'd seen Drusilla going up to heaven and, for all that marvellous news, no one believed him, he has solemnly sworn that he personally will never reveal what he's seen, even if it's a murder in the middle of the Forum. I am here setting down clearly and precisely what I got from him at the time, so help him God!

2. Now Phoebus[4] had made short the arc of day,
    Shortening his road, and Sleep extends its sway;
    Now vaster realms hear Cynthia's conquering call;
    Foul Winter plucks the crown from wealthy Fall;
    Bacchus is told, Grow old; no vine escapes,
    As the tardy vintner[5] plucks the few last grapes.

I think it'll be better understood if I put it this way: it was the month of October, the thirteenth day of October. The hour I can't say for certain – it's easier to get philosophers to agree than clocks.[6] Anyway, it was between twelve and one o'clock. 'That's too crude!' you say. 'No poet is content to describe just dawn and sunset. They all like those descriptions so much that they make midday miserable too. Will you pass up such a good hour like this?'

> Now the chariot of Phoebus had passed mid-orbit;
> Closer to Night, he shook his tiring reins,
> Sending the curving light down paths oblique.

Claudius began to gasp his last breath, but he could not find the proper exit.

3. At that point Mercury,[7] as he had always enjoyed his wit, took one of the three Fates aside[8] and said: 'Why are you allowing that poor man to be tortured, you cruel woman? After all his long agony, isn't he ever going to get peace? It's sixty-four years since he began fighting against his breath. Why the malice against him and the state? Let the astrologers[9] be right for once: ever since he became emperor they've been burying him off every month of every year. Of course, it's not surprising they make mistakes and that none of them can predict his last hour – they all thought he'd never been born. Do what has to be done:

> Let him be slain,
> That he who best deserves alone may reign.'[10]

Clotho however said: 'Well, for Hercules' sake! I was going to give him a bit of time until he could grant citizenship to the handful left without it: he'd made up his mind to see every Greek, Gaul, Spaniard and Briton in a toga.[11] But since you like the idea of leaving a few aliens to start the next crop and you insist on it that way, so be it.' She opens a little box and brings out three spindles. One was for Augurinus,[12] the second for Baba and the third for Claudius. 'I'll make these three die in one year at very short intervals – I won't send him off without company. For a man who used to see so many thousands following him, so many thousands in front of him, and so many thousands around him, it's not right to be left suddenly on his own. He'll be happy in the meantime with these close old friends.'

4. This said, she twirled the thread on an ugly spool,
   Cut from the imperial line one doddering life.
   But Lachesis, locks looped, with tresses dressed,

Pierian crown of laurel on forehead and hair,
Takes from the snowy fleece the bright white yarn,
Shaping with happy touch; new colours now dawn.
The sisters look at their work in awed surmise,
To see cheap wool turn into a mass of gold.
The Ages of Gold[13] spin out in a lovely line.
No limits are set. They teaze the favoured fleece,
Filling their hands in joy, so sweet their task.
As if by itself, the work went on, with ease;
Softly the threads turn on to the twirling spool –
Tithonus? his eons – Nestor? his years surpassed.
Phoebus is by to assist and the decades to come
Gladden his heart, so he helps with a song,
Now plucking the strings, now happily passing the wool.
He keeps them to work with his song, beguiling their labour,
No praise too much for his lyre, his brotherly songs.[14]
Their hands spin more than they used; and the work he salutes
Surpasses the lot of a man. 'Stint not, o ye Fates!'
Says Apollo, 'Let him surpass by far a mortal span,
Image of me in looks and beauty as well,
In song and voice no less. To a weary folk
He brings glad times, to muted law a tongue.
Like the Morning Star, setting the stars to flight,
Like the Evening Star, rising with the stars' return,
As the shining Sun, whenso the ruddy Dawn,
The shades of night dispersed, brings back the day,
Looks on the world and starts his chariot off:
So Caesar comes, so Nero appears to Rome,
His bright face fired with gentle radiance,
His neck all beauty under his flowing hair.'

This was Apollo. For her part, Lachesis, being herself on the side of such a handsome mortal, did her job with generous hands and gave Nero a lot of years from her own stock. As for Claudius, however, they commanded that all

> in joy and holy awe bear him from the house.[15]

And he did indeed gurgle out his last breath and from that moment stopped even appearing to be alive. However, when he expired he was listening to some comic actors, so you can understand that my fear of them is not unfounded. His last words heard on earth came after he'd let off a louder noise from his easiest channel of communication: 'Oh my! I think I've shit myself.' For all I know, he did. He certainly shat on everything else.

5. An account of what happened after that on earth is superfluous. My readers are perfectly familiar with the events, and there is no danger of people forgetting what national celebrations impress on the memory. No one forgets his own good luck. Here is what happened in heaven: my informant will be responsible for the reliability of the account.

An announcement was made to Jupiter that there was a visitor of a respectable size and with very white hair. He was making some sort of threat, as he kept shaking his head; he was also dragging his right foot. When asked his nationality, he had made some answer with a confused noise and in indistinct tones. It was impossible to understand his language: he was neither Greek nor Roman, nor of any known race.

Jupiter then instructed Hercules,[16] who had travelled the whole world over and seemed familiar with every nationality, to go and find out his nationality. Hercules was badly shaken by the first sight of him – he hadn't been scared by all possible monsters yet. Seeing the strange sort of appearance and the weird walk and hearing the hoarse and incomprehensible voice that belonged to no land creature but seemed more appropriate to a sea-monster, he thought his thirteenth labour had arrived. On a closer inspection, it appeared to be something like a man. So he came nearer and asked in the language these little Greeks find easiest:

> Who art thou? Whence? Thy city and thy kin?[17]

Claudius was glad there were scholars there. He had hoped that there would be a place for his Histories.[18] And so, using himself another line from Homer to indicate he was Caesar, he said:

> The winds from Ilion to the Cicons' shore,
> Beneath cold Ismarus, our vessels bore.[19]

The line after that, however, would have been more correct and equally Homeric:

> We sack'd the city and destroy'd the race.

6. He would have put it over on Hercules, who is not at all sharp, if the goddess Fever[20] had not been there. She was the only goddess to leave her temple and come with him: she had left all the other gods in Rome. 'This man is telling you absolute lies,' she said. 'I'll give you the

truth, since I've lived with him all these years. He was born at Lyons.[21] You see in front of you one of Munatius' fellow townsmen.[22] I tell you, he was born at the sixteenth milestone from Vienne, a *Bruder* Gaul. And so, as a Gaul should, he captured Rome.[23] I assure you, this man was born at Lyons, where Licinus[24] ruled for years. Now you've tramped over more places than any long-haul mule driver and you ought to know that there are many miles between the Xanthus[25] and the Rhone.'

Claudius flared up at this point and fumed as loudly as he could. No one understood what he was saying. He was, in fact, giving orders for the goddess Fever to be taken away. With his shaky hand, which was steady enough only on these occasions, making the familiar gesture with which he had people's heads cut off, he had ordered her to be decapitated. You'd have thought they were all his freedmen the way no one took any notice of him.

7. 'Listen to me,' says Hercules then, 'and stop playing the fool. You've come where mice chew iron. Out with the truth, quick, before I knock this nonsense out of you.' To make himself more terrifying, he speaks in tones of high tragedy:

> Say, sirrah, quick, what country hail'st thou from,
> Or, smitten by this bough, thou sink'st to earth,
> A club that oft hath butchered savage kings.
> Why mumble now thy words in tones unclear?
> What land, what nation, raised that shaking head?
> Speak out. I once did seek the far-flung realms
> Of triform Geryon,[26] whose most noble herd
> I drove from Western seas to Argos town.
> While homeward bound, I saw a mountain crest,
> O'erlooking two great rivers, which the sun
> Faces direct when first he rises up.
> There mighty Rhone with rapid current flows;
> Hard by the Saône, in doubt where it should run,
> With hushed and quiet shallows laps its banks.
> Is this the soil that nursed thee into life?

This is delivered with some vigour and courage. None the less he is out of his mind and is nervous of some *coup de fou*.[27] Claudius, seeing his physique, cut out the nonsense, realizing that though he had no one equal to him in Rome, up there he did not have the same prestige: whatever your gall, you're cock-of-the-walk only on your own dungheap. And so, as far as he could be understood, he apparently said: 'Hercules, strongest of all the gods, I hoped you would stand up for me among the others, and if anyone asked me for a person to vouch for me, I was going to name you, as you know me best. If you recall, I was the one who used to preside in court in front of *your* temple for whole days at a time in the months of July and August.[28] You know what misery I went through there, listening to lawyers day and night. If you'd been dropped into that, mighty tough as you think you are, you'd have preferred to clean out the Augean sewers: I threw out a lot more bullshit. But since I'd like . . .[29]

*

8. '. . . it's no surprise that you've come charging into the Senate: nothing is barred to you. Just tell us what sort of god you want him to be. He can't be an Epicurean god: he'd be "untroubled and troubling none".[30] A Stoic god? How can he be "globular", as Varro says "with no head, no foreskin"?[31] There *is* something about him of the Stoic god, I now see. He's got neither a heart nor a head.

'For Hercules' sake, if he'd asked this favour from Saturn, he wouldn't have got it, even though he celebrated his month all year round, a proper Saturnalian emperor.[32] Still less would he get that favour from Jupiter, after he condemned him for incest, as far as he could: he killed his son-in-law Silanus.[33] Why, I ask you? Because his sister, who was the most delightful girl in the world, he preferred to call Juno, when everyone called her Venus. You say "Why his own sister, I wonder?" Get back to school, you idiot! In Athens you can go halfway, in Alexandria the whole way.[34] Just because in Rome, you say, "the mice lick the millstones", is he the one to set crooked things straight with us? He won't know what he does in his own bedroom: already "he keeps his eye on regions in the sky".[35] He wants to become a god, does he? Isn't it enough for him to have a temple in Britain, have savages worship him,[36] and pray they'll find in him a Merciful Clod.'

9. Jupiter finally recollected that with members of the public in the Senate-house it was out of order for senators to offer a motion or debate. 'Gentlemen of the senate,' he said, 'I permitted you to put some questions, but you're making the whole thing an absolute shambles. I request you to observe the rules of order of the House. What will this man think of us, whatever he is?'

Once Claudius was dismissed, Father Janus[37] was given the floor first. He had been appointed consul for the afternoon of the first of July;

he was – at least in his own street – always forward-looking and watching his rear at the same time. As he lived in the Forum, he made a long and eloquent speech, which the recorder could not keep up with and which I therefore will not report in case I substitute other words for what he actually said. He spoke at length about the high status of gods. This honour should not be granted to ordinary people. 'Once,' he said, 'it was a great thing to become a god. Now you've made it a farce – not worth a bean.[38] Therefore, to avoid any appearance of speaking against the person involved and not for the principle of the thing, I move that from this day forth no one who "eats the harvest of the tilth" or lives off "the grain-bearing tilth"[39] shall become a god. Any person who is declared a god or so spoken of or so depicted in contravention of this decree of the senate shall be handed over to gladiatorial managers and at the next show in the arena shall be beaten with rods along with the new recruits.'

Diespiter[40] was next recognized. The son of the goddess Vica Pota, he was also consul elect and a moneylender in a small way. He made his living at this and used to sell bits and pieces of citizenships. Hercules daintily approached him and touched his ear-lobe.[41] Diespiter accordingly phrased his motion as follows:

'Whereas the Divine Claudius is related by blood to both the Divine Augustus and equally to the Divine Augusta, his grandmother, whom he personally had declared a goddess, and whereas he is far superior intellectually to all other mortals, and whereas it is in the interest of the state that there should be someone who can "swallow boiling turnips" with Romulus,[42] I hereby propose that the Divine Claudius be a god from this day forth with the privileges accorded to those of his predecessors with the most unquestionable qualifications and that an account of the matter be appended to Ovid's *Metamorphoses*.'[43]

Motions were made of various kinds and Claudius seemed to be winning. For Hercules, who saw his own irons were in the fire, rushed here and there on the floor, and kept saying: 'Don't turn me down, my own interests are involved. Next time you want a favour, I'll do the same for you. You scratch my back, I'll scratch yours.'

10.   Then the Divine Augustus rose to his feet when his turn to speak came and delivered a highly eloquent oration. 'Gentlemen of the senate,' he said, 'you are witness that, since I became a god, I have not uttered a word. I always mind my own business. Yet I cannot hide my feelings any longer or conceal the pain, which my sense of honour aggravates.

Was it for this that I brought peace to land and sea? Was this why I put an end to civil war? Was this why I laid a foundation of laws for Rome, beautified the city with public works – in order to ... I can't think of what to say, gentlemen. No words can be equal to my indignation. I must fall back on the remarks of that great orator, Messala Corvinus, and say, "I am disgusted with power."[44] This man, gentlemen, who seems to you incapable of shooing a fly, killed men as easily as you get a low roll of the dice. But why am I talking about all those important victims? When a man looks at the troubles in his own house, he has no time to shed tears over national calamities. So I'll pass over them and talk about my domestic problems. Even if my ankle doesn't know it, the knee is nearer than the shin.[45] That man you see in front of you, after all those years of hiding under my name,[46] thanked me by killing my two great-granddaughters, one Julia with cold steel, the other Julia by starving her to death, and by killing one of my great-great-grandsons, Lucius Silanus.[47] You will decide, Jupiter, whether it was for an unjustified cause. Certainly it was one which reflects on you, if you are to be fair. Tell me, Divine Claudius, for what reason did you condemn any one of the men and women you killed, before specifying the charges, and before ascertaining the facts? Where is this usual? It doesn't happen in heaven.

11. 'Take Jupiter, who has held supreme power all these years. In Vulcan's case alone did he break his leg, whom

Taking by the foot he flung from heaven's threshold.[48]

He was also angry with his wife and hung her up. Did he ever kill? You killed Messalina, whose great-great-uncle I was as well as yours. "I don't know about it," you say. God damn you! Not to know about it is worse than killing her.[49]

'He didn't stop dogging Gaius Caesar's footsteps even after he was dead. Gaius had killed his father-in-law: Claudius killed a son-in-law too.[50] Gaius wouldn't allow Crassus' son to be called Magnus: Claudius returned his title and removed his head. In one household he killed Crassus, Magnus, and Scribonia. Three lightweights, but they *were* aristocracy – Crassus in fact was so stupid he could even have been an emperor.[51] Do you now want to make this man a god? Look at his body – the gods were angry when it came into the world. In short, let him say three words one after the other and he can drag me off as his slave. Who's going to worship him as a god? Who'll believe in him?

While you create such gods, no one will believe that you yourselves are gods. To get to the point, gentlemen of the senate, I ask you, if I have been an honest man while with you, if I have been too blunt to no one, make him pay for the wrongs he has done me. I put this motion to the House.'

And then he read as follows from a notebook: 'Whereas the Divine Claudius has murdered his father-in-law, Appius Silanus,[52] his two sons-in-law, Magnus Pompeius and Lucius Silanus, his daughter's father-in-law, Crassus Frugi, a man as like him as two peas, his daughter's mother-in-law, Scribonia, his wife Messalina and others too numerous to go into, I move that he be severely punished, that he be denied any immunity from trial, and that he be deported as soon as possible, leaving heaven within thirty days and Olympus within three.'

On the division there was general support for this motion. Without delay, Mercury seized him, twisting his neck, and hauled him off from heaven to hell,

that bourne from which, they say, no man returns.[53]

12. While they were going down by way of the Via Sacra, Mercury inquired the meaning of the great crowd: was it Claudius' funeral? And it was the most handsome cortège ever, with no expense spared to let you know that a god was being buried. There was such a mob, such an orchestration of trumpeters, horn players, and every kind of brass instrumentalist that even Claudius could hear it. Everyone was happy and gay. The Roman people walked about like free men. Agatho[54] and a few barristers were in tears, but they were clearly sincere. Legal authorities were emerging from the shadows, pale, thin, and scarcely breathing, like men who had just come back to life. One of them, seeing the barristers with their heads together, crying over their bad luck, went up and said: 'I told you it won't always be carnival time.'

When Claudius saw his funeral, he realized he was dead. For a dirge[55] was being sung with a huge choir *en masse*:

> Mourn, mourn
> Ye Roman lads and lasses!
> Sound, sound
> The sad and gloomy brasses!
> In the Forum,
> Sound them for him.
> Brave heart ever,

Now he passes,
Braver never,
Who surpasses
Him for racing
Or for warring
Parthians chasing?
His light spears
Hit the Persians,
His sure bow
Made swift incursions,
Lightly pricking
All attacks,
Routing Medes
With painted backs.
Beyond the seaways
That we knew
He made Britons,
Brigantes too,
Drop blue targes,
Be our charges
In the chains of
Romulus.
He brought the Ocean
Roman *Pax*,
Spread devotion
With our axe.

Weep, weep
For the man's good judgements.
Who could master
Lawsuits faster,
Hearing either
One or neither.
Who will warm
The bench and dock
Through the year
And round the clock?
Minos, retire for him,
Let Claudius instead,
O Cretan lawgiver,
Be judge of the Dead.

Pound, pound
Your breasts
In solemn mourning,
Lawyers for retainers
And all the other gainers!
Weep, weep,
Ye new poetic prattlers
And ye tribes of
Lucky dice box rattlers!

13. Claudius was delighted to hear his praises sung and wanted to watch longer. The heavenly herald got a grip on him and hauled him along through the Campus Martius, his head wrapped up so that no one could recognize him. And between the Tiber and the Via Tecta he descended into the infernal regions. Claudius' freedman Narcissus had already gone on ahead by a short cut to make his master welcome.[56] As Claudius arrived, he met him, gleaming because he'd come straight from a bath.

'What are gods doing with men?' he asked. 'Get a move on!' said Mercury, 'and announce our arrival.' Quicker than the words, Narcissus flew off. Everything slopes downward and the descent is easy.[57] And so, despite his gout, he arrived in an instant at the gate of Dis, where lay Cerberus, or, as Horace calls him, 'the hundred-headed monster'.[58] He was a bit frightened – he'd been used only to a little off-white bitch as a pet – when he saw that black, shaggy dog, which was certainly not the sort of thing you'd like to meet in the dark, and in a loud voice he cried out: 'Claudius is on his way!'

People came out clapping and chanting in Greek, 'We have found Him, let us rejoice!'[59] Here was Gaius Silius, a consul designate, Juncus, a former praetor, Sextus Traulus, Marcus Helvius, Trogus, Cotta, Vettius Valens, Fabius – all Roman knights whom Narcissus had ordered executed.[60] In the centre of this singing crowd was the ballet-dancer, Mnester,[61] whom Claudius had cut down to size for the sake of appearances, as regards Messalina. The rumour spread quickly that Claudius had arrived. Up rushed first of all the freedmen Polybius,[62] Myron, Arpocras, Ampheus and Pheronactus – all of whom Claudius had dispatched ahead to avoid being anywhere without attendants. Then came the two Praetorian Prefects, Justus Catonius[63] and Rufrius Pollio. Then Claudius' Cabinet members, Saturninus Lusius, Pedo Pompeius, Lupus, and Celer Asinius, all men of consular rank. Finally, the daughter of his brother, the daughter of his sister, his sons-in-law, his fathers-in-law, his mothers-in-law, all obviously close kin.[64] And forming into a line they came to meet Claudius.

When he saw them, Claudius cried out: '*Tout le monde mes amis!*[65] How did *you* get here?' Pedo Pompeius then spoke: 'What do you mean, you cruel bastard? You ask *how*? Who else sent us here but *you*, you butcher of every friend you had? Let's go into court. *I*'ll show *you* the bench down here.'

14. He leads him before Aeacus' tribunal;[66] he sat on cases that fell under the Cornelian legislation on murder.[67] Pedo requests that Claudius be charged and he lays out the indictment: 'Executed 30 Senators, 221 Roman knights, and others "to the number of the grains of sand and the specks of dust".'[68] Claudius finds no counsel. Finally, an old crony of his, Publius Petronius,[69] comes forward, a master of Claudian-style eloquence, and he requests an adjournment. It is not granted. Pedo Pompeius opens for the prosecution amid acclamation. The defence starts wanting to reply. The superbly impartial Aeacus denies the request, and with only one side of the case heard, finds Claudius guilty and quotes in Greek:

> 'What thou hast wrought shouldst thou suffer,
> Straight would justice be done.'[70]

There was a profound silence. Everyone was stupefied, thunderstruck by the strange procedure: this had never happened before. Claudius found it more unjust than unprecedented. As for the type of punishment, there was a long argument about what penalty should be imposed upon him. There were those who said that Sisyphus had been carrying his burden for a long time, that Tantalus would die of thirst unless relieved, and that sometime or other the brake had to be put on poor Ixion's wheel.[71] It was decided that none of these old lags should be pardoned, in case even Claudius had his hopes raised for something similar.

It was decided that a new punishment should be instituted, some useless labour should be thought up, an illusory hope of gratifying some desire. Aeacus then orders him to throw dice from a dicebox with a hole in it. And he was off hunting already for the continually falling dice, and getting nowhere.

> When from the rattling cup he seeks to throw
> The dice, they trickle through the hole below,
> And when he tries the recovered bones to roll –

> A gambler fooled by the eternal goal –
> Again they fool him: through his finger-tips
> Each time each cunning die as cruelly slips,
> As Sisyphus' rocks, before they reach the crest,
> Slip from his neck and roll back to their rest.

15. Suddenly Gaius Caesar[72] turned up and starts claiming him as his slave. He produces witnesses who had seen him being beaten by Gaius with whips, rods and his fists. The judgement is in his favour. It is to Gaius Caesar that Aeacus awards him. He in turn hands him over to his freedman Menander to put him to work as legal secretary.[73]

1. Julia Drusilla was the sister and, very probably, paramour of the emperor Gaius (Caligula). He granted her divine honours on her early death in A.D. 38 and found a senator, Livius Geminius, who, for a million sesterces, attested to her assumption into heaven (see Dio 59.11).

2. An ironic glance at the *Aeneid* (2.724), where Virgil describes the tiny Ascanius unable to keep up with his father Aeneas. Claudius had weak legs and tended to totter (Suetonius, *Claudius* 21.6).

3. The Via Appia was the main Roman road to the south of Italy and would pass close to the most famous entrance to the Underworld, at Cumae. The officials responsible for its maintenance were experienced administrators of consular rank, nominated of course by the emperor. Both Augustus and Tiberius had died in Campania and were brought up to Rome for burial, although only Augustus was granted the divine honours referred to here. The unjustified compliment to Tiberius is to accentuate Claudius' unworthiness for deification, even though it was granted him.

4. Phoebus (Cynthius) and Cynthia, that is, Diana, represent the sun and the moon in poetry, while Bacchus represents the vine. These lines and those following are tame parodies of epic circumlocutions for expressing time. Seneca, like Abraham Cowley, ridicules the practice elsewhere (*Epistles* 122.11-13; see *Letters from a Stoic*, pp. 223 f.).

5. Perhaps the star Vindemitor in the constellation Virgo, which supposedly affects grapes, although it has no astronomical prominence at this time; otherwise the somewhat prosaic 'grape harvester'.

6. Roman water-clocks were highly unreliable because of evaporation and the seasonal variability of the Roman hour, as well as their elementary construction, and the Romans as philosophers were highly eclectic in their views.

7. An ironic touch. Mercury is above all the god of craftiness and subtlety, hence his supposed enthusiasm for Claudius' wit. It has been suggested by Athanassakis that Seneca is here playing on a possible double meaning for *anima* (soul/wind) and is caustically alluding to Claudius' notorious propensity to meteorism (or flatulence). Mercury thus becomes a more appropriate god

to aid Claudius since in the Homeric Hymn he escaped Apollo by 'a terrible working of the belly, a reckless messenger' (ll. 295–6). But Mercury also has his appropriate role as the conductor of dead souls to the underworld or, as here, to Olympus.

8. Clotho, whose name points to the spinner among the three *Parcae*, is elsewhere described as the one who holds the distaff, while Lachesis teases out the thread and Atropos breaks it. In c. 4 below Clotho is given also the last two tasks in the case of Claudius, and all three cooperate in the case of Nero.

9. Astrologers were prevalent among the superstitious Romans. Frequently expelled from Rome by imperial decree as subversives, because of their sought-after predictions of imperial destinies and deaths, they tended to drift back to their lucrative practice.

10. A quotation from Virgil (*Georgics* 4.90); the original advises the be-ekeeper to kill off the worse, if there are two 'kings' in the hive.

11. A snobbish reflection on Claudius' generous policies of granting citizenship to Roman subjects, which gave them the right to wear the toga. His generosity in this is considerably exaggerated here; citizenship for all free men in the empire was not awarded until A.D. 212, during the reign of Caracalla.

12. Augurinus (a little augur or prophet) is unknown although it was a surname of the Minucii. Baba is mentioned by Seneca (*Epistles* 15.9) as a proverbial idiot and is connected with a Greek exclamation of wonderment. The three are offered as a sort of ABC of stupidity.

13. The theme of the Golden Age inaugurated by the new emperor is not infrequent in Neronian propaganda, being used also by Calpurnius Siculus in nis *Eclogues* and perhaps reflected in Nero's Golden House. Virgil had used the theme, originally enunciated clearly by Hesiod, to eulogize Augustus' principate. In each case Apollo is the tutelary deity. Perhaps the chief credit for the exploitation of the idea should go to Seneca, who was an admirer of both Augustus and Virgil. Nero, even more than Augustus, tended to identify with Apollo because of his interests in poetry and music.

14. Apollo was the half-brother of the Fates, their common father being Jupiter and their mothers Latona and Themis respectively.

15. A quotation from Euripides' lost *Cresphontes* (Nauck[2], Fgt. 449). The original context implied that the friends of the deceased should be glad that he had finished with the sorrows of life.

16. Hercules is the logical choice for this job because of his experience in ridding the world of monsters as part of his twelve labours. Seneca then draws on a long anti-heroic tradition about Hercules as the bibulous, buffoonish braggart, which goes back to Aristophanes and even Euripides. Representations of Hercules in comic situations, looking drunk or ridiculous, were popular in Greek and Roman art. The part he comes to play as Claudius' advocate is also appropriate since Hercules himself had been a mortal who was elevated to

divine status. As a frequent subject of serious dramas, including Seneca's, his mock-tragic address in the next chapter provides a nice occasion for literary parody.

17. A quotation from Homer (*Odyssey* 1.170), where Telemachus is speaking to the disguised Athene.

18. Suetonius provides a good deal of information on Claudius' historical and other works (*Claudius* 33; 40; 42). He wrote a history of Rome from the assassination of Julius Caesar, which, because of family pressure, skipped the period of the civil wars and continues the story from their conclusion to the death of Augustus; he also wrote twenty volumes of Etruscan history and eight of Carthaginian in Greek. He perhaps has all of these in mind here. He also produced a manual on dice-playing, an *apologia* for Cicero, a proposal to augment the Latin alphabet, and a lengthy and indiscreet autobiography. The regrettable loss of the last prompted Robert Graves to write *I, Claudius* and *Claudius the God*.

19. *Odyssey* 9.39. Odysseus is describing his adventures to King Alcinous.

20. The goddess Fever, as the Averter of Fever, was a genuine divinity in Rome with three sanctuaries, the most ancient standing on the Palatine, and so near Claudius' own palace. She was an appropriate deity for Rome with its high frequency of malaria, and a suitable companion for the emperor who perhaps suffered from the disease as well as from a natural palsy (Suetonius, *Claudius* 30).

21. Claudius was born at Lugdunum, the modern Lyons, on the northern border of Gallia Narbonensis, in 10 B.C. His mother, Antonia, was accompanying his father, Drusus, on a campaign against the Germans at the time. The modern Vienne (*Vienna*), the capital of the Allobroges, was also a Roman colony in Claudius' time and did not enjoy good relations with Lugdunum, which, being situated in Transalpine Gaul, could be regarded as more crudely Gallic than Vienna in Gallia Narbonensis; hence the sneer at the town and Claudius.

22. L. Munatius founded the colony about 44 B.C., when he was governor of Transalpine Gaul.

23. The Gauls captured Rome in 390 B.C., but they were regarded as a constant threat until late in Republican times. In the Latin there is an untranslatable pun on *germanus*, which can mean 'sibling', 'genuine' or 'German'.

24. Licinus was a Gaul, the slave and later freedman of Julius Caesar; he became procurator of the area under Augustus and his record of rich vulgarity and despotic behaviour was almost proverbial. The implication is that some of his qualities rubbed off on Claudius.

25. The Xanthus is a small river near Troy, frequently mentioned by Homer. It would be over a thousand miles away. It might be noted that

Claudius' boyhood tutor had been a superintendent of mule drivers according to Suetonius (*Claudius* 2). The goddess Fever cannot understand Claudius' Homeric pleasantries and Claudius' reaction seems very understandable. Claudius was regarded as subservient to his freedman secretaries, a fact much resented by upper-class Romans, not least by Seneca, who had had to fawn on Polybius during his exile in hopes of securing his return from exile.

26. This was the labour of Hercules that seemed to involve most wandering. After getting the red oxen of the monster Geryon from the fabulous western island of Erythea, he is supposed to have passed the Alps and Pyrenees, founded the towns of Alesia and Nemausus, and fathered the race of Celts. He might therefore plausibly be expected to come across Mt Fourvière, upon which Lyons is built, and which overlooks the confluence of the Rhone and Saône. The latter river was noted by Julius Caesar as having an almost imperceptible current.

27. The original is a derisive adaptation of a frequent Greek tragic phrase meaning 'the stroke of a god'. My adaptation of *coup de foudre* gives the real meaning.

28. Bücheler suggested reading *Tiburi* for *tibi* here. There was a temple of Hercules at Tibur, a Roman resort, and Augustus used to hear trials there (Suetonius, *Augustus* 72). July and August were more or less a continuous legal vacation at Rome. Claudius might have been taking a busman's holiday. On the other hand, there were two temples of Hercules in Rome and that of Hercules Victor was near the Palatine. Claudius' reference to 'sewers' in his speech alludes to another Labour of Hercules, when he cleaned the cattle stables of King Augeas, which had not been cleaned for thirty years, by diverting the rivers Alpheus and Peneus through them.

29. A considerable lacuna follows (see the Introduction, p. 211). It is easy enough to surmise however that Claudius wins over Hercules, who forces his way into the Senate of Olympus, and pleads the cause of Claudius' deification. Jupiter throws the matter open to the House amid uproar and when the text resumes, we find one of the gods addressing Hercules and throwing cold water on Claudius' pretensions.

30. Epicurus had to admit that the gods existed, because we had mental images of them, but he argued that they lived carefree lives in the clear spaces between the worlds, giving no thought or trouble to men. Claudius had had troubles and caused them.

31. The god or *logos* of the Stoics permeated the world and therefore could be regarded as having the same spherical shape. The quotation from Varro is taken from his Menippean satires (583 B). The *logos* was not a personal deity, and so would be without intellect.

32. Saturn was the father and displaced predecessor of Jupiter. His month was December, a season of licence and carnival. The glance at Claudius'

drinking and other habits is perhaps reinforced by the fact that he added an extra day to the traditional four days of the Saturnalia (Dio 60.25). The implication is that he ran Rome as though he were King of Carnival all the year long.

33. Lucius Junius Silanus Torquatus was engaged to Claudius' daughter, Octavia. In A.D. 48, at the instigation of Agrippina, who wished Octavia to marry her son, Nero, he was accused of incest with his very attractive sister, Junia Calvina, and forced to commit suicide. Claudius even carried out a ceremonious purification. The reference to Juno, Jupiter's sister and wife, points up the implicit reflections on Jupiter himself.

34. One could marry one's half-sister (on the paternal side) at Athens and of course the Ptolemies of Alexandria frequently married their full-sisters.

35. Adapted from a line in the *Iphigenia* of Ennius. Claudius' ignorance about his own private affairs, his general 'star-gazing' and obliviousness to daily life are commented on by Suetonius (*Claudius* 39).

36. There was a temple and a priesthood established for Claudius in 49 at Camelodunum, the modern Colchester. A traditional Greek prayer is parodied here by the substitution of *fool* for *god*.

37. Janus was an important and ancient Roman deity who presided over the beginnings of everything. He was supposed to have power over the entrance to heaven and his month began the year. His name is related to the Latin word for 'door'. It is appropriate therefore that he should be one of the two consuls elect who traditionally would open the debate, particularly when the question was whether Claudius should be allowed into heaven. For various historical reasons his statues often had two faces back to back. The reference to the Forum may be explained by the existence there of a passage with two entrances called the *Janus Medius*. July was the beginning of the second half of the Roman calendar year, but also a month for vacation and practically no public business took place in the afternoon in any month. Janus would therefore be consul-designate when the position was totally honorific. There is also a satiric allusion to the often short tenure of the consulship, particularly in the imperial period.

38. In the original Janus talks of a 'Bean' farce (*mimus*), which, according to Eden (*op cit*. p. 109), may have dealt with survival after death in the form of the lowly bean, which was closely connected with the Roman cult of the dead. The Pythagorean cult, which believed in the transmigration of souls, had *tabus* about beans.

39. Janus used Homeric phraseology to add further solemnity to the technical legislative language he is adopting.

40. The revival of this old Italian sky-god, the meaning of whose name is identical with that of Jupiter's, perhaps hints at Claudius' interest in archaic religion. Vica Pota was also an ancient divinity, the goddess of conquests and lucky acquisitions. Unless Seneca, like many ancient writers, is confusing

Diespiter with Dis pater or Pluto, god of the underworld and then of wealth, who is sometimes described as a son of Fortuna, the relationship is invented to explain Diespiter's lucrative occupations. Selling citizenships was a thriving business with Claudius' entourage.

41. The lobe of the ear was regarded by the ancients as the seat of memory. Hercules is presumably reminding Diespiter of some past favour. This would lessen the value of his pro-Claudian proposal.

42. According to Ennius, Romulus, the first King of Rome, was in heaven where he continued to live his old simple life. Turnips would be unwelcome fare for a gourmand such as Claudius. The source of the quotation may be from the satirist Lucilius (Fr. 1375 Krenkel).

43. A humorous touch; Ovid's *Metamorphoses* already contained the apotheoses of Romulus and Julius Caesar and predicted that of Augustus.

44. The circumstances in which Valerius Messala Corvinus (64 B.C.–A.D. 8) uttered these words are unknown. Perhaps it was when he resigned from his post of city prefect in 25 B.C. after a few days in office, protesting that the power involved was unconstitutional.

45. The original proverb is Greek and is the equivalent of our 'charity begins at home'.

46. Most emperors were granted (or took) the title *Augustus*.

47. The daughter of Drusus was killed through the jealousy of Messalina; Julia Livilla, daughter of Germanicus, was accused in A.D. 41 of adultery with Seneca, and her death seems also due to the jealousy of Messalina. On Lucius Silanus, see n. 33 above. It may be noticed below that Claudius seems now to be present in the senate. If this is not a rhetorical device, it may indicate the haste of the composition of the pamphlet. Possibly he is in the vestibule and visible from the floor of the senate.

48. Homer *Iliad* 1. 591. Hephaestus (Vulcan) is reminding his mother Hera of Zeus' action to warn her. The reference to Zeus' suspension of his wife in the sky is *Iliad* 15.18 ff.

49. Narcissus gave the orders for Messalina's death in the name of Claudius. The emperor's absent-mindedness perhaps gave rise to the story that after her execution he asked why she was not at dinner.

50. Gaius had killed Marcus Junius Silanus, father of his wife, Junia Claudilla, in A.D. 38. Claudius had killed Appius Silanus, actually his stepfather, not his father-in-law, in A.D. 42, L. Junius Silanus, his intended son-in-law, in A.D. 49, and Cn. Pompeius Magnus, who married Claudius' daughter, Antonia, in A.D. 47.

51. M. Licinius Crassus Frugi was consul in A.D. 27, Cn. Pompeius being his son and Scribonia his wife. Crassus was engaged to Claudius' daughter, although he never married her. Caligula, according to Suetonius, stripped a number of families of their historical distinctions, including the descendants

of the great Pompey. Claudius restored the title *Magnus*. It is fairly obvious that Claudius suspected Crassus of pretensions to the purple, not an impossible idea if we consider the disillusionment with the Julian line and the career of Pompey himself, who might well have been the founder of a line of emperors.

52. C. Appius Junius Silanus, consul in A.D. 28, governor in Spain in A.D. 40–41, had married Domitia, mother of Messalina, so becoming Claudius' father-in-law. He was executed on flimsy grounds through the instigation of Messalina. For the others mentioned in this indictment see the notes above.

53. Catullus 3.12, from one of the poems on Lesbia's dead sparrow.

54. Agatho is obviously a lawyer, but otherwise an unidentifiable Greek. He and his friends are deploring the drop in legal business that they can expect now that Claudius is dead. The legal experts, who had been starved of employment because of Claudius' disregard for legal interpretations other than his own, naturally show no sympathy.

55. The Latin metre is anapaestic dimeters, favoured by Seneca for the choruses of his tragedies and suitable for dirges. For an analysis of the dirge and its conformity with Seneca's metrical practice in his tragedies, see Eden (*op. cit.* p. 131). Its form follows the traditional arrangement for a funeral oration; as for its satiric content, one might note the unjustified emphasis on his wisdom, bravery and justice, all qualities in which his hostile contemporaries found him lacking; his military achievements, all vicarious, of course; and the contemptible types of people, lawyers, modernist poets, and gamblers, who are expected to miss him most.

56. When Claudius died, Narcissus, his powerful freedman, and confidential secretary, was taking a cure for gout at the baths of Sinuessa in Campania. He was put out of the way almost immediately on Nero's accession. The short cut was suicide.

57. A glance at Virgil's *facilis descensus Averno* (*Aeneid* 6.126).

58. *Odes* 2.13.34.

59. A ritual cry from the Egyptian cult of Isis, uttered on the finding of her husband Osiris. Claudius was interested in oriental religions.

60. Those we can identify seem to have been Messalina's lovers or involved in the scandal of her mock marriage to Gaius Silius in A.D. 48 Narcissus was mainly responsible for their punishment.

61. Mnester was a famous pantomime actor, who had been a great favourite of the emperor Caligula and retained his popularity at Claudius' court, particularly with Messalina, whose lover he was, until he was replaced by Gaius Silius. He was involved in the great scandal also and was executed. The meaning of the sentence is perhaps deliberately obscure. Claudius had earlier ordered Mnester to do whatever Messalina commanded; he later had him executed, perhaps by decapitation.

62. Polybius was an important freedman of Claudius' and was his literary

secretary. He was forced to commit suicide in A.D. 47 through Messalina. About the others little or nothing is known.

63. Catonius was an army officer, who became Prefect of the Praetorian Guard under Claudius and was destroyed by the machinations of Messalina in A.D. 43. Pollio became Prefect in A.D. 41 and was still popular with Claudius in 44. The circumstances of his death are unknown. Lusius Saturninus and Cornelius Lupus were victims of the intrigues of an informer Publius Suillius. Asinius Celer was consul in 38. Pompeius is unknown outside this satire.

64. These are (in order) Julia, daughter of Germanicus, Julia, daughter of Livia and Drusus, L. Silanus and Pompeius Magnus, Appius Silanus and Crassus Frugi, Domitia Lepida, Messalina's mother, and Scribonia, mother of his son-in-law Magnus.

65. An adapted Greek quotation: see Eden (*op. cit*. p. 143). Claudius is not yet aware of his plight.

66. Aeacus, son of Jupiter and Aegina, was so just in life that he was appointed one of the judges in the underworld; the others, Minos and Rhadamanthus, are less often cited by Roman authors.

67. The dictator L. Cornelius Sulla in 81 B.C. had set up a number of permanent courts for different offences. The judicial system of Hades is humorously based on Roman legal procedures. This particular court dealt not only with murder and poisoning but also with those who had given unfair sentences in capital cases. Pedo Pompeius is initiating the prosecution, as was the right of any private citizen.

68. A Homeric tag, *Iliad* 9.385.

69. Publius Petronius was consul in A.D. 19, and later proconsul in Asia and an imperial deputy in Syria.

70. Aeacus is quoting a traditional Greek tag, first recorded in Hesiod.

71. These inhabitants of Hades are the unredeemable sinners of classical myth. Sisyphus was a rapist, murderer and thief, but his chief crimes were accusing Jupiter of the abduction of Aegina and insulting Pluto; he was punished by having to push a large stone up a hill, from which it promptly rolled down again. Tantalus had stolen nectar and ambrosia from heaven and given it to mortals, and had also served up his son Pelops to the gods for a meal; his punishment therefore had strong oral connections: he was tormented by fruit he couldn't eat and water he couldn't drink, while an ever-threatening stone hung over his head. Ixion, king of Thessaly, had murdered his father-in-law, and tried to seduce Juno; he was tied to a perpetually revolving fiery wheel and lashed with snakes. Tityus has also been detected in the text instead of Sisyphus. The former, another unredeemable sinner, was a Giant who insulted Latona, mother of Apollo and Artemis, who killed him; he was placed in Tartarus, where vultures gnawed his liver, which grew again once devoured.

72. Caligula, while alive, had been the bane of Claudius' life.

73. As this is probably not the comic writer, Menander's identity remains unknown. The point, however, is that Claudius is under the thumb of a freedman as usual and continues with legal work, presumably in the intervals of his punishment.

FOR THE BEST IN PAPERBACKS, LOOK FOR THE 🐧

In every corner of the world, on every subject under the sun, Penguin represents quality and variety – the very best in publishing today.

For complete information about books available from Penguin – including Pelicans, Puffins, Peregrines and Penguin Classics – and how to order them, write to us at the appropriate address below. Please note that for copyright reasons the selection of books varies from country to country.

In the United Kingdom: For a complete list of books available from Penguin in the U.K., please write to *Dept E.P., Penguin Books Ltd, Harmondsworth, Middlesex, UB7 0DA*

In the United States: For a complete list of books available from Penguin in the U.S., please write to *Dept BA, Penguin, 299 Murray Hill Parkway, East Rutherford, New Jersey 07073*

In Canada: For a complete list of books available from Penguin in Canada, please write to *Penguin Books Canada Ltd, 2801 John Street, Markham, Ontario L3R 1B4*

In Australia: For a complete list of books available from Penguin in Australia, please write to the *Marketing Department, Penguin Books Australia Ltd, P.O. Box 257, Ringwood, Victoria 3134*

In New Zealand: For a complete list of books available from Penguin in New Zealand, please write to the *Marketing Department, Penguin Books (NZ) Ltd, Private Bag, Takapuna, Auckland 9*

In India: For a complete list of books available from Penguin, please write to *Penguin Overseas Ltd, 706 Eros Apartments, 56 Nehru Place, New Delhi, 110019*

In Holland: For a complete list of books available from Penguin in Holland, please write to *Penguin Books Nederland B.V., Postbus 195, NL–1380AD Weesp, Netherlands*

In Germany: For a complete list of books available from Penguin, please write to *Penguin Books Ltd, Friedrichstrasse 10 – 12, D–6000 Frankfurt Main 1, Federal Republic of Germany*

In Spain: For a complete list of books available from Penguin in Spain, please write to *Longman Penguin España, Calle San Nicolas 15, E–28013 Madrid, Spain*

PENGUIN CLASSICS

Aeschylus	The Oresteia (Agamemnon/Choephori/Eumenides) Prometheus Bound/The Suppliants/Seven Against Thebes/The Persians
Aesop	Fables
Apollonius of Rhodes	The Voyage of Argo
Apuleius	The Golden Ass
Aristophanes	The Knights/Peace/The Birds/The Assembly Women/Wealth
	Lysistrata/The Acharnians/The Clouds
	The Wasps/The Poet and the Women/The Frogs
Aristotle	The Athenian Constitution
	The Ethics
	The Politics
Aristotle/Horace/ Longinus	Classical Literary Criticism
Arrian	The Campaigns of Alexander
Saint Augustine	City of God
	Confessions
Boethius	The Consolation of Philosophy
Caesar	The Civil War
	The Conquest of Gaul
Catullus	Poems
Cicero	The Murder Trials
	The Nature of the Gods
	On the Good Life
	Selected Letters
	Selected Political Speeches
	Selected Works
Euripides	Alcestis/Iphigenia in Tauris/Hippolytus/The Bacchae/Ion/The Women of Troy/Helen
	Medea/Hecabe/Electra/Heracles
	Orestes/The Children of Heracles/ Andromache/The Suppliant Woman/ The Phoenician Women/Iphigenia in Aulis

PENGUIN CLASSICS

Hesiod/Theognis	**Theogony and Works and Days/Elegies**
'Hippocrates'	**Hippocratic Writings**
Homer	**The Iliad**
	The Odyssey
Horace	**Complete Odes and Epodes**
Horace/Persius	**Satires and Epistles**
Juvenal	**Sixteen Satires**
Livy	**The Early History of Rome**
	Rome and Italy
	Rome and the Mediterranean
	The War with Hannibal
Lucretius	**On the Nature of the Universe**
Marcus Aurelius	**Meditations**
Martial	**Epigrams**
Ovid	**The Erotic Poems**
	The Metamorphoses
Pausanias	**Guide to Greece** (in two volumes)
Petronius/Seneca	**The Satyricon/The Apocolocyntosis**
Pindar	**The Odes**
Plato	**Georgias**
	The Last Days of Socrates (Euthyphro/The Apology/Crito/Phaedo)
	The Laws
	Phaedrus and Letters VII and VIII
	Philebus
	Protagoras and Meno
	The Republic
	The Symposium
	Timaeus and Critias
Plautus	**The Pot of Gold/The Prisoners/The Brothers Menaechmus/The Swaggering Soldier/Pseudolus**
	The Rope/Amphitryo/The Ghost/A Three-Dollar Day

PENGUIN CLASSICS

Pliny	**The Letters of the Younger Pliny**
Plutarch	**The Age of Alexander** (Nine Greek Lives)
	The Fall of the Roman Republic (Six Lives)
	The Makers of Rome (Nine Lives)
	The Rise and Fall of Athens (Nine Greek Lives)
Polybius	**The Rise of the Roman Empire**
Procopius	**The Secret History**
Propertius	**The Poems**
Quintus Curtius Rufus	**The History of Alexander**
Sallust	**The Jugurthine War** and **The Conspiracy of Cataline**
Seneca	**Four Tragedies** and **Octavia**
	Letters from a Stoic
Sophocles	**Electra/Women of Trachis/Philoctetes/Ajax**
	The Theban Plays (King Oedipus/Oedipus at Colonus/Antigone)
Suetonius	**The Twelve Caesars**
Tacitus	**The Agricola** and **The Germania**
	The Annals of Imperial Rome
	The Histories
Terence	**The Comedies (The Girl from Andros/The Self-Tormentor/The Eunuch/Phormio/The Mother-in-Law/The Brothers)**
Thucydides	**The History of the Peloponnesian War**
Tibullus	**The Poems** and **The Tibullan Collection**
Virgil	**The Aeneid**
	The Eclogues
	The Georgics
Xenophon	**A History of My Times**
	The Persian Expedition

Saint Anselm	**The Prayers and Meditations**
Saint Augustine	**The Confessions**
Bede	**A History of the English Church and People**
Chaucer	**The Canterbury Tales**
	Love Visions
	Troilus and Criseyde
Froissart	**The Chronicles**
Geoffrey of Monmouth	**The History of the Kings of Britain**
Gerald of Wales	**History and Topography of Ireland**
	The Journey through Wales and **The Description of Wales**
Gregory of Tours	**The History of the Franks**
Julian of Norwich	**Revelations of Divine Love**
William Langland	**Piers the Ploughman**
Sir John Mandeville	**The Travels of Sir John Mandeville**
Marguerite de Navarre	**The Heptameron**
Christine de Pisan	**The Treasure of the City of Ladies**
Marco Polo	**The Travels**
Richard Rolle	**The Fire of Love**
Thomas à Kempis	**The Imitation of Christ**

ANTHOLOGIES AND ANONYMOUS WORKS

The Age of Bede
Alfred the Great
Beowulf
A Celtic Miscellany
The Cloud of Unknowing and Other Works
The Death of King Arthur
The Earliest English Poems
Early Christian Writings
Early Irish Myths and Sagas
Egil's Saga
The Letters of Abelard and Heloise
Medieval English Verse
Njal's Saga
Seven Viking Romances
Sir Gawain and the Green Knight
The Song of Roland

PENGUIN CLASSICS

John Aubrey	**Brief Lives**
Francis Bacon	**The Essays**
James Boswell	**The Life of Johnson**
Sir Thomas Browne	**The Major Works**
John Bunyan	**The Pilgrim's Progress**
Edmund Burke	**Reflections on the Revolution in France**
Thomas de Quincey	**Confessions of an English Opium Eater**
	Recollections of the Lakes and the Lake Poets
Daniel Defoe	**A Journal of the Plague Year**
	Moll Flanders
	Robinson Crusoe
	Roxana
	A Tour Through the Whole Island of Great Britain
Henry Fielding	**Jonathan Wild**
	Joseph Andrews
	The History of Tom Jones
Oliver Goldsmith	**The Vicar of Wakefield**
William Hazlitt	**Selected Writings**
Thomas Hobbes	**Leviathan**
Samuel Johnson / James Boswell	**A Journey to the Western Islands of Scotland / The Journal of a Tour to the Hebrides**
Charles Lamb	**Selected Prose**
Samuel Richardson	**Clarissa**
	Pamela
Adam Smith	**The Wealth of Nations**
Tobias Smollet	**Humphry Clinker**
Richard Steele and Joseph Addison	Selections from the **Tatler** and the **Spectator**
Laurence Sterne	**The Life and Opinions of Tristram Shandy, Gentleman**
	A Sentimental Journey Through France and Italy
Jonathan Swift	**Gulliver's Travels**
Dorothy and William Wordsworth	**Home at Grasmere**

PENGUIN CLASSICS

Matthew Arnold	Selected Prose
Jane Austen	Emma
	Lady Susan, The Watsons, Sanditon
	Mansfield Park
	Northanger Abbey
	Persuasion
	Pride and Prejudice
	Sense and Sensibility
Anne Brontë	The Tenant of Wildfell Hall
Charlotte Brontë	Jane Eyre
	Shirley
	Villette
Emily Brontë	Wuthering Heights
Samuel Butler	Erewhon
	The Way of All Flesh
Thomas Carlyle	Selected Writings
Wilkie Collins	The Moonstone
	The Woman in White
Charles Darwin	The Origin of the Species
Charles Dickens	American Notes for General Circulation
	Barnaby Rudge
	Bleak House
	The Christmas Books
	David Copperfield
	Dombey and Son
	Great Expectations
	Hard Times
	Little Dorrit
	Martin Chuzzlewit
	The Mystery of Edwin Drood
	Nicholas Nickleby
	The Old Curiosity Shop
	Oliver Twist
	Our Mutual Friend
	The Pickwick Papers
	Selected Short Fiction
	A Tale of Two Cities

PENGUIN CLASSICS

Benjamin Disraeli	**Sybil**
George Eliot	**Adam Bede**
	Daniel Deronda
	Felix Holt
	Middlemarch
	The Mill on the Floss
	Romola
	Scenes of Clerical Life
	Silas Marner
Elizabeth Gaskell	**Cranford** and **Cousin Phillis**
	The Life of Charlotte Brontë
	Mary Barton
	North and South
	Wives and Daughters
Edward Gibbon	**The Decline and Fall of the Roman Empire**
George Gissing	**New Grub Street**
Edmund Gosse	**Father and Son**
Richard Jefferies	**Landscape with Figures**
Thomas Macaulay	**The History of England**
Henry Mayhew	**Selections from London Labour** and **The London Poor**
John Stuart Mill	**On Liberty**
William Morris	**News from Nowhere** and **Selected Writings and Designs**
Walter Pater	**Marius the Epicurean**
John Ruskin	**'Unto This Last' and Other Writings**
Sir Walter Scott	**Ivanhoe**
Robert Louis Stevenson	**Dr Jekyll and Mr Hyde**
William Makepeace Thackeray	**The History of Henry Esmond**
	Vanity Fair
Anthony Trollope	**Barchester Towers**
	Framley Parsonage
	Phineas Finn
	The Warden
Mrs Humphrey Ward	**Helbeck of Bannisdale**
Mary Wollstonecraft	**Vindication of the Rights of Women**

PENGUIN CLASSICS

Arnold Bennett	**The Old Wives' Tale**
Joseph Conrad	**Heart of Darkness**
	Nostromo
	The Secret Agent
	The Shadow-Line
	Under Western Eyes
E. M. Forster	**Howard's End**
	A Passage to India
	A Room With a View
	Where Angels Fear to Tread
Thomas Hardy	**The Distracted Preacher and Other Tales**
	Far From the Madding Crowd
	Jude the Obscure
	The Mayor of Casterbridge
	The Return of the Native
	Tess of the d'Urbervilles
	The Trumpet Major
	Under the Greenwood Tree
	The Woodlanders
Henry James	**The Aspern Papers** and **The Turn of the Screw**
	The Bostonians
	Daisy Miller
	The Europeans
	The Golden Bowl
	An International Episode and Other Stories
	Portrait of a Lady
	Roderick Hudson
	Washington Square
	What Maisie Knew
	The Wings of the Dove
D. H. Lawrence	**The Complete Short Novels**
	The Plumed Serpent
	The Rainbow
	Selected Short Stories
	Sons and Lovers
	The White Peacock
	Women in Love

PENGUIN CLASSICS

Horatio Alger, Jr.	**Ragged Dick** and **Struggling Upward**
Phineas T. Barnum	**Struggles and Triumphs**
Ambrose Bierce	**The Enlarged Devil's Dictionary**
Kate Chopin	**The Awakening and Selected Stories**
Stephen Crane	**The Red Badge of Courage**
Richard Henry Dana, Jr.	**Two Years Before the Mast**
Frederick Douglass	**Narrative of the Life of Frederick Douglass, An American Slave**
Theodore Dreiser	**Sister Carrie**
Ralph Waldo Emerson	**Selected Essays**
Joel Chandler Harris	**Uncle Remus**
Nathaniel Hawthorne	**Blithedale Romance**
	The House of the Seven Gables
	The Scarlet Letter and Selected Tales
William Dean Howells	**The Rise of Silas Lapham**
Alice James	**The Diary of Alice James**
William James	**Varieties of Religious Experience**
Jack London	**The Call of the Wild and Other Stories**
	Martin Eden
Herman Melville	**Billy Budd, Sailor and Other Stories**
	Moby-Dick
	Redburn
	Typee
Frank Norris	**McTeague**
Thomas Paine	**Common Sense**
Edgar Allan Poe	**The Narrative of Arthur Gordon Pym of Nantucket**
	The Other Poe
	The Science Fiction of Edgar Allan Poe
	Selected Writings
Harriet Beecher Stowe	**Uncle Tom's Cabin**
Henry David Thoreau	**Walden** and **Civil Disobedience**
Mark Twain	**The Adventures of Huckleberry Finn**
	A Connecticut Yankee at King Arthur's Court
	Life on the Mississippi
	Pudd'nhead Wilson
	Roughing It
Edith Wharton	**The House of Mirth**

PENGUIN CLASSICS

Honoré de Balzac	**Cousin Bette**
	Eugénie Grandet
	Lost Illusions
	Old Goriot
	Ursule Mirouet
Benjamin Constant	**Adolphe**
Corneille	**The Cid / Cinna / The Theatrical Illusion**
Alphonse Daudet	**Letters from My Windmill**
René Descartes	**Discourse on Method and Other Writings**
Denis Diderot	**Jacques the Fatalist**
Gustave Flaubert	**Madame Bovary**
	Sentimental Education
	Three Tales
Jean de la Fontaine	**Selected Fables**
Jean Froissart	**The Chronicles**
Théophile Gautier	**Mademoiselle de Maupin**
Edmond and Jules de Goncourt	**Germinie Lacerteux**
J.-K. Huysmans	**Against Nature**
Guy de Maupassant	**Selected Short Stories**
Molière	**The Misanthrope / The Sicilian / Tartuffe / A Doctor in Spite of Himself / The Imaginary Invalid**
Michel de Montaigne	**Essays**
Marguerite de Navarre	**The Heptameron**
Marie de France	**Lais**
Blaise Pascal	**Pensées**
Rabelais	**The Histories of Gargantua and Pantagruel**
Racine	**Iphigenia / Phaedra / Athaliah**
Arthur Rimbaud	**Collected Poems**
Jean-Jacques Rousseau	**The Confessions**
	Reveries of a Solitary Walker
Madame de Sevigné	**Selected Letters**
Voltaire	**Candide**
	Philosophical Dictionary
Émile Zola	**La Bête Humaine**
	Nana
	Thérèse Raquin

PENGUIN CLASSICS

Pedro de Alarcon   **The Three-Cornered Hat and Other Stories**
Leopoldo Alas   **La Regenta**
Ludovico Ariosto   **Orlando Furioso**
Giovanni Boccaccio   **The Decameron**
Baldassar Castiglione   **The Book of the Courtier**
Benvenuto Cellini   **Autobiography**
Miguel de Cervantes   **Don Quixote**
    Exemplary Stories
Dante   **The Divine Comedy** (in 3 volumes)
    La Vita Nuova
Bernal Diaz   **The Conquest of New Spain**
Carlo Goldoni   **Four Comedies (The Venetian Twins/The Artful
       Widow/Mirandolina/The Superior Residence)**
Niccolo Machiavelli   **The Discourses**
    The Prince
Alessandro Manzoni   **The Betrothed**
Giorgio Vasari   **Lives of the Artists** (in 2 volumes)

and

**Five Italian Renaissance Comedies (Machiavelli/The Mandragola;
    Ariosto/Lena; Aretino/The Stablemaster; Gl'Intronatie/The
    Deceived;Guarini/The Faithful Shepherd)**
The Jewish Poets of Spain
The Poem of the Cid
**Two Spanish Picaresque Novels (Anon/Lazarille de Tormes; de
    Quevedo/The Swindler)**